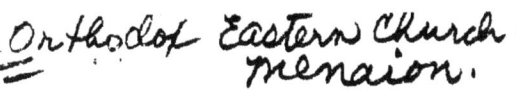

THE GENERAL MENAION

OR

THE BOOK OF SERVICES

COMMON TO THE

FESTIVALS OF OUR LORD JESUS CHRIST

OF THE HOLY VIRGIN

AND OF

THE DIFFERENT ORDERS OF SAINTS

TRANSLATED
FROM THE SLAVONIAN SIXTEENTH EDITION OF 1862
PRINTED IN MOSCOW AND PUBLISHED BY
THE MOST HOLY GOVERNING SYNOD OF RUSSIA

ALL RIGHTS RESERVED

LONDON
J. DAVY & SONS
DRYDEN PRESS 137 LONG ACRE.
1899

TO
THEIR EMINENCES
THE RIGHT REVEREND NICHOLAS
NOW LORD BISHOP OF TAURIDA & SYMPHEROPOL,
late of Aleut and Alaska, and
THE RIGHT REVEREND TIKHON,
PRESENT LORD BISHOP OF ALEUT AND ALASKA,

WHOSE FATHERLY SOLICITUDE, FOR THE SPIRITUAL WELFARE OF THE FLOCK OF THIS UNIQUELY EXTENDED DIOCESE, MOVED THE FIRST TO SUGGEST THE TRANSLATION, AND THE SECOND TO CALL HIS BLESSING UPON THE WORK,

IS

THIS BOOK

IN A BOLD, BUT HEARTFELT AND PRAYERFUL TRUST OF FURTHERING, UNDER GOD, A GOOD CAUSE,

Most gratefully and humbly Dedicated
BY
PROFESSOR N. ORLOFF,
THE TRANSLATOR.

The Feast of SS. Peter and Paul. KING'S COLLEGE,
LONDON, W.C.
$\frac{\text{29th June}}{\text{11th July}}$ 1899.

PREFACE.

The Orthodox Eastern Church undoubtedly possesses the most abundant hymnology for her services. Special entire services date their origin as far back as the fourth if not the third century. But the greatest impetus to their production was given by the sweet melodies of St. John of Damascus (a substantial part of the Octoechos). The rich harvest of about two centuries' work appears in the shape of 12 books, one Menaion for each month, with at least one service for every day. At the time when everything had to be copied by hand, such a wealth could of course be found in large monasteries only; almost from the beginning therefore a want was felt and supplied later on by a book, of which the translation is now offered and which had and has to be used, even where the Menaia are found, in cases *e. g.* of the newly canonized saints until special services are composed in their honour.

The present editions of the Greek Anthologion and of the Menaia, under the title Anonymoi, viz., in those parts which exactly correspond to the Slavonic General Menaion, contain only the Stichera for "O Lord, I have cried," and the Canons; but the style, the disposition of the words in sentences, even the language itself, do not leave the slightest doubt in the translator's mind that the fuller Slavonian Book is only a translation from Greek manuscripts, not an independent composition. The absence of the originals has made the translator's work doubly more difficult and anxious, on account of mostly fruitless search, only occasionally rewarded with a Sticheron here and Troparion there; but he sincerely trusts that the present work is also free from such blunders as those made by an English translator of other Liturgical Books, who, a formidable List of Books supposed to have been consulted notwithstanding, had *e. g.* empowered an arch-priest to ordain, called a scribe a martyr whose countenance and body was branded with hot iron, and dwindled down the number of martyrs from twenty thousand to a mere bagatelle of two thousand (not knowing the Slavonian word "tma" = 10,000).

THE CONTENTS

OF

THE GENERAL MENAION.

CHAPTER.	PAGE.
I. THE FESTIVALS OF OUR LORD JESUS CHRIST	1
II. THE FESTIVALS OF THE HOLY VIRGIN	13
III. THE FESTIVALS OF THE CROSS	24
IV. THE GENERAL SERVICE TO THE HOLY ANGELS AND OTHER BODILESS ONES	34
V. THE GENERAL SERVICE TO JOHN THE BAPTIST	47
VI. THE GENERAL SERVICE OF THE HOLY FATHERS	58
VII. THE GENERAL SERVICE TO A PROPHET	69
VIII. THE GENERAL SERVICE TO ONE APOSTLE	79
IX. THE GENERAL SERVICE TO APOSTLES	89
X. THE GENERAL SERVICE TO ONE HIERARCH	99
XI. THE GENERAL SERVICE TO HIERARCHS	110
XII. THE GENERAL SERVICE TO A MONK	119
XIII. THE GENERAL SERVICE TO TWO OR MORE MONKS	129
XIV. THE GENERAL SERVICE TO ONE MARTYR	139
XV. THE GENERAL SERVICE TO TWO OR MORE MARTYRS	150
XVI. THE GENERAL SERVICE TO ONE HIEROMARTYR	160
XVII. THE GENERAL SERVICE TO TWO OR MORE HIEROMARTYRS	170
XVIII. THE GENERAL SERVICE TO A MONK-MARTYR	181
XIX. THE GENERAL SERVICE TO TWO OR MORE MONK-MARTYRS	192
XX. THE GENERAL SERVICE TO A FEMALE MARTYR	203
XXI. THE GENERAL SERVICE TO TWO OR MORE FEMALE MARTYRS	213
XXII. THE GENERAL SERVICE TO A NUN	223
XXIII. THE GENERAL SERVICE TO TWO OR MORE NUNS	232
XXIV. THE GENERAL SERVICE TO A NUN-MARTYR	242
XXV. THE GENERAL SERVICE TO A HIERO-CONFESSOR OR MONK-CONFESSOR	253
XXVI. THE GENERAL SERVICE TO THE UNMERCENARIES AND WONDER-WORKERS	263
XXVII. THE GENERAL SERVICE TO THE FOOLISH FOR CHRIST'S SAKE	272
APPENDIX	282

CHAPTER I.

GENERAL SERVICE FOR THE FESTIVALS OF OUR LORD JESUS CHRIST,

AS WELL AS PREPARATIONS THERETO AND OCTAVES THEREOF.

At the Vespers, for O Lord, I have cried, the Stichera, Tone 6.
Similar to : O Lord, the grave of Lazarus...

Thou, O Lord, that dost fill up every thing with Thy Divinity and through Thy clemency hast united Thyself unto men, one of the two natures being invisible,—hast become visible after Thy coming out of the pure one and dost shew the image of Thy bodily form in Thy (*name of the event*); thereunto having come we adore Thee, O Master, and knowing Thee as the Maker, we pray: Blessed art Thou, O Saviour, have mercy upon us. *Twice.*

O Lord, the incomprehensible mystery of Thine economy which was forecast from the beginning, Thou dost in Thy coming make known and in assurance thereof hast Thou shewn unto the world Thy divine (*name of the event*); Thou hast filled everything with joy and renewed afresh the nature of man, desiring to save him: Blessed art Thou, O God, have mercy upon us. *Twice.*

O Lord, most glorious is the condescension of Thy compassion! Dwelling on high in the bosom of the Father as indescribable and incomprehensible, on Thy coming to the earth-born Thou wast seen now; wherefore we honour Thy festival (*name of the event*), that Thou mayest deliver us from passions who on account of it honour Thee, the Master, that hast revivified us from death through sins. Blessed art Thou, O Saviour, have mercy upon us. *Twice.*

O Lord, Thou didst become incarnate as Thou desiredst, having been pleased to show both our indigence and abundance of Thy compassion, whereby Thou hast deified me—the earth. We glorify Thee, O Lover of man, seeing the example of Thine economy in Thy (*name of the event*). Do grant therewithal unhindered entry into Eden unto Thy servants, overlooking all their sins. *Twice.*

Glory...Both now... Tone 8:

O Master, Lover of man! Great is the depth of Thine economy; from generation to generation dost Thou benefit Thy creation; without forsaking the bosom of the Father, as man in the flesh didst Thou appear on earth and hast come calling all to repentance. As the King and God we adore Thee, since Thou destroyest our enemies and savest Thine endurable people who celebrate Thy honoured (*name of the event.*) *The Prokeimenon of the day.*

The Reading from the Book of Exodus (20, 12-18).

The Lord said unto Moses: Come up to Me into the mount and be there; and I will give thee tables of stone, and a law, and commandments which I have written that thou mayest teach them. And Moses and his minister Joshua rose up and went up into the mount of God, and Moses said unto the elders: Tarry ye here for us until we come again unto you; and, behold, Aaron and Hur are with you; if any man have any matters to do, let him come unto them. And Moses went up into the mount, and a cloud covered the mount. And the glory of the Lord came down upon Mount Sinai, and the cloud covered it six days. And the seventh day the Lord called unto Moses out of the midst of the cloud. And the sight of the glory of the Lord was like a devouring fire on the top of the mount in the eyes of the children of Israel. And Moses went into the midst of the cloud and gat him up into the mount; and was in the mount forty days and forty nights.

The Reading from the Book of Deuteronomy (4, 1. 6-15).

Moses said unto the people: Now hearken, O Israel, unto the statutes and unto the judgments which I teach you for to do them, that ye may live. Keep therefore and do them; for this is your wisdom and your understanding in the sight of the nations, which shall hear all these statutes and say: surely this great nation is a wise and understanding people, as the Lord our God is in all things that we call upon Him for. And now take heed to yourselves, all ye the house of Israel, and keep your souls diligently, lest ye forget the things which your eyes have seen, and lest they depart from your hearts all the days of your life. But teach them your sons and your sons' sons, specially the day that ye stood before the Lord your God in Horeb, when the Lord said unto me: Gather me the people together and I will make them hear my words, that they may learn to fear me all the days that they shall live upon the earth, and that they may teach their children. And ye came near and stood under the mountain, and the mountain burned with fire unto the midst of heaven, with darkness, clouds and thick darkness. And the Lord spake unto you out of the midst of the fire: ye heard the voice of the words, but saw no similitude, only ye heard a voice. And He declared unto you His covenant, which He commanded you to perform. And the Lord commanded me at that time to teach you statutes and judgments that ye might do them in the land. The Lord spake unto you in Horeb out of the midst of the fire.

The Reading from the Book of Deuteronomy (5, 1-7. 9. 10. 23-26. 28; 6, 1. 2. 4. 5. 13. 18).

Moses called all Israel, and said unto them: Hear, O Israel the statutes and judgments which I speak in your ears this day, that ye may learn them and keep and do them. The Lord God made a covenant with you in Horeb, not with your fathers alone did the Lord make His covenant, but with you also. The Lord talked face to face in Horeb out of the midst of the fire, and I stood between the Lord and you at that time to declare unto you the words of the Lord saying: I am the Lord thy God, which brought thee out of the land of Egypt, from the house of bondage; there are no others gods beside Me, for I the Lord thy God am a jealous God, shewing mercy unto thousands of them that love Me and keep My commandments. And it came to pass when ye heard the voice out of the midst of fire, and the mountain did burn with fire, that ye all came near unto me, and ye said: Behold, the Lord our God hath shewed us His glory, and we have heard His voice out of the midst of the fire. We have seen this day that God doth talk with man and he liveth. Now, why should we die? for this great fire will consume us; if we hear the voice of the Lord our God any more, then we shall die. For who is there of all flesh, that hath heard the voice of the Lord speaking out of the midst of the fire, and liveth? And the Lord heard the voice of your words, when ye spake unto me, and I said unto you all the commandments, the statutes and the judgments which the Lord commanded you that ye might fear all His statutes, that He may be merciful unto you and that ye may increase in the land. Hear, O Israel, the Lord your God is one Lord. And thou shalt love the Lord thy God with all thy thought, with all thy heart, with all thy soul and with all thy might; thou shalt fear Him and serve Him alone, cleave unto Him, thou shalt swear by His name and shalt do that which is good in His sight, that it may be well with thee.

With the Versicles, the Stichera, Tone 2. Similar to : O house of Ophrah...

The illumination hath come; the grace appeared and the deliverance arrived, the world hath been enlightened; be filled with joy, O ye people.

The Verse: *God came from Teman, and the Holy One from mount Paran.* O sing ye, the kindreds of the nations, sending up praise and glory unto Christ the God, diligently hasting and glorifying Thy (*name of the event*)

The Verse: O Lord, I heard Thy speech and feared. The word of God by Whom all things were made, the Impassive and Ineffable, in one Hypostasis, but in two natures, hath come to save humanity.

Glory...Both now...Tone 8 : O Lord, desiring to fulfil what Thou hast ordained from the beginning, Thou hast selected from among all Thy creatures ministers of Thy mystery: from angels —Gabriel, from man—the Virgin, from heavens—the star, from earth—the mountain, from wilderness—the manger, from waters —the Jordan in which Thou hast destroyed the impious deeds of all; O our Saviour, glory to Thee. *The Troparion of the Festival, but if there be none, say the general Troparion, Tone* 2: Thine undefiled Icon we adore...

At the Matins, for God is the Lord, the same Troparion thrice.

After the 1st Stichologia, the Cathisma, Tone 1. Similar to: Thy sepulchre...

Thy grace hath been poured upon us, O Saviour, when Thou, Incomprehensible One, becamest visible, and the darkness of illusion hath disappeared. Wherefore do Thou set our steps in the light of Thy countenance, so that, walking in accordance with Thy commandments, we may be made worthy to see Thee, the Light unapproachable. [*Glory...Both now...the same.*

After the 2nd Stichologia, the Cathisma, Tone 5. Similar to:
The Co-unoriginate...

The Co-unoriginate Son of the Father and Ever-existing, Invisible in Thy nature and Intactable, having come under the conditions of time, Thou hast, through Thine ineffable goodness, left us, O Master, of Thy circumscribed body the sweet image in (*name of the event*) for the salvation of our souls. *Glory ...Both now...the same.*

The Refrain (Magnificat) of the Festival.
After the Polyleon, the Cathisma, Tone 4. Similar to:
Thou that hast ascended...

There is no longer lamentation in the countenance of Adam, since Adam was put on by His Maker, Who appeareth unto all in the likeness of Adam's countenance and moveth the communities of the pious unto love that they may with one voice hymn: Glory, O Master, Lover of man, to Thine extreme condescension.

Glory...Both now...the Graduals, the 1st Antiphon of the 4th Tone. The Prokeimenon:

O Lord, we shall walk in the light of Thy countenance, and in Thy name shall we rejoice unto the ages. *The Verse:* All the ends of the earth have seen the salvation of our God. *The Gospel of the Festival that happeneth to be. After the 50th Psalm, the Sticheron, Tone* 8. O Lord, desiring to fulfil...(*see Glory ...with the Versicles*).

The Canon, Tone 4. *The Heirmoi twice and the Troparia in* 12. *Ode* 1. *The Heirmos:*

Unto Him that of old hath instructed Israel running away from Pharaoh's bondage, and hath fed them in the wilderness, unto our God, the Deliverer, let us sing; for He is glorified.

On the day set apart for our festival let us, O people, open our mouths and expound with our tongues the divine manifestation of Christ our God in (*name of the event*) cheerfully singing: For He is glorified.

The Light Ever-existing, carrying out the words of the Father and desiring to shew His grace, hath taken the form of a servant for our sake and manifested Himself in the manner of His divine (*name of the event*), highly illumining us with light.

O come ye all, let us in faith celebrate Christ's (*name of the event*), and intelligently offering the divine melody, let us glorify Him and vociferate harmoniously: Christ is come unto the restoration of the darkened. Let us sing unto Him, for He is glorified. [*The Theotokion:*

This day's manifestation of the birth of the God incarnate we have truly learned through thee, O all-pure one, and honouring thee were accounted worthy to behold (*name of the event*) of thy Son; Whom supplicate to save us from every danger.

For the Catabasia either the Heirmoi of the Festival or the following:

Covered with divine darkness, the one slow of speech hath proclaimed the God-written law, for, having thrown the mire off his mental eye, he doth see the Existing One and acquireth knowledge of the Spirit, praising with divine songs.

Ode 3. *The Heirmos:*

Neither in wisdom, nor in power and riches we glory, but in Thee, O Christ, the Hypostatic Wisdom of the Father, for there is no one more holy than Thou art, O Lover of man.

Master by nature, Thou, O Christ, didst unite Thyself unto

Thy servants and becamest visible, working for us various forms of salvation which we now glorify in Thy (*name of the event*), for there is no one more holy than Thou art, O Lover of man.

Thy people, O Christ, who are enlightened by the faith in Thee, brightly celebrate Thy divine festival (*name of the event*); honouring which we get delivered from dangers; vouchsafe unto us, O Saviour, the Kingdom of heaven also.

O Life Hypostatical! Having now tasted of death in the flesh and thereby made life to flow unto the dead, Thou hast, O Christ, granted us as meditator of life Thine awaking and Thy (*name of the event*).   [*The Theotokion* :

The salvation hath before shone forth in the flesh out of thee in the world, and now unto the faithful through thee, O God's Mother, the life appeared in Christ's light-bearing (*name of the event*) ; for the sake thereof do, O Theotokos, supplicate thy Son to deliver us from dangers and from everlasting torments.

The Catabasia : The fetters of the childless womb, and the unbearable insults from a fruitful foe have of old been done away with in the case of Anna the prophetess solely by her prayer, brought with an afflicted spirit unto the Mighty One and God of wisdom.

The Cathisma, Tone 4. *Similar to :* Thou that wast lifted up on the cross...

We implore Thee, O Master and Merciful Saviour, to deliver from all enemies both visible and invisible, from incursions of other nations and from all manner of dangers and confusion, us who in faith and with love celebrate Thy divine (*name of the event*) ; for the sake thereof do vouchsafe that we may obtain the enjoyment of eternal good things.   [*Glory...Both now...the same.*

Ode 4. *The Heirmos* :

Perceiving the unfathomable divine council with regard to the incarnation from the virgin of Thee, the High One, the prophet Habbakuk called out : Glory to Thy might, O Lord.

The divine festival of One Who in the flesh drew so near unto men, as a light hath come to the newly elected Israel and enlighteneth to day the ends of the whole world by His (*name of the event*): Glory to Thy might, O Lord.

Having been illumined, Moses was of old made worthy to see God's glory in Thy signs, and the new Israel doth now behold Thee, the Deliverer, clearly face to face: Glory to Thy might, O Lord.

Behold, all ye people, the wonderful things, rejoice now in spirit, hymning (*name of the event*) of Christ, Who hath appeared on earth unto men for their salvation: Glory to Thy might, O Lord. [*The Theotokion:*

O most pure Theotokos, save us that flee unto thee and celebrate Thy Son's divine (*name of the event*), and always supplicate Him to grant us remission of sins. [*The Catabasia:*

O King of Kings, Sole from the only One, the Only Word of the Uncaused Father, Thou in Thy bounty hast truly sent down Thy Co-equal in might Spirit upon the apostles that hymn Thee: Glory to Thy might, O Lord.

Ode 5. *The Heirmos:*

Thou Who hast dispersed the primordiate light that the works may in the light hymn Thee, O Christ, as the Creator, do in Thy light direct our paths.

Let us to-day clap our hands and shout with our voices the praises of the Lord, for, behold, He hath truly appeared, enlightening all the faithful with the divine (*name of the event*) of His most pure body.

The assemblies of the faithful are to-day enlightened and the bands of heretics put to shame at the sight of the adoration of (*name of the event*) of Christ, the Deliverer having assumed the bodily form.

The festivity is come and the great mystery hath shone forth light from the countenance of the Lord in the well-arranged festival of the divine (*name of the event*) of the Lord, for therewithal were granted unto all the captives peace and joy.

The Theotokion: Let the clouds drop sweetness from above unto the earthly, at thine intercession, O most holy Virgin; having taken compassion of the world, thy Son and our God hath to-day raised the horn of the christians; to-day hath He granted salvation unto the faithful by his divine (*name of the event*). [*The Catabasia:*

O ye, illustrious children of the church! Receive the fire-breathing dew of the Spirit for the perfect purification of sins, for now from Zion hath gone forth the law—the grace of the Spirit in the shape of the tongues of fire.

Ode 6. *The Heirmos:*

Celebrating this divine and all-honourable feast of the Mother of God, come ye Godly-wise, let us clap our hands, glorifying the God that was born of her.

Life hath shone forth unto the dead, and light hath come unto those that were already blind, and unto those grievously afflicted hath sprung up a cure, and salvation hath come nigh unto all through the lightbearing (*name of the event*) of Christ.

Let every intelligence rejoice, now clearly seeing the spiritual festival of the divine (*name of the event*), which doth shed enlightenment unto those that adore Him.

O Lord, the heavens, seeing Thee, declare Thy glory, O Jesus Christ, they call together all Thy faithful to the hymning of Thy divine (*name of the event*), and those that are to come unto the knowledge of true repentance. [*The Theotokion:*

O Mother of God! there appeared unto the nations a sign and sure salvation, O pure Virgin, in the light of the honoured (*name of the event*) of Thy Son; Him supplicate to save us that recall Thee, and deliver from dangers and incursions of pagans with thine intercessions. [*The Catabasia:*

O Christ! Thou hast shone forth from the Virgin unto us, O Master, as propitiation and salvation, that, just as once the prophet Jonah out of the belly of a sea-monster, Thou mightest rescue from corruption Adam, fallen with all his race.

The Contakion of the Festival; but if there be none, say the following Contakion, Tone 2:

O uncircumscribed Word of the Father! knowing Thine undrawn by hand, but God-made icon to be the trophy of Thine ineffable and divine economy respecting men and of Thine undoubted incarnation, we honour Thee in kissing it.

The Oikos: Giving assurance unto men of the mystery of His incarnation, the Lord becometh Himself circumscribed by His God-and-man form; the Archetype thereof doth He seat on the Father's throne to be worshipped of the bodiless angels, and the adoration of an image of the Archetype hath He granted unto us; which embracing with our souls and hearts, we honour Him in kissing it.

FESTIVALS OF OUR LORD JESUS CHRIST.

Ode 7. The Heirmos:

The Abrahamic youths have once in Babylon trodden under their feet the flame of the furnace, calling out in songs: O God of our fathers, blessed art Thou.

Every city and country rejoice together with the new Zion in faithful celebration; for the King of her glory, Christ, hath come in the form of His venerable festival (*name of the event*) and saveth those that adore Him and vociferate: O God of our fathers, blessed art Thou.

The sayings of the God-voiced prophets have been fulfilled in the Holy Scriptures, for now we see the accomplishment in Christ's (*name of the event*); thereby is the world enlightened and with its brilliant shine are saved those that sing: O God of our fathers, blessed art Thou. [*The Theotokion:*

With the earthly the heavenly are rejoicing, and the multitude of all the saints participate in the rejoicings; both the kings and princes, the rich and poor—we are all celebrating; for Christ hath prepared for us an enlightenment in the picture of His festival—the god-effecting similitude which He hath received from the Virgin. [*The Catabasia:*

Harmoniously have once resounded the instruments in honour of the golden-made, lifeless idol, and the light-bearing grace of the Comforter doth animate to the vociferation: O Sole Trinity, equal in might, unoriginate, blessed art Thou.

Ode 8. The Heirmos:

The youths in Babylon, burning with the divine zeal, have manfully scorned both the tyrant and the flame, and being thrown into the midst of the fire, but bedewed, sung: Bless the Lord, all ye the works of the Lord.

Being perfect God by nature, Thou wast seen a perfect man also, preserving in both natures their properties, and as God giving assurance of the divine (*name of the event*) in the flesh; Him adoring we sing: Bless the Lord, all ye the works of the Lord.

Exalt the horn, O Word of God, of those who confess Thee to be God and man and who glorify Thy (*name of the event*), wherewith Thou hast vouchsafed unto all the faithful the life eternal and made of no effect the rage of the pagans, haters of Thy divine might.

The new law shineth and the church is adorned, for the light of Thy divine glory, O Christ the God, hath gone forth and manifested Thy light-like countenance in Thy (*name of the event*) unto the salvation of Thy people that vociferate unto Thee: Bless the Lord, all ye the works of the Lord. [*The Theotokion:*

O Thou, restoration of the fallen, joy of the despairing, instructress of those gone astray, healer of the sick and salvation for all Christians—do preserve, O Sovereign-Lady Theotokos, us that honour [*name of the event*) of Thy Son; supplicate of Him that we may be delivered from the incursions of foreign nations.

The Catabasia: The triply-shining form of Godhead looseth the chains and bedeweth the flame; the youths hymn and the whole creation blesseth the Only Saviour and Maker as Benefactor.

Ode 9. The Heirmos:

Thy bringing forth hath proved incorrupt: God hath passed out of thy loins, as flesh-bearer did He appear on earth and hath lived among men; wherefore we all magnify thee, O Theotokos.

Let us sing an ode of thanksgiving unto the Lord who was pleased to grant us exceedingly abundant riches in (*name of the event*) of His divine flesh which in battles affordeth so strong a support and honouring which we the faithful magnify Thee.

O the wonders above understanding which Thou, O Lord, hast made for us that trust in Thee! For just as (*name of the event*) was, Thou hast ineffably and awfully shown unto all the image thereof; do deliver those that honour it, from every anger and fall.

O Word of God, Wisdom and Might and Image of the Father! O God comprehensible! Do make us worthy to accomplish the joyful celebration of Thy festival (*name of the event*) in the light of good works, spiritually magnifying Thee.

The Theotokion: Truly thy height, O most pure one, is that of the mystery of God and the depth that of the divine and ineffable wisdom. For the Most High was unspeakably born of thee and the Invisible One became Visible in His fleshly (*name of the event*); adoring which we the faithful magnify thee.

The Catabasia: Hail thou, O Queen, the glory of both mother and maiden, for no mouth, however fluent and well-spoken, can be so eloquent as worthily to hymn thee, and every mind faileth to comprehend thy bringing forth; wherefore we with one voice glorify thee.

The Photagogicon. Similar to: Hear, O ye women...

A mystery—the greatest and withheld from angels, through the benevolence of the Father and the working of the Holy Spirit was accomplished as a fulfilment of prophecy: the Unoriginate Word having accepted an origin, as a man was born of the Virgin for the salvation of the world and unto the redemption of mankind. [*Thrice.*

With the Lauds, the Stichera. Tone 1. Similar to: Of the heavenly orders...

O come ye all, let us in faith celebrate Christ's (*name of the event*), and offering intelligent hymns expressive of divine doxology, let us with one voice call out: Christ is come—the salvation and restoration unto the earth. [*Twice.*

O come, let us with festive odes and mental rectitude glorify the (*name of the event*) of Christ, for being of equal honour with the Father and the Holy Spirit, He hath put on our compound on account of His commiseration; which we unspeakably celebrate together with the angels.

Let us with our mouths proclaim, on cymbals and in odes acclaim: The (*name of the event*) of Christ hath appeared; the preaching of the prophets hath found its fulfilment, since they foreannounced His appearance in the flesh among men, for our salvation and restoration.

Glory...Both now... Tone 1. The Idiomelic Sticheron:

O come, let us, O people, celebrate Christ's (*name of the event*), let us concentrate our minds and feelings and we shall see Him who hath taken His flesh from the pure Virgin, being perfect Son both in his Godhead and humanity; wherefore let us call: O Holy God—the Father Unoriginate, O Holy Mighty—the Son Incarnate, O Holy Immortal—the Comforting Spirit—the Holy Trinity—glory to Thee.

The great Doxology and the Dismission. At the Liturgy, with the Beatitudes, the Odes 3rd and 6th of the Canon.

CHAPTER II.

THE SERVICE COMMON TO THE FESTIVALS OF THE HOLY VIRGIN.

For O Lord, I have cried, the following Stichera Tone 4.
Similar to : Thou hast given a token...

With divine workings dost Thou preserve and shelter from incursions of the enemy those that lovingly celebrate Thine all-glorious (*name of the event*) and call unto Thee : Thou art our strength and stablishment and Thy Son our God is the God-becoming delight, Whom adoring we say: O Jesu all-powerful, save our souls as Compassionate One!

To-day being divinely gathered together let us praise the Theotokos. O most holy Virgin, many are thy grandeurs and abyss-full are thy wonders, for thou art holy protection, praise and glory and source of healing unto us also that celebrate thy holy (*name of the event*); wherefore praying we say: O Jesu all powerful, save our souls as Compassionate One.

Do thou, O most holy one, with thy honourable supplications both shelter and preserve, and unto the enemies—as fearful and unsubduable shew those that make a festival of thy (*name of the event*), that we may call unto thy Son: O Jesu all-powerful, save us as Compassionate One! [*Glory...Both now...Tone* 6.

As with a most brilliant circle, with thy (*name of the event*), O most holy Theotokos, the Church of God hath been surrounded and shining for joy and secretly exulting doth to-day call aloud unto thee, O Sovereign-Lady : Hail thou—O precious diadem and crown of God's glory ; hail—the only fulfilment of the glory and the eternal gladness ; hail—the haven unto those that flee to thee, mediatrix and the salvation of our souls.

The Entrance. The Prokeimenon of the day.
The Reading from the Book of Genesis (28, 10-17).

Jacob went out from Beersheba, and went toward Haran. And he lighted upon a certain place, and tarried there all night, because the sun was set; and he took of the stones of that place, and put them for his pillows, and lay down in that place to sleep. And he dreamed, and, behold, a ladder set up on the earth, and the top of it reached to heaven; and, behold, the angels of God ascending and descending on it. And, behold, the Lord stood above it, and said: I am the Lord God of Abraham thy father and the God of Isaac; be not afraid: the land whereon thou liest, to thee will I give it, and to thy seed; and thy seed shall be as dust of the earth, and thou shalt spread abroad to the west, and to the east, and to the north, and to the south; and in thee and in thy seed shall all the families of the earth be blessed. And, behold, I am with thee, and will keep thee in all places whither thou goest, and will bring thee again into this land; for I will not leave thee, until I have done that which I have spoken to thee of. And Jacob awaked out of his sleep and he said: Surely the Lord is in this place, and I knew it not. And he was afraid, and said: How dreadful is this place! this is none other but the house of God, and this is the gate of heaven.

The Reading from the prophecy of Ezekiel (43, 27. and 44, 1-4).

Thus saith the Lord: upon the eighth day and so forward, the priests shall make your burnt offerings upon the altar, and your peace offerings, and I will accept you, saith the Lord God. Then He brought me back the way of the gate of the outward sanctuary which looketh toward the east; and it was shut. Then said the Lord unto me: This gate shall be shut, it shall not be opened, and no man shall enter in by it; because the Lord, the God of Israel hath entered in by it, therefore it shall be shut. As for the Prince, he shall sit in it to eat bread before the Lord; he shall enter by the way of the porch of that gate, and shall go out by the way of the same. Then brought He me the way of the north gate before the house, and I looked, and, behold, the glory of the Lord filled the house of the Lord.

The Reading from the Proverbs (9, 1-11).

Wisdom hath builded her house, and hath fixed the seven pillars thereof. She hath killed her beasts; she hath mingled her wine; she hath also furnished her table. She hath sent forth her maidens. She crieth upon the highest places of the city: whoso is single, let him turn in hither; as for them that want understanding, she saith unto them: come, eat of my bread and drink of the wine which I have mingled. Forsake foolishness, and ye shall live, and go in search of understanding that ye may live, and improve understanding in knowledge. He that reproveth a scorner getteth to himself shame; and he that rebuketh a wicked man getteth himself a blot, for rebukes unto the wicked are as wounds to him. Reprove not a scorner, lest he hate thee; rebuke a wise man, and he will love thee. Give instruction to a wise man, and he will be yet wiser; teach a just man, and he will increase in learning. The fear of the Lord is the beginning of wisdom, and the knowledge of the holy is understanding. For understanding of the law proceedeth from a good thought, for in this wise thy days shall be multiplied, and the years of thy life shall be increased.

For Versicles, the Stichera, Tone 3.

Come, O ye all the ends of the earth, and the honourable (*name of the event*) of the Mother of God let us glorify, for lifting up her hands to her Son doth she pray; wherefore with her holy (*name of the event*) the world is revivified; with psalms, and hymns and spiritual odes, let us joyfully celebrate with all the saints.

The Versicle: Unto the King shall virgins be brought in her train, and her companions shall be brought unto thee. Greatly hath God adorned thee with beauty since in the midst of men He placed the Light in thine arms. Do thou, that art alone in His light, the hope of Christians, the help unto those afflicted with wants and sorrows, and the haven for those labouring in the deep, entreat that may be delivered from afflictions those who lovingly hymn thy (*name of the event*) all-honoured.

The Versicle: Hearken, O daughter, and look and incline thine ear. Thine all-honoured (*name of the event*), O all-holy and pure Virgin, is glorified both by angels in the heavens and by the race of man on earth, for thou wast the Mother of the Maker of all, Christ the God. Him to entreat for us do not cease, pray we, that have in thee, next to God, placed our trust, O Theotokos, most highly praised and innocent of marital intercourse.

Glory...Both now...Tone 2. Having purged our thoughts and minds, we, together with angels, joyfully celebrate the Virgin— the Bride of the King of all, Christ our God, beginning with the David's hymn and saying: Arise, O Lord, in Thy repose, Thou and the ark of Thy sanctuary. As a beautiful chamber hast Thou adorned her and numbered her unto Thy city, O Master, to rear and to shelter from the inimical pagans, by the mighty power, through her entreaties.

The Troparion of the Festival from the Typicon. If there be no Typicon, say the following Troparion, Tone 4.

To the Theotokos let us, sinners and humbled, now flee and in penitence fall down before her calling out of the depth of our souls: O Sovereign Lady, help us taking pity on us, do hasten to our assistance as we are perishing from the multitude of our transgressions; neither turn thy servants empty away, for thou art the only hope that we have.

Glory...Both now... We shall never cease, although unworthy, to proclaim thy powers, O Theotokos; for if thou didst not intercede with thine entreaties, who should have delivered us from so many dangers? and who should have preserved us in freedom until now? we shall never turn away from thee, for thy servants dost thou always deliver from all manner of evils.

At the Matins, for " God is the Lord," the Troparion twice; Glory...Both now : We shall never cease...Once.

After the 1st Stichologia, the Cathisma, Tone 4. Similar to : Thou hast appeared to-day...

Auroras like hath shone forth the world-wide joy of thy (*name of the event*), O Virgin Mother, Mary. Do thou enlighten on earth the thoughts of those who lovingly hymn thee.

Glory...Both now...the same.

After the 2nd Stichologia, the Cathisma, Tone 4. Similar to :
Amazed...

The Virgin Mary that is truly Theotokos hath shone forth unto us as a bright cloud; therewithall Adam is no longer condemned and Eve is released from bonds; wherefore we also cry out unto the only pure one, with boldness vociferating: O most holy Virgin, entreat thy Son to grant us remission of sins.

Glory...Both now...the same. After Praise ye the name of the Lord...the Refrain:

Let us bring unto the Theotokos every spiritual hymn. *The selected Psalm:* Remember David, O Lord, and all his affliction. *...After the Polyeleon, the Cathisma, Tone* 1. *Similar to:* The angelic hosts were upon Thy tomb-stone...

The ear of thy virginal womb proved to be beautiful, for thou hast given birth unto the Life of the world; wherefore the heavenly powers vociferate unto thee, O Theotokos, praising thy venerated festival, O most pure one. Glory unto thy (*name of the event*); glory to thy virginity, O Mother, that knewest not a man. [*Glory...Both now...the same.*

The Graduals, the 1st Antiphon of the 4th Tone. The Prokeimenon, Tone 4:

I will make thy name to be remembered in all generations. *The Verse:* My heart hath poured forth a good word, I speak of my doings unto the King. Every breath...

[*The Gospel, St. Luke* 10, 38-42; 11, 27-28.

After the 50th Psalm, the Sticheron, Tone 6:

To-day the gates of heaven are opening and the divine door moveth forth. To-day the grace of gladness beginneth, shewing forth unto the world (*name of the event*) of the Mother of God, through whom the earthly things become united with the heavenly, unto the salvation of our souls.

The Canon of the All-holy Theotokos, Tone 8. *The Heirmoi to be said twice; the Troparia* 12 *times. Ode* 1. *The Heirmos.*

Having crossed the water as if it were dry land and having escaped the evils of Egypt, the Israelites cried out: Let us sing unto our Deliverer and our God.

Do thou graciously strengthen me with God's power joyfully to sing thy (*name of the event*), O most pure one,—the protection of thy city, and unto all thy people, O all-holy one, invincible dominion and stability unto thy flock.

Benignity and mercy do we draw with thine entreaties, for thou hast brought forth God, the Mighty One, Who saveth all the pious through thine intercessions, O most spotless one; for His sake we all glorify thee, O Sovereign-Lady.

Thy divine (*name of the event*) do we celebrate, since through thee, O most pure Theotokos, have been granted incorruptible salvation, indestructible joy and hope, shelter and dominion and a refuge unto our souls.

Under thy shelter, O Sovereign-Lady, do we—thy people—flee. Be thou, O most spotless one, a help unto us, thy servants, and transmit supplication for salvation of those that lovingly hymn thee.

The Catabasia : I will open my mouth.

Ode 3. The Heirmos.

O Lord, the roofer of the heavenly firmament and the founder of the church, do Thou stablish me in Thy love, Thou—the end of the desires, the stablishing of the faithful, the only Lover of man.

Let us with faith renew the hearts on (*name of the event*) of the holy Theotokos. Vouchsafing unto all that in faith pray for deliverance, do thou, O most pure one, protect us from the enemies, both visible and invisible.

Thou dost graciously sanctify those that in faith flee into thy temple and in love fall down before thy (*name of the event*). Do thou deliver us from all dangers and grant victories unto our Emperor (*mentioned by name*) over the pagans, and make gracious unto us thy Son and our God.

Having become incarnate of thee, God the Word hath made a house for Himself in thy holy womb and was pleased to be born, as He desired, and granted unto us to see the day of thy (*name of the event*); which lovingly celebrating, we do send our supplications unto thee.

With gladsome souls and joyful hearts we have directed our intelligence unto thy honoured and divine (*name of the event*), and we all the faithful, pray unto thee, O Theotokos, since thou hast suckled with thy milk thy most pure Son that feedeth us with His mercy.

The Cathisma, Tone 4:

Thy church doth festively celebrate thy glorious (*name of the event*), and we, all the faithful, in hymning thee, diligently call unto thee, O pure Virgin, to strengthen all the faithful against the power of the enemy, to destroy the counsels of the wicked, and to direct our lives so that we do the divine will of thy Son.

Glory...Both now...the same.

Ode 4. The Heirmos:

I have hearkened, O Lord, unto the mystery of Thine Economy, comprehended Thy works and glorified Thy Godhead.

Since thou, O Virgin pure, hast passed over unto the never-setting Light, in praying unto thy Son and our God, remember also us who are celebrating thy honoured (*name of the event*) that He may grant us the remission of sins.

As the resplendent sun, in crossing the horizon, shineth forth, so doth also thy divine festival emit the rays, and driving away from us the darkness of passions, imparteth cleansing unto our souls and deliverance from dangers.

Now the darkness of the evil is dispersed and as light both of the sun and soul the festival of thy honoured (*name of the event*), O all-spotless Mother of God, shineth forth, which we do piously celebrate.

Thou art, O most pure and most spotless Mother hymned of all, the great refuge and praise, thou art the ark of the intellectual sanctity and the inexhaustible source of cures unto those that venerate thy honoured (*name of the event*).

Ode 5. The Heirmos.

Wherefore hast Thou driven me away from Thy presence, O never-setting Light, and a strange darkness hath overcome me, the wretched one? Do, however, turn me and set my paths unto the light of Thy commandments, I implore Thee.

Unto those that flee to thee for refuge everything becometh full of holiness, and we, faithful, obtaining pardon, celebrate thy honoured (*name of the event*), whereon we entreat thee to grant us grace and mercy in the day of judgment.

Adorned with the purity of virginity wast thou that gavest birth unto the Fair One, thy Son and our God; do thou adorn the festival of thy honoured (*name of the event*) and gladden the hierarchical order; subdue unto our Emperor the foreign races and deliver from all dangers thy people.

As another paradise possessing in its midst the flower of sweet smell, becometh known thy honoured festival; with a divine sweet smell doth it fill the hearts of the faithful that lovingly venerate thee, O most spotless Sovereign-Lady.

A cloud wast thou, O Virgin, unto the divine rain, O most spotless Sovereign-Lady, pouring down the water of salvation with which was filled the earth dried with sins, and bringing unto the creation the fruit of virtue; wherefore we glorify thee.

Ode 6. *The Heirmos:*

Cleanse me, O Saviour, for many are my transgressions, and lead me up from the depth of evils, I implore Thee, for unto Thee have I cried, and hearken to me, O God of my salvation.

Him that existed before all ages, hast thou as a babe brought forth and hast rejuvenated our hearts which were decayed through many sins; accept also the renewal of our hymnology which is being offered unto Thy festival, O all-holy Theotokos.

Holy is thy temple and truly wonderful is thy most honoured (*name of the event*) which we celebrate therein; granting unto all that glorify thee, O most pure one, the cures for their hearts, do also preserve thy servants from all dangers.

Every soul rejoiceth at coming together in thy temple, and thy festival we celebrate, hymning, O Virgin Theotokos, thy honoured (*name of the event*) that is resplendent as a sun and shineth with light through the grace of God's Spirit. Do thou illumine us also and enlighten our hearts, O Virgin-Mother, Sovereign-Lady.

We hymn thy most honoured (*name of the event*) and reverence thy spotless conception and birth, O God's Bride and Maiden; with us do the angelic orders and the choirs of all saints glorify thee. *Thereupon the Contakion of the Festival which happeneth to be. But if there be none, say the following Contakion, Tone 1.*

Thou that wast above word and understanding the honoured dwelling of the ineffable divine nature and art the joint security for sinners, that grantest grace and cure as the Mother of the

King of all, do thou entreat thy Son that we may obtain mercy in the day of judgment.

Another Contakion, Tone 6:

We have no other help, we have no other hope but thee, O Sovereign-Lady; do thou help us, in thee we trust, and in thee we glory; since we are thy servants, let us not be put to shame.

The Oikos: Let us lovingly cry unto the Theotokos: Hail thou, O Lord's city; hail thou, O David's sceptre; hail thou, O intellectual palace; hail thou, O pot of the divine manna; hail thou, O unconsumed bush; hail thou, O golden candlestick; hail thou, O inextinguishable candle; hail thou, O God's overshadowed mountain; hail thou, O fire-bearing throne; hail thou, O heavenly ladder and door; hail thou, O Aaron's rod that sprouted without moisture; hail thou that savest all from all dangers and afflictions. Do entreat, O most pure one, thy Son that we may obtain mercy in the day of judgment.

Ode 7. *The Heirmos:*

Through God's descent the fire in Babylon did once become softened; wherefore the youths dancing with joyful step in the furnace as if it were a flowery lawn, sung: Blessed art Thou, O God of our fathers.

As the Queen of all having come, thou hast set unto our glory the heavenly shelter of thy divine festival (*name of the event*); therewith we obtain deliverance from the irruption of the invisible enemies, crying out unto thy Son: Blessed is the God of our fathers.

With thy nativity, O Sovereign Theotokos and Virgin, and with all thy festivals the cycle of the year is crowned. Do now adorn also the day of thy honoured (*name of the event*) by outpouring grace, while we all the faithful are flocking into thy temple.

All the heavenly powers praise her that bare the Lord and the races of men glorify her that shewed unto us the day of her honoured (*name of the event*): she is our refuge, hope and protection, and the shelter from the incursions of the enemy.

O gracious cloud, do thou sprinkle from above with the dew of thy grace and mercy us that venerate the day of thy glorious festival (*name of the event*), which every soul gladly hymneth and glorifieth : Blessed art thou among women and blessed is the fruit of thy womb.

Ode 8. The Heirmos:

The Unoriginate King of glory, before Whom tremble the heavenly hosts, sing ye the priests and ye the peoples extol unto all the ages.

The only Queen of all before God art thou, O pure parent of God, both holy throne and the palace of Christ the God. Him entreat for those that venerate thy honoured (*name of the event*) to grant us the remission of sins.

In holy arms truly hast thou carried on earth the Lord Who of thee became incarnate, O all-glorious, and now hast thou ascended above heavens and left unto men the most joyous day of thy honoured (*name of the event*), whereon we also glorify thee, singing: Sing unto the Lord and exalt Him unto the ages.

Rejoice, O ye divine prophets, venerating the honoured (*name of the event*) of the Virgin Theotokos; for she has fulfilled the sayings of you all, having brought forth Christ the King of all; Whom we exalt unto the ages.

O thou, raising of the fallen, gladness of the despondent, instructress of the wandering, unto the sick visitation and cure and salvation unto all christians; do, O Sovereign-Lady, preserve us that cry unto thee and venerate thy (*name of the event*) and deliver us from the incursion of other nations.

Ode 9. The Heirmos:

Everyone became terrified at hearing of the ineffable God's condescension, that the Most High did voluntarily come down even unto the flesh itself, having become man in a virgin's womb; wherefore we the faithful magnify the most pure Theotokos.

Glorious things were said of thee, O city of God and of Him Who ever reigneth over the heavenly and earthly things, was born of thee and raised thee from the earth into heaven. Do unceasingly entreat Him for those that venerate thy honoured (*name of the event*), with Whom we magnify thee.

O ye the incorporeal orders, the assembly of the patriarchs and of apostles the godly compound, the prophetic choir, and the army of martyrs, the companies of hierarchs and of pious fathers, and ye all the saints—do rejoice with us celebrating (*name of the event*) of the Mother of God and magnifying her.

Thou hast sanctified everything with thy bringing forth, O most pure Virgin, and caused to appear a yet greater illumination—the all honourable day of thy (*name of the event*), which celebrating we magnify thee.

Exalt the horn of our right pious Emperor and put down the ragings of other nations, O most pure Parent of God; keep free from wars thy cities and preserve all the christian countries wherein is magnified and faithfully glorified by all thy great and multiglorious name, O pure Sovereign-Lady.

The Photagogicon. Similar to : Hearken ye women...

Revive, O Adam, and thou Eve, rejoice, exalt ye—prophets together with apostles and martyrs and be glad—ye ascetics and hierarchs; for joy and gladness is both unto the angels and men the (*name of the event*) of the most pure Theotokos Mary. *Thrice.*

With the Lauds the Stichera. Tone 1.

Since unto the source of light and the inexhaustible stream of sereneness we offer the festival (*name of the event*), Him entreat, O Theotokos, to deliver us from the darkness of ignorance and from passions both spiritual and bodily, and in the world to come to save us from endless torment. *Twice.*

Being the source of benign wisdom and the gulf of understanding and grace, He that was born of thee in the flesh hath shewn thee, O Theotokos, as an abyss of the Hypostatical Wisdom of God in the festival (*name of the event*); for His sake do grant me a drop of thy wisdom and understanding, and instruct me with regard to the life.

The head of the mysterious wonders of Christ—that awful commencement—having seen, we honour and adore the venerable accomplishment — the festival (*name of the event*) of thy O Sovereign-Lady, venerated image and of the divine wonders; do visit us as instructress in sicknesses and sorrows and deliver us, O Theotokos, from the torment to come.

Glory...Both now...Tone 8 :

Let us all sing unto the Theotokos Mary : Hail thou O Mother of God ; hail,—the ladder animated and reasonable ; hail—the bush unconsumed; hail,—the all-holy pot; hail,—the flower of the faith; hail,—the rod that sprouted; hail,—the golden censer; hail,—the God's overshadowed mountain, the Virgin; hail, —the loosening of the first Eve; hail,—the throne of God; hail, —the multimerciful beauty; hail,—the Sovereign-Lady.

The Great Doxology...and the Dismission.

CHAPTER III.

THE GENERAL SERVICE TO THE VENERATED AND VIVIFYING CROSS.

For, " O Lord, I have cried," the Stichera, Tone 7. Similar to
Called from above...

To-day rejoiceth the divine multitude of the faithful; for unto the ends of the world there appeareth the cross, illumineth the firmament with light unapproachable, brighteneth the air and adorneth the face of the earth. The church of Christ hymneth with songs divine and in venerating serveth the divine and most wonderful cross which from above doth preserve her; by its power strengthened, let us approach the Master calling out and saying: pacify the world and enlighten our souls.

Let the creation rejoice and dance; for the cross to-day from heaven shineth forth in the ends of the world, enlightening the earthly and shewing united those that are scattered; to-day men exult together with the choirs of angels, for the cross having destroyed the forbidding call of separation, hath now joined all openly into one. Wherefore shining brighter than the sun it enlighteneth with grace the whole creation, and maketh clear and saveth those that faithfully honour it.

Shining brighter than the sun and shewing itself unto the world as the revered sceptre of Christ, the King, and as His end is the divine cross. It shineth clearly forth unto the ends of the world. It hath brought out of the hades the race of man and having greatly despoiled the hades and overturned the enemy did utterly destroy the arrogance of the demons. And now doth it declare the resurrection of the Saviour and saveth those that call: pacify the world and enlighten our souls.

Glory...Both now... Tone 8.

That which Moses of old did prefigure, whilst vanquishing Amalek and obtaining victory over him, and that which David the Psalmist, calling it as Thy footstool, enjoined to adore,— Thy venerable cross, O Christ the God, we sinners do this day adore, and with our unworthy lips extolling Thee Who hast deigned to be crucified thereon, we entreat: O Lord, with the malefactor of Thy kingdom do make us worthy.

The Entrance. The Prokeimenon of the day.

The Reading from the Book of Exodus (15, 22-27; 16, 1).

Moses brought Israel from the Red Sea, and they went out into the wilderness of Shur; and they went three days in the wilderness, and found no water. And when they came to Marah, they could not drink of the waters of Marah, for they were bitter; therefore the name of it was called Marah. And the people murmured against Moses, saying: What shall we drink? And he cried unto the Lord, and the Lord shewed him a tree, which when he had cast into the waters, the waters were made sweet; there He laid for them statutes and ordinances, and there He proved them, and said: If thou wilt diligently hearken to the voice of the Lord thy God, and wilt do that which is right in His sight, and wilt give ear to His commandments, and keep all His statutes, I will put none of these diseases upon thee which I have brought upon the Egyptians; for I am the Lord that healeth thee. And they came to Elim, where were twelve wells of water, and three score and ten palm trees; and they encamped there by the waters. And they took their journey from Elim, and all the congregation of the children of Israel came unto the wilderness of Sin, which is between Elim and Sinai.

The Reading from the Book of Proverbs (3, 11-18).

My son, despise not the chastening of the Lord; neither be weary of his correction; for whom the Lord loveth He correcteth,—even as a father the son in whom he delighteth. Happy is the man that findeth wisdom, and the man that getteth understanding. For the merchandise of it is better than the merchandise of silver, and the gain thereof than fine gold. She is more precious than costly stones: no evil can withstand her, she is well known to those who approach her, and everything that is honoured cannot be compared unto her. Length of days, and years of life are in her right hand, and in her left hand riches and honour. Out of her mouth truth proceedeth, and law and mercy she carrieth on her tongue. Her ways are ways of pleasantness, and all her paths are peace. She is a tree of life to them that lay hold upon her and unto those that trust in her as in the Lord, she is steadfast.

The Reading from the Book of Isaiah (60, 11-16).

Thus saith the Lord: thy gates shall be open continually; they shall not be shut day nor night, that men may bring unto thee the forces of the Gentiles, and that their kings may be brought. For the nation and kingdom that will not serve thee shall perish, yea, those nations shall be utterly wasted. The glory of Lebanon shall come unto thee, the fir tree, the pine tree, and the box together, to beautify the place of My sanctuary, and I will make the place of My feet glorious. The sons also of them that afflicted thee shall come bending unto thee; and all they that despised thee shall bow themselves down at the soles of thy feet, and they shall call thee, the city of the Lord, the Zion of the Holy One of Israel. Whereas thou hast been forsaken and hated, so that no man went through thee, I will make thee an eternal magnificence, a joy of many generations. Thou shalt also suck the milk of the Gentiles, and shalt consume the riches of kings; and thou shalt know that I the Lord am thy Saviour and thy Redeemer, the Mighty One of Israel.

For Versicles, the Stichera, Tone 2. Similar to: O house of Ophrah...

With the deified water and Thy blood, O Word, is the church brightly ornamented as a bride, praising the glory of the cross.

The Versicle: Exalt ye the Lord our God and bow down before His footstool, for it is holy.

Let us bow down whilst exalting the spear with the cross, the nails and other things with which the life-bearing body of Christ was affixed. *The Versicle: And God our King before the ages hath wrought salvation in the midst of the earth.*

When Moses was vanquishing Amalek and holding his hands in the air, he did prefigure in the form of the cross the most pure passion of Christ. [*Glory...Both now...*

Prefiguring Thy cross, O Christ, Jacob, the patriarch, whilst blessing his grand children laid his hands upon their heads in the form of the cross, which to-day exalting we cry out, O Saviour: Grant victories unto the Christ-loving Emperor as Thou didst grant the overcoming unto Constantine. Now Thou lettest...*The* Trisagion. *And after* Our Father...*the Troparion:* O Lord, save Thy people. *And the Dismission.*

At the Matins, for God is the Lord, the same Troparion thrice.
After the 1st Stichologia, the Cathisma, Tone 6:

No sooner was the tree of Thy cross, O Christ, fixed, the very foundations of death, O Lord, were shaken; for Him Whom the hades so greedily engulfed it had with dread to disgorge. Thou, O Holy One, hast declared unto us Thy salvation and we glorify Thee, O Son of God; have mercy upon us.

Glory...Both now...the same.

After the 2nd Stichologia, the Cathisma, Tone 6:

To-day is fulfilled the prophetic saying, for we bow down upon the spot on which stood Thy feet, O Lord, and having received the tree of salvation, we obtained the freedom of sinful passion, through the supplications of the Theotokos, O Only Lover of men. [*Glory...Both now...the same.*

After Praise ye the name of the Lord, the Refrain:

We magnify Thee, O Life-giver, Christ, and we venerate Thy holy cross with which Thou hast delivered us from the thraldom of the enemy. [*The selected Psalm:*

Judge, O Lord, those who offend me, vanquish those who fight against me...

After the Polyeleon the Cathisma, Tone 8. Similar to:
That which was secretly ordained...

In paradise a tree hath once made me naked, the enemy through eating bringing about death, and when the tree of the cross, bringing the vestment of life unto men, hath been fixed on earth, the whole world was filled with every manner of joy. This seeing lifted up, let us, O people, with one voice and one faith cry out unto God: Filled is Thy house with glory. *Glory...Both now... the same.*

The Graduals, the 1st Antiphon of the 4th Tone.

The Prokeimenon, Tone 4:

All the ends of the world have seen the salvation of our God. *The Verse:* Sing unto the Lord a new song. Let every breath... *The Gospel St. John 12, 28-36.*

After the 50th Psalm the Sticheron, Tone 6:

O cross of Christ—the hope of christians, the instructor of the straying, the haven of the assaulted, the victory in wars, the stablishment of the universe, of the infirm the healer, the resurrection of the dead, have mercy upon us.

The Canon of the venerated and life-giving Cross—the work of Gregory the Sinaiate. The Heirmoi—twice each, and the Troparia 12 times in all. Tone 4: Ode 1. The Heirmos: I will open my mouth...

O cross all-powerful! Thou art the boast of the apostles, the stablishing of the ascetics and the sign of the faithful, the glory of both the hierarchs and of the martyrs, the victory and stablishing of all those that praise thee.

O cross most venerated! Thou hast proved to be four-ended power, the adornment of the apostles and of martyrs the strength, the health of the infirm, of the dead the resurrection and of the falling the raising.

O cross! Be unto me the might, the strength and the power, the deliverer and foremost defender against my assailants, the shield and protector, my victory and stablishing, ever preserving and sheltering me. [*The Theotokion:*

When thou, O all-spotless one, saw on the cross thy Son, a painful weapon did lacerate thy breast, thou hast given way to exclamations, lamenting in thy pain, but soon didst thou glorify the might of the cross. *The Catabasia*: Having delineated the cross, Moses...

Ode 3. The Heirmos: Thy hymnologists, O Theotokos...

O cross most venerated! Thou art the weapon of the ascetics —the two-edged sword of Christ, the adornment of the faithful, of ailing the cure and protection and raising of the dead.

O cross! Thou hast proved to be the foundation of piety, the destroyer of demons, the ornament of churches, the ruin of the wicked and humiliation of the enemies in the day of judgment.

O cross the life-bearing! Be unto me the strength and victory, the shield and wall unassailable, the driving away of demons and the extinguishing of bad thoughts and preservation unto my mind. [*The Theotokion*.

The crucifixion most humiliating did thy Son, O Virgin Sovereign-Lady, suffer as well as the death most unsuitable; but exalted hath He become and hath overturned the antagonistic forces of the enemy, as Immortal One. *The Catabasia*: A staff as type of mystery...

The Cathisma, Tone 8. Similar to: That which was secretly ordained...

The form of the cross did of old mysteriously typify Joshua the son of Nun, when he cruciformly spread his arms, O my Saviour, and the sun stood until the enemies that fought against Thee, O God, were overpowered; and now seeing Thee on the cross the sun set, and having destroyed the power of death, Thou hast raised with Thyself the whole world. *Glory...Both now...the same.*

Ode 4. The Heirmos: He that sitteth in glory on the throne of the Godhead...

The world being four-ended, thou, O cross, art represented by us, and as a three-edged sword dost thou cut off the principles of darkness, being the great weapon of Christ and an invincible and all-powerful victoriousness.

Thy height, O life-bearing cross, striketh the prince of the air, and thy depth slayeth the serpent of the whole abyss, and thy width doth again appear in putting down the prince of the world by thy might.

Being raised, thou hast attracted the fallen together with thee, thou hast exalted the earthly nature and art praised equally with the throne of God; O cross—the great height, bridge for the world, do speedily bring up my soul from the depth of passions. *[The Theotokion:*

Having cruciformly stretched out thy hands, O most pure Maiden-Theotokos, unto Him Who was lifted on the cross, do now, O Virgin, bring also thine entreaties for all those that in faith pray unto thee. *The Catabasia:* Having heard, O Lord, the mystery of Thine œconomy.

Ode 5. The Heirmos: Amazed were all things at thy divine glory...

O cross! Thou art the heavenly ladder of the sanctuary, the indicator of steps, the height and glory of Christ, the image of God equally significative unto the world both visible and invisible.

O cross! A form indescribable in power, sanctification of waters, purification of the air, consecration and enlightenment; thou hast appeared as a sign of every valour and as Christ's immutable sceptre that hurleth to the ground every adversary.

O cross all-powerful! Do put down the wicked enemies that foolishly hate and denounce thee; set fire to the heathen and extinguish their rage. O cross, all-holy and Christ-bearing, preserve us by thy might.

The Theotokion: O Queen of all, Sovereign-Lady, by the sceptre of thine Offspring, do, O Virgin, destroy the revolt of those who denounce the might of the cross, do grant strength and cleansing, victory and help unto our Faithful Emperor. *The Catabasia:* O most highly praised tree...

Ode 6. The Heirmos: Celebrating this divine and most honourable feast...

Cross is the resurrection of all, cross is the raising of the fallen, the mortification of passions and subjugation of the body, cross is the glory of souls and light eternal.

Cross is the destroyer of enemies, cross is the overthrow and captivation of the wicked and of the faithful the might, the preserver of the pious, and the driver away of the demons.

Cross is the destruction of passions, cross is the driving away of bad thoughts, cross is the ruin of the crafty heathen and hath proved to be the captor of spirits.

No sooner the cross is lifted, the orders of the spirits of the air fall, and when the cross descendeth, all the impious fear, seeing as lightning the power of the cross.

The Catabasia: The sea monster...*The Contakion,* Tone 4.
Similar to:

Thou that wast of Thine own will lifted up on the cross, do grant Thy bounties, O Christ the God, to Thy new community named after Thee; make glad in Thy power our Faithful Emperor (*mentioned by name*), conferring victories over his enemies upon him who hath Thine assistance, the armoury of peace—an unconquerable trophy.   [*The Oikos:*

He that was caught up to the third heaven into paradise and heard unspeakable and godly words which may not be uttered by (human) tongues—what doth he write unto the Galatians which the zealots of scriptures read and understood? As to me, saith he, God forbid, that I should glory, save in the cross alone of Christ, Who hath suffered thereon and hath slain the passions; that cross of the Lord we all therefore also hold in glory, for this tree of salvation is unto us the armoury of peace, an unconquerable trophy.

Ode 7. The Heirmos: The godly-minded ones worshipped not the creature...

The Undivided and Unmixed Trinity let us theologize as One in nature—the Father Unbegotten and the Begotten Son and the Holy Proceeding Spirit of God, singing in hymns: Blessed art Thou, O God of our fathers.

With the never-setting lightnings of Thine, O Three-hypostatic One, do enlighten our mental eyes that we may see Thy transcendent beauty, O Triluminar One, which is incomprehensible unto men and to angels inaccessible.

With the rays of Thy light, O gracious God, most-hymned and all-powerful, do Thou raise up from the depth my fallen soul that was ensnared away from the light of grace and precipitated into the darkness. [*The Theotokion:*

Crosswise stretching thine arms, O pure one, unto Him Who had stretched His arms on the tree of the cross and exalted our nature as well as slain the armies of the enemies, cease not in thy supplications. *The Catabasia:* The senseless order of the tyrant...

Ode 8. *The Heirmos:* The pious youth in the furnace...

The height of Christ's passion, the bow and arrow and a sword—an unassailable weapon and unconquerable power, Christ's footstool and victory over the enemies, symbol of reign and sceptre of the faithful—hast thou proved to be, O victorious cross.

Thou hast raised up our fallen nature, having restored us together with and through Christ crucified, O height divine and depth unspeakable! Thou art the symbol of Christ, O most precious cross, and the breadth without measure as well as the symbol of the Incomprehensible Trinity, O life-bearer.

Embracing the cross of the Lord with our lips, souls and hearts, let us all come now together, exalt and magnify it, and adoring it let us sing together the purest hymn, exclaiming: Hail thou, O cross, that art the greatest riches, the adornment of the church.

It is the tree of life and of salvation, the tree of immortality, the tree of knowledge, the tree thrice-beloved, incorruptible and inexhaustible—that cross tripartite, the honoured tree, for it bears the image of the three-hypostatical Trinity.

The Catabasia: Bless ye, O youths...

Ode 9. *The Heirmos:* Let every earth born one leap in spirit...

Who will be able in writing to proclaim thy works, O cross dear to the world, thy powers and wonders—the raising of the dead? Howbeit the whole world hath exalted together with Himself He, the greatly desired One, Who hath ascended unto God.

Stablishing of the faithful is the thrice-blessed cross, their sign and glory, the tree all-powerful; the cross of Christ is great and perfect, it is the glory of the apostles, stablishment of the ascetics and of martyrs the strength and might, of kings the victory and glory.

Hail thou, O cross, the image uncircumscribed and most eminent, the thrice-rich tree both fearful and all-blessed; hail thou, O all-holy and all-powerful cross; hail, the preserver of our lives—thou, O all-hymned cross of the Lord.

O honoured cross! Be unto me the preserver of my soul and body, with thy form putting down demons, driving away mine enemies, destroying passions and granting me blessing, life and strength by the co-operation of the Holy Ghost and through the honoured entreaties of the all-pure one.

The Catabasia: Mysterious paradise art thou,
O Theotokos...*The Photagogicon*:

The cross is the preserver of the universe; the cross is the adornment of the Church; the cross is the might of kings; the cross is the stablishment of the faithful; the cross is the glory of angels and the sore of demons. *Thrice.*

With the Lauds the Stichera, Tone 1. Similar to:
Of the heavenly orders the joy...

The way to heaven the venerable cross prepareth unto all that adore it, in undoubted faith; and unto the choirs of the bodiless powers coupleth those that lovingly hymn it, He Who was nailed thereon.

Adoring in faith the venerable cross, let us hymn the Lord crucified thereon; purifying both our lips and souls at the bidding of that one, we shall become enlightened with the spiritual brightness of This one, in praising Him.

Sweetening the bitterness, Moses hath of old saved Israel by making the form of the cross, and we all the faithful, mystically and divinely impressing it in our hearts, are always saved by its power.   [*Glory...Both now...Tone* 4:

Having helped meek David to subdue the stranger, do Thou, O Lord, succour our faithful Emperor (*mentioned by name*) and with the arm of the cross put down our enemies; make shine upon us, O Bounteous, Thy mercies of old, that they may truly understand that Thou art God, and that trusting in Thee we may obtain victories, whilst we customarily pray unto Thy most pure Mother that great mercy may be granted unto us.

The great Doxology...And the Dismission. At the Liturgy for the Beatitudes Ode 3 and 6 of the Canon.

CHAPTER IV.

THE SERVICE COMMON TO THE HOLY ANGELS AND OTHER BODILESS ONES.

For, O Lord, I have cried, the Stichera, Tone 4.
Similar to : As a virtuous...

Of the thrice-sunny Godhead the most illustrious attendants, —ye, angels, that appear as chief-captains, joyfully shout with the powers above: Holy art Thou, O Father, Holy art Thou, O Unoriginate Word, Holy art Thou also, O Holy Spirit, one glory, one kingdom and nature, one Godhead and power.

As your appearance is fiery, so is your virtue wonderful, O Michael and Gabriel—the first among angels, for in your unearthly nature ye traverse the ends of the world, carrying out the behests of the Creator of all, being acknowledged powerful in your strength and making sources of healings the temples dedicated to you and venerated on account of your holy calling.

Thou, O Lord, that makest, as hath been written, Thine angels spirits and Thy ministers flames of fire, hast shewn pre-eminent amongst the orders Thine Arch-angel Michael together with Thy chief-captain Gabriel that at a sign from Thee obey Thee, O Word, and the trisagion hymn, with fear, vociferate unto Thy glory. [*Glory, Tone* **6**:

Rejoice with us, all ye angelic orders, for your chiefs and our intercessors—the great chief-captains,—gloriously appearing to-day in their honourable temple, are blessing us; wherefore in dutifully hymning them we cry unto them: Shelter us with the shadow of your wings, O ye the greatest chief-captains.

Both now...the Theotokion: Rejoice with us, all ye the choirs of virgins, for our intercessor and mediatrix, shelter and great refuge doth to-day in her honourable and divine temple comfort the afflicted; wherefore let us, in dutifully hymning her, cry out: Shelter us with thy divine intercession, O most pure Theotokos, Sovereign-Lady.

The Entrance. The Prokeimenon of the day.

The Reading from Joshua the son of Nun (5, 13-15).

It came to pass, when Joshua was by Jericho, that he lifted up his eyes and looked, and, behold, there stood a man over against him with his sword drawn in his hand; and Joshua went up to him and said unto him: Art thou for us, or for our adversaries? And he said, As Captain of the host of the Lord am I now come. And Joshua fell on his face to the earth, and said unto Him: What saith my Lord unto His servant? And the Captain of the Lord's host said unto Joshua: Loose thy shoe from off thy foot; for the place whereon thou standest is holy. And Joshua did so.

The Reading from the Book of Judges (6, 2. 7. 11-24).

It came to pass in those days that the hand of Midian prevailed against the children of Israel, and they cried unto the Lord God. And there came an angel of the Lord, and sat under an oak which was in Ophrah, that pertained unto Joash the Abi-ezrite; and his son Gideon threshed wheat by the wine-press to hide it from the Midianites. And the Angel of the Lord appeared unto him, and said unto him: The Lord is with thee, thou mighty man of valour. And Gideon said unto him: O, my Lord, if the Lord be with us, why then is all this befallen us? and where be all the miracles which our fathers told us of, saying: Did not the Lord bring us up from Egypt? but now the Lord hath forsaken us, and delivered us into the hands of the Midianites. And the Lord looked upon him and said: Go in this thy might, and thou shalt save Israel from the hand of the Midianites, and, behold, I have sent thee. And Gideon said unto Him: O my Lord, wherewith shall I save Israel? behold, my family is poor in Manasseh, and I am the least of my father's house. And the Lord said unto him: Surely I will be with thee, and thou shalt smite the Midianites as one man. And Gideon said unto Him: If now I have found grace in Thy sight, then shew me a sign that Thou talkest with me. Depart not hence, until I come unto Thee, and bring forth my present and set it before Thee. And the angel of the Lord said unto him: It is I and I will tarry until thou come again. And Gideon went in, and made ready a kid and unleavened cakes of an ephah of flour: the flesh he put in a basket, and he put the broth in a pot, and brought it out unto Him under the oak and worshipped Him. And the angel of the Lord said unto him: Take the flesh and the unleavened cakes and lay them upon this rock and pour out the broth. And he did so. Then the angel of the Lord put forth the end of the staff that was in His hand, and touched the flesh and the unleavened cakes; and there rose up fire out of the rock, and consumed the flesh and the unleavened cakes. Then the angel of the Lord departed out of his sight. And when Gideon perceived that He was an angel of the Lord, Gideon said: Alas, O Lord God! for because I have seen an angel of the Lord face to face. And the Lord said unto him: Peace be unto thee, fear not; thou shalt not die. Then Gideon built an altar there unto the Lord, and called it Jehovah-shalom even unto this day.

The Reading from the Book of the Prophet Isaiah (14, 7-20).

Thus saith the Lord: Let the whole earth break forth into singing; yea, let the fir trees rejoice at thee, and let the cedars of Lebanon say: Since thou art laid down, no fitter has come up against us. Hell beneath is vexed at meeting thee, at thy coming; it stirreth up all the giants against thee, even the chief ones of the earth; it hath raised up from their thrones all the kings of the nations. All they shall speak and say unto thee: Art thou also become weak as we? art thou become like unto us? Thy pomp is brought down to the grave, and all thy noise; the worm is spread under thee and the worms cover thee. Thou art fallen from heaven, O Aurora, shining in the morning. Thou art broken down against the ground, thou which didst weaken the nations! For thou hast said in thy heart: I will ascend into heaven, I will exalt my throne above the stars of heaven, I will sit also upon the high mount in the midst of mountains that are in the north; I will ascend above the heights of the clouds, I will be like the Most High. Yet thou shalt be brought down to hell, to the foundations of the earth. They that see thee shall wonder and say of thee: This is the man that made the earth to tremble, that did shake kingdoms, that made the universe a wilderness, and destroyed the cities thereof, that loosed not his prisoners into their houses. All the kings of the nations lie in glory, yea every one in his own house, but thou shalt be cast out of thy grave like an abomination of the dead, with those dead that are slain, thrust through with a sword, that go down to the pit. As the raiment steeped in blood cannot be clean, so also thou wiltst not be clean, for thou hast destroyed My laws and slain My people, and thou shalt never be renowned.

For the Versicles, the Stichera, Tone 1.

O ye chief-captains of the intellectual hosts, ever standing before the throne of the Most High, do entreat the Lord to grant peace unto the world and unto our souls great mercy.

The Versicle: He maketh His angels spirits and His ministers flame of fire:

The chief of the powers on high, Michael, the first amongst the divine orders, that ever accompanieth us and preserveth all from every attack of the devil, hath called us to-day unto the feast. Wherefore come, O ye lovers of feasts and lovers of Christ, and taking with us the flowers of virtues, let us, with pure thoughts and ever-clear conscience, do homage unto the assembly of archangels, for standing continually before God and singing the trisagion hymn, they pray that our souls may be saved.

The Versicle: Praise ye Him, all His angels, praise ye Him, all His hosts:

O chief-captains of the intellectual hosts, that stand before the Immaterial Being and with the splendours of the thrice-sunny glory illumine the universe, with an unceasing voice ye sing the trisagion hymn; wherefore pray that our souls may be saved. [*Glory...Both now...Tone* 8.

As the chief defender and leader of angels, do, O chief-captain, deliver from every want and tribulation, from wickedness and mortal sins those that hymn thee and implore thee, O glorious one, since, as bodiless, thou seest the Immaterial One and art illuminated with the unapproachable light of the glory of the Most High; for He out of love to mankind and for our sake hath taken the flesh from the Virgin, being desirous of saving the race of man.

The Troparion: Tone 4. Of the heavenly hosts the chief-captains we, the unworthy ones, do ever entreat you, that through your prayers ye may protect us with a shelter of the wings of your immaterial glory, preserving us who assiduously fall down before you and cry out unto you: From dangers do deliver us as the chiefs of the powers on high.

Glory...Both now...the Theotokion or the Stavro-theotokion:

At the Matins, for God is the Lord, the same Troparion twice. Glory...Both now...the Theotokion. After the 1st Stichologia, the Cathisma, Tone 6:

The angelic hosts standing before Thy throne, O Christ, are praying for the race of man; granting therefore peace unto all through their intercessions, do Thou subdue the insolence of foreigners. *Twice.*

Glory...Both now...The Theotokion: Having at the archangel's salutation conceived in thy womb, O Theotokos, the Word, Co-unoriginate with the Father and the Holy Spirit, thou hast appeared higher than the cherubim and seraphim and the thrones.

After the 2nd Stichologia, the Cathisma, Tone 6:

Around the throne of the King of all ever rejoicing, O ye all the orders of angels, do preserve us, that in faith invoke you, and deliver us from sufferings.

Twice. Glory...Both now...the Theotokion. Hail thou—the door open unto God Who unspeakably entered in, and passed out of, thee, O Ever-Virgin.

After Praise ye the name of the Lord, the Refrain:

We magnify you, O archangels and angels and all the hosts, cherubim and seraphim, that glorify the Lord. [*Another:*

We magnify you, O archangels, angels, principalities, authorities, thrones, dominions, powers, cherubim and fearful seraphim that glorify the Lord.

The selected Psalm: I will confess unto Thee, O Lord, with all my heart...

After the Polyeleon the Cathisma, Tone 6:

O ye, shining angels of God that stand before the divine throne of grace, obtaining the true humility and real enlightenment from the divine light, do look down with the heavenly lovers of men upon us that suffer from the terrible persecution of the prince of the world and sleep in darkness. Come then, O archangels, to our assistance and deliver us from the snares of the origin of evil—the enemy, for unto your shelter, O most praised ones, we all have recourse. [*Twice.*

Glory...Both now...the Theotokion:

The hope and shelter and refuge of those who trust in thee, O tender God's Mother and intercessor for the world, do thou assiduously entreat with the bodiless ones man-loving God Whom thou hast brought forth, O only blessed one, that our souls may be delivered from every threatening.

The Graduals, the 1st Antiphon of the 4th Tone. The Prokeimenon: He that maketh His angels spirits and His ministers flames of fire. *The Verse:* Bless the Lord, O my soul; O Lord my God, Thou art become exceedingly exalted. Let every breath...*The Gospel, St. Luke* 10, 16-21. *Glory*...Through the intercessions of the archangels...*Both now:* Through the intercessions of the Theotokos...*After the 50th Psalm the Sticheron, Tone* 6:

Thine angels, O Christ, that stand in fear before the throne of the majesty and with the outpouring of Thy light are ever illuminated, Thy heavenly psalmodists and ministers of Thy council who are sent down by Thee,—they enlighten our souls.

The Canon, Tone 8. Ode 1. The Heirmos:

Let us, O people, send up a song unto our marvellous God Who delivered Israel from thraldom, chanting a song of victory and vociferating : We sing unto Thee, our only Lord.

Let us, O ye faithful, hymn the uncreated Trinity that ruleth all the immaterial orders of the heavenly choirs, vociferating: Holy, Holy, Holy art Thou, O God Almighty.

The beginning of creation, bodiless substance that surroundeth Thy most precious throne, Thou, the Creator of angels, hast set to cry unto Thee: Holy, Holy, Holy art Thou, O God Almighty.

Hail, Gabriel, witness of the mystery of God's incarnation, and Michael—the foremost amongst the orders of the immaterial, that ceaselessly cry: Holy, Holy, Holy art Thou, O God Almighty.

The Theotokion: I tremble before the mystery of Thy condescension, O Christ, for being God by nature, Thou wast pleased to be born as man of a virgin, that Thou mayest save the world from the thraldom of the enemy.

Ode 3. The Heirmos:

Thy fear, O Lord, do Thou plant in the hearts of Thy servants and be Thou the strength of those that in truth invoke Thee.

In strength hast Thou, O Immortal One, set the mighty ones that perform Thy most holy will, that ever stand above before Thee.

The initiates of Thine incarnation and august awakening—the chief of the angels interceding for us, do Thou, O Christ, receive.

Angels hast Thou, as Compassionate One, set guardians of men and hast shewn them, O Christ, ministers of the salvation unto Thy holy ones. [*The Theotokion:*

Ineffably hast Thou, O God's Bride, conceived the Lord and Saviour Who delivereth from terrible things us that invoke thee in truth.

The Cathisma, Tone 8. Similar to: What was commanded...
The chiefs of the heavenly ones and the foremost that stand before the highest and dreadful throne of the divine glory, Michael and Gabriel, the chief captains of angels, together with all the bodiless ones,—O ye ministers of the Most High, whilst you incessantly pray for the world, do obtain by your entreaties the remission of our transgressions and that we may meet with mercy and grace in the day of judgment.

Twice. Glory...Both now...The Theotokion:
Having woefully fallen into the slough of despondency through the multitude of my wicked and lawless deeds, I reached the stage of perplexity and am now holden of by despair. O Theotokos, Sovereign-Lady, do thou save me, do thou help me, for unto sinners thou art the cleansing and saving purification. [*The Stavro-theotokion:*
Seeing Him Who was incarnate of thy pure blood and past all understanding was born of thee, O pure one, hanging on the tree in the midst of malefactors, thy heart sickened and motherly lamenting thou didst cry out: Woe unto me, O my child! how divine and ineffable is Thine economy wherewith Thou hast revivified Thy creation! I hymn Thy commiseration.

Ode 4. The Heirmos:
Thou hast mounted the horses—Thine apostles, O Lord, and hast taken up in Thy hands their reins and Thy riding is become salvation unto those that in faith sing : Glory to Thy might, O Lord.

Thou hast sat upon angels as on horses, O Lover of men, and hast taken up with Thy hand their reins, and Thy riding is become salvation unto those that unceasingly cry out: Glory to Thy might, O Lord.

Thy virtue, O Lover of men, covereth the angels and filleth up the ends of the world with Thy glorious and divine praise, O Unoriginate One, and with them vociferateth unto Thee: Glory to Thy might, O Lord.

Thou, O compassionate One, didst come for the salvation of Thy people, O Christ, calling unto Thee the friends of Thy might, and Thy coming is become joy unto those that in faith cry out unto Thee: Glory to Thy might, O Lord.

The Theotokion. As Virgin and Mother hast thou, O most pure one, supernaturally appeared, since as both God and man hast thou brought forth Christ, to Whom the angelic orders with fear cry out: Glory to Thy might, O Lord.

Ode 5. *The Heirmos*:

Having enlightened with the knowledge of God the ends of the world that was in the night of ignorance, do Thou, O Lord, illumine me with the morning of Thy love to man.

Ever carried by irrevocable desire unto the height, unto Thee, O Christ, that art the extremest end of all desires, the angelic hosts do unceasingly glorify Thee.

The intellectual by nature Thou hast, O Christ, made the psalmodists of Thy majesty incorruptible by Thy grace, having shaped Thine angels in the image, O Incomprehensible One.

Thou hast, O Christ, preserved Thy servants from being inclined to the evil by keeping them near unto Thee, for being the Source of goodness, Thou dost do good unto those that worthily serve Thee. [*The Theotokion*:

Do Thou, O all-spotless one, who broughtest forth the Preserver of life, revive my soul that hath been deadened with vile passions and set me into the path eternal unto the blessed life.

Ode 6. *The Heirmos*:

Thou hast, O Lord, settled Jonah alone in the whale; do Thou save me, burdened with trammels of the enemy, from corruption as Thou didst him.

God-beseemingly hast Thou, O Lord, by Thy word brought out of nothing into existence the heavenly immortal hosts, making them luminous.

Honourable initiates of the praising of God you have become, O bodiless ones, the dwellers of the heavenly and truly divine tabernacle, worthily serving the Creator.

The intellectual orders of the bodiless Thee, O Son of God, truly Unoriginate, ceaselessly praise and glorify as Maker and Architect of all things. *The Theotokion*:

Him that from eternity sitteth on high with the Father, thou, O all purest one, wast made worthy to lay down in thine arms; vouchsafe, O pure one, to make Him merciful unto thy servants.

The Contakion, Tone 2. O ye chief captains of God, ministers of the divine glory, superiors of angels and guides of men, do as the chief captains of the incorporeal ones, entreat for us what is profitable and great mercy.   [*The Oikos*:

In Thy writings, O Lover of men, hast Thou said, there is great joy among angels in heaven on account of one repenting man, O Immortal One; wherefore we that are in sins, always make bold, O Thou the only Sinless One and Searcher of hearts, to implore Thee, as One abounding in mercy, to commiserate and to send down unto us, unworthy, compunction, granting us pardon, for for us all intercede before Thee, O Master, the chief captains of the bodiless ones.

Ode 7. *The Heirmos.*

The Hebrew youths have boldly trodden the flame in the furnace and have changed the fire into dew, crying out : Blessed art Thou, O Lord the God, unto the ages.

Luminaries hast Thou, O Compassionate, shewn the immaterial nature of Thine angels, constantly filled with the ineffable light and calling: Blessed art Thou, O God, unto the ages.

Before Thee continually stand myriads of angels serving Thee, without being able to bear the sight of Thy countenance, and calling : Blessed art Thou, O Lord the God, unto the ages.

By Thy Hypostatic Word hast Thou made the multiplicity of angels and having hallowed them with the Divine Spirit, has taught them, O God, to bless the Trinity unto the ages.

Of the Trinity : Meditating on the three Hypostases, we glorify the uncircumscribed nature of the Father, Son, and Holy Ghost, crying out : Blessed art Thou, O Lord the God, unto the ages.

Ode 8. *The Heirmos:*

Unto Him that was glorified on the holy mount and in the bush through the flame unto Moses the mystery of the Ever-virgin hath shewn, sing unto the Lord and extol Him unto all the ages.

Let us emulate the life of angels and directing our thoughts on high let us with the angels mentally sing, hymning the Lord and extolling Him unto all the ages.

44 THE SERVICE COMMON TO THE HOLY ANGELS, ETC.

Participators of the heavenly rejoicings, standing around the throne of the glory and continually moving before God, the angels hymn and extol Him unto all the ages.

Unto the Trinity that maketh those continually serving on high a flame of immaterial fire and the angels—spirits, let us bow down and let us doxologize It unto all the ages. [*The Theotokion* :

Before Whom in heaven stand with fear myriads of angels and archangels, Him wast thou, O Theotokos, made worthy to carry in thine arms; do entreat Him that may be saved those who doxologize Him unto all the ages.

Ode 9. The Heirmos:

Thou hast passed the limits of nature, having conceived the Maker and Lord, and wast unto the world the door of salvation; wherefore we do unceasingly magnify thee, O Theotokos.

Thee, O Christ, Who didst ineffably unite the earthly things unto the heavenly and hast of angels and men perfected one Church, we do unceasingly magnify.

O ye both angels and archangels, the thrones, authorities and dominions, principalities and powers, cherubim and seraphim—do with the Theotokos intercede for the world.

Shewing yourselves as the protectors of all, O Michael and Gabriel, do visit those that lovingly honour your all-festive memory, and deliver from every calamity those that are in faith hymning you.

The Theotokion: Hail, O holy Bride of God! Hail thou that broughtest forth unto the faithful the Light of the world; hail thou—the wall and shelter of us all! do unceasingly entreat for us God as Benefactor.

The Photagogicon. Similar to: With the spirit in the sanctuary...

Thou, Michael, the chief-captain of the ministers of fire, hast obtained from the Father the foremost place amongst the lights; wherefore dost thou possess also the brightness of His glory, standing, as the first of the immaterial orders, around the most pure throne. [*The Theotokion*:

The orders of the bodiless ones honour thy birth, for thou alone hast filled the earthborn with joy; wherefore we the faithful glorify thee, the all-spotless one, doxologizing in hymns, for unto those in darkness hast thou kindled a light as an advanced morning day. [*With the Lauds, the Stichera. Tone 2.*

O intellectual beings, divine and incorporeal! surrounding the immaterial throne, with flaming lips ye sing the trisagion hymn unto God the Ruler: Holy God, the Father Unoriginate, Holy Mighty the Son Co-unoriginate, Holy Immortal-Spirit of the same substance, glorified together with the Father and the Son. *Twice.*

With immaterial lips and intellectual mouths the orders of the angels an unceasing doxology bring unto Thine unapproachable Godhead, O Lord; and the pure minds and ministers of Thy glory praise Thee, O Lord; with whom Michael the bodiless and Gabriel the greatly resplendent and the foremost of the powers on high, the chief-captains of angels are this day our instructors, enjoining us to sing the song of songs unto Thine unapproachable glory, O Lover of man; before which they also unceasingly entreat for our souls. *Tone 4.*

With lips of fire the cherubim hymn Thee, O Christ the God, and with immaterial mouths incessantly doxologizeth Thee the choir of archangels, and Michael, the chief-captain of the powers on high, unceasingly bringeth unto Thy glory the victorious hymn; he it is also who enlightened us this day with our perishable lips worthily to strike in psalmody the trisagion praise on the occasion of the bright festival, for everything hath been filled with Thy praise and Thou dost grant therewith unto the world great mercy!

Glory...Tone 5. Idiomelic:

Wherever thy grace overshadoweth, O archangel, therefrom is driven the power of the devil, for the fallen morning star cannot bear to see thy light; wherefore we entreat thee his fire-bearing arrows which are directed against us, to extinguish with thine intercession, delivering us from his temptations, O worthily-praised (*mentioned by name*), the chief-captain. *Both now...the Theotokion:*

We bless thee, O Theotokos Virgin, and we the faithful praise thee as in duty bound, O city unassailable, wall impregnable, sure intercession and refuge for our souls.

[*The Stavro-theotokion:*

A lamb, seeing once her Lambkin go to be slaughtered, intently followed, thus calling out after Him: Whither goest Thou, O my sweetest Child, Jesus? Why dost Thou make this swift progress, O Long-suffering One, unsluggishly? O Jesu, most desired Lord, sinless, plenteous in grace! Give me, Thy servant, a word of reply; O my most beloved Son, do not despise, O Compassionate, with Thy silence, me that hath so strangely given birth unto Thee, O God All-compassionate, granting unto the world great mercy.

For the Versicles. Glory...Tone 4.

Ye that are illumined with the sun-rays of God's light, the chief-captains, you do illuminate the ranks of the immaterial ones, and forming up on high a brilliant light, you enlighten the world with the fire of the unapproachable Godhead; wherefore also the trisagion hymn ye with fiery mouths do incessantly sing: Holy, Holy, Holy art Thou, our God, glory to Thee. [*Both now...The Theotokion:*

O Theotokos, Sovereign of all, the glory of the orthodox, put an end to the machinations of the heretics and their countenances to shame, since they neither adore, nor honour thy honourable image, O all-pure one. [*The Stavro-theotokion:*

Seeing Christ, the Lover of men, crucified and with a spear pierced in His side thou, O all-pure one, didst lament, crying out: What is this, O my Son? What did the ungrateful people render Thee in return for the good Thou hast done unto them? And yet so lovingly Thou dost take care that I may bear my childlessness. I wonder, O Compassionate One, at Thy voluntary crucifixion.

CHAPTER V.

GENERAL SERVICE TO JOHN, PRECURSOR, PROPHET AND BAPTIST OF THE LORD.

For O Lord, I have cried, the Stichera, Tone 8. *Similar to :* O most glorious wonder...

O blessed John the precursor, sincere friend of the Master, who in the waters of the Jordan didst touch with thy hand His all-purest crown, do thou always bring up in love to the Lord my humble soul by thy holy intercessions, extinguish the fire of things that are sweet unto me, leading me to the performance of the divine injunctions and truly cleansing the senses of my heart, that I may glorify thee.

O thou, offspring of barrenness and Master's garden of purity, of men the ornament, the baptist of the Lord, all-praised John the precursor, the divine guardian of my humble soul, do vouchsafe unto me graciousness through thine intercessions, delivering me from the serpent, his crafty and wily slanders and attacks.

Thou art the sweetest of all and full of the divine sweetness, O prophet ever-glorious, and thou makest glad all those who come unto thee in faith, sweetening their senses both of the soul and body, and undoing for us the bitterness of maladies and afflictions, of attacks from the evil one, and of all the soul-destroying dainties. [*Glory...Tone* 4 :

To-day appeared the great precursor, that hath come from the barren womb of Elizabeth, a prophet, the greatest of all the prophets, there is no other, nor hath one ever arisen ; since after the precursor—the lamp there followed Light the most resplendent, and after the voice the Word, and after the Bridegroom's leader the Bridegroom. He was preparing for the Lord the multitude of people and was preliminarily cleansing them with water unto the Spirit; he was Zacharia's offspring and good pupil of wilderness, the preacher of repentance and of transgressions the cleansing. He hath announced unto those in the hades the resurrection from the dead and doth intercede for our souls. *Both now...The Theotokion of the resurrection:* The Prophet David, that through thee hath become God's ancestor ...*The Entrance. The Prokeimenon of the day.*

The Reading from the Prophet Isaiah (40, 1-3, 9; 41, 17-18; 45, 7-8; 48, 20-21; 54, 1).

Thus saith the Lord: Comfort ye, comfort ye My people, saith the God. Speak ye, priests, unto the heart of Jerusalem, cry unto her that her humiliation is at an end, since her iniquity is pardoned, for she hath received of the Lord's hand double for her sins. The voice of him that crieth in the wilderness: Prepare ye the way of the Lord, make straight the paths for our God. Get thee up into the high mountain, O Zion, that bringest good tidings; lift up thy voice with strength, O Jerusalem, that bringest good tidings, lift it up, be not afraid: I am the Lord God, I will hear the poor of Israel and will not forsake them, but will cause rivers to flow in high places and fountains in the midst of the fields. I will turn the wilderness into meadow and the dry land into water-springs. Let heaven above rejoice and let clouds sprinkle down righteousness; let the earth shine and let mercy shoot forth and let righteousness spring up together. With a voice of singing declare ye, and let it be heard, utter it even to the end of the earth, say ye: The Lord hath redeemed His servant Jacob, and if they thirst in the wilderness, He will cause water to flow out of the rock for them. Sing, O barren one, thou that didst not bear, break forth into singing and cry aloud, thou that didst not travail, for more are the children of the desolate than the children of the married wife.

The Reading from the Prophet Malachi (3, 1-7. 12, 18; 4, 4-6).

Thus saith the Lord Almighty: Behold I will send My messenger before Thy countenance, and he shall prepare the way before Thee. And the Lord, Whom ye seek, shall suddenly come to His temple, but who may abide the day of His coming? for He shall come like a refiner's fire and like fuller's soap, and He shall purify by consuming and purging as gold and silver. And He shall come unto you for judgment, and will be a swift witness against the evil ones, and against the adulterers, and against false swearers, and against those that deprive the hireling of his wages, and against those that oppress the widows and push away the fatherless, and that turn aside the stranger from his right, and fear not Him, saith the Lord Almighty, for I am the Lord your God and I will not change. And ye the sons of Jacob are gone away from the law and have not kept it. Wherefore return unto Me and I will return unto you, saith the Lord Almighty, and all nations shall call you blessed. Learn ye that I am the Lord that doth discern between the righteous and the wicked, in that day wherein I shall affectionately meet those that love Me. Learn then and remember ye the law of Moses, My servant, which I commanded unto him in Horeb for all Israel, with the statutes and judgments. Behold, I will send you Elijah the Tishbite before the coming of the great and illustrious day of the Lord; and he shall turn the heart of the father to his son and the heart of man unto his neighbour, lest I come and smite the earth swiftly, saith the Lord Almighty, the Holy God of Israel.

The Reading from the Wisdom of Solomon
(Chapters 4, 7. 16. 17. 19-20; 5, 1-7).

The righteous man if he happen to die early shall be at rest, and the dying righteous man shall bring judgment unto the wicked living, for they will see the end of the righteous one and will not understand what is destined for him. And the Lord will hurl the wicked down voiceless and will remove them from their foundations, and they shall pass away unto the last in sorrow and their memory shall vanish, for they shall come in dread unto the realization of their sins, and their transgressions shall convict them to their faces. Then the righteous man will stand up in great boldness before those who offended him and despised his works. At the sight of him they will be agitated with great fear and will feel astonished at his glorious salvation; for, repenting and sighing from the oppression of the spirit, they shall speak within themselves, saying: this is he whom we laughed at and held in scorn; we were so foolish as to account his life as madness and his end dishonourable;

how, then, is he now numbered unto the sons of God and his lot is cast among the holy? We have therefore wandered away from the right path, and the light of truth hath not illumined us, and the sun hath not shone unto us; we were full of the wicked ways and perdition, and walked in the unpassable paths, but did not comprehend God's ways.

For Versicles the Stichera, Tone 2:

Do thou, O proclaimer of Christ and baptist, angel, apostle, martyr, prophet, precursor, lamp, nearest friend, of prophets the seal, the most honoured among the born ones, mediator of both the ancient and the new covenant, joyful voice of the Word,—with thy holy intercessions·support our prayerful exertions before the Merciful God.

The Versicle: Blessed be the Lord God of Israel. He hath visited and hath wrought the deliverance unto His people. Behold the Lamb of God that taketh away the sins of the world,—hast cried out thou, O blessed precursor, when thou didst see Christ walking on earth; Him, therefore, entreat to grant the remission of sins unto those that honour thee, for thou, O baptist, dost truly possess a great boldness as the mediator of the law and the grace.

The Versicle: And thou, O youth, shalt be called blessed. Make haste and snatch me away from temptation, O glorious prophet of the Lord, I implore thee, for in vain have arranged themselves against me the bitter demons that are fighting me and seeking to seize up the soul of thy servant as a poor bird,—do not forsake me to the end, but rather let them understand, O most blessed one, that thou art my refuge.

Glory...Tone 4: O Godly illustrious voice, lamp of the Light, precursor of the Lord, testified to by Christ, the first among the prophets! Whilst interceding with thine entreaties for the world, do thou particularly remember thy flock in order to preserve it in safety. *Both now...the Theotokion of the resurrection:* Behold fulfilled is now the prophecy of Isaiah...*The Troparion, Tone 2*:

The memory of a righteous one calleth forth for praises, and as to thee, O precursor, the Lord's testimony alone sufficeth; for thou didst truly shew thyself to be even more honourable than the prophets, since thou wast found worthy to baptize in the streams Him Whom thou hadst preached ; therefore, having joyfully suffered for the truth, didst thou announce also to those in hades the glad tidings of God that was manifested in flesh, that took up the sin of the world and granteth us great mercy.

Glory...Both now...the Theotokion.

At the Matins, for God is the Lord, the same Troparion. After the 1st Stichologia, the Cathisma, Tone 4. Similar to: Amazed was Joseph...

To-day hath unto us sprouted forth the off-spring of Zachariah and bringeth intellectual joy unto the thoughts of the faithful, —an ornament of the desert and the basis of the prophets, wherefore he appeared as the precursor of Christ and true witness of His coming; let us therefore harmoniously cry out unto the baptist in spiritual odes: O prophet and proclaimer of the Truth, supplicate that we may be saved. *Twice. Glory... Both now...the Theotokion:*

We hymn thee, O God's Bride, Mother of Christ the God, glorifying thine incomprehensible bringing forth, wherewith we were delivered from the deceit of the devil and from every misfortune, and in faith we cry out unto thee, O Sovereign-Lady Theotokos: Have mercy upon thy flock, O all-hymned one.

After the 2nd Stichologia, the Cathisma, Tone 2. Similar to:
Being of the mercy...

For the sake of compassion through mercy, hast Thou, O Good One, come down to save Thy creation, and inclined down the heavens in Thy descent, wherefore hymning Thine awful economy, we cry out unto Thee, O Christ: Through the intercessions of Thy precursor grant us the cleansing of sins, as the only Compassionate One. *Twice. Glory...Both now...the Theotokion:*

As a warm defence of Christians, do, O Theotokos, ever pray unto Thy Son, that we may be rescued from every evil deed and affliction of the wrestler, and that He may grant us the remission of transgressions for the sake of abundance of mercies, through thine entreaties, O Mother Virgin.

THE SERVICE OF THE PRECURSOR.

After Praise ye the name of the Lord, the following Refrain for the Nativity of the Precursor:
We magnify thee, the precursor of the Saviour, John, and honour thy most glorious birth from a barren one.

The selected Psalm: Blessed be the Lord God of Israel.

For the Conception the same Psalm, but for the Decollation and the Finding this Psalm: Blessed is the man that feareth God... *The end of the Refrain:* and all honour the decollation of the venerable head. *For the Finding:* And all honour the finding of thy venerable head. *For the Assembly:* and all honour thine all-venerable assembly. *After the Polyeleon, the Cathisma, Tone 5. Similar to:* The Word Co-unoriginate...

Let us loudly praise in hymns him that from the womb was manifested as God's prophet and as a lamp of the world came out of a barren one, the baptist of Christ and victorious sufferer —the precursor John, for he entreats God that our souls may be saved. *Twice. Glory...Both now...the Theotokion:* O bride, pure of marital intercourse, O most pure God's parent, that hast changed Eve's sorrow into joy, we always hymn thee and glorify, since thou hast delivered us from the first curse; do also now unceasingly entreat, O most hymned one, thy Son and God to save us.

The Graduals, the 1st Antiphon of the 4th Tone. The Prokeimenon: And thou, O youth, shalt be called prophet of the Most High. *The Verse:* Blessed be the Lord God of Israel... Let every breath...*The Gospel,* Matth. 11, 2-15.

After the 50th Psalm the Sticheron, Tone 1.
Proclaimer wast thou of the Lamb of God the Word, O John the prophet and precursor, for thou dost foretell the future and declareth unto the ends beforehand: Behold, the Lamb of God that taketh away the sins of the world and granteth unto all peace and great mercy.

The Canon of the Theotokos in 6, and of the Precursor in 8. Tone 4. Ode 1, the Heirmos:

Do Thou that wast born of the Virgin, drown in the depth of impassivity the triformity of my soul—those mighty strongholds, I implore Thee, that in the mortification of flesh as on a tymbal I may melodize a triumphant hymn unto Thee.

As a great star of the Sun, hast thou, O precursor, illumined the earth with thy brightness, O baptist; wherefore I call unto thee: enlighten also my heart blinded with the dark shadows of the numberless transgressions.

Thou hast once, O blessed one, loosed in thy birth the bonds of barrenness; wherefore I implore thee, through thine intercessions, to make my soul, desolate through the barrenness of passions, appear fruitful, bringing forth offsprings of virtues.

Thou hast prepared the ways for the Redeemer, going before Him in the power of Elijah, O most glorious baptist; do thou direct also to Him the emotions of my soul, delivering me with thine intercessions from every temptation and the flame of passions. [*The Theotokion:*

Do thou, O cloud of light, dispel, through thy bright mediations, the many and dark clouds from off my soul, that I may see the dawn of Him Who hath shone forth from thee, and that I may with light receive the Light never setting.

Ode 3. *The Heirmos:*

The bow of the mighty hath become impotent and the infirm have girded themselves with strength; wherefore my heart hath become strengthened in the Lord.

Every virtue hast thou manifested, and every evil deed hast thou heartily hated, and shewn unto man the path of penitence, O all-blessed one.

Of the incarnate Word great precursor didst thou appear; wherefore I implore thee to free me from irrational passions, by leading me to impassiveness.

Whilst still living in the flesh, thou, O precursor, hast made the life of the bodiless manifest, and to approach that hast thou, O God-bearing one, with thine intercessions strengthened us. [*The Theotokion:*

The world that through transgression hath become worthless, was pardoned through thee, O Mother-Virgin; wherefore as in duty bound it doth bless thee in hymnal odes. [*The Cathisma, Tone* 1: In the wilderness hast thou dwelled, O precursor of Christ, just as did Elijah; wherefore, O all-blessed one, do establish my heart. [*Twice. Glory...Both now...the Theotokion:*

As Queen and pure Virgin doth David proclaim thee, O most

pure one; wherefore I implore thee do make me the heir of the heavenly Kingdom, that I may bless thee.

Ode 4. The Heirmos:

For the sake of Thy love, for Thine image hast Thou, O Compassionate One, ascended the cross and the nations were moved, for Thou, O Lover of man, art my strength and praise.

As a dove that announceth beforehand unto the world the true spring in the truest words, accounting thee, we bless thee, O ever-glorious precursor.

Utterly wrecked with the temptations of the deceitful one, do thou as the mediator of the old and the new covenant, wholly renew me hymning thee, O precursor.

Do thou that wentest into the wilderness to lead the irreproachable life, call up with thy divine intercessions, O precursor, my mind, made desolate with all kinds of transgressions. *The Theotokos:* As cleansing and redeeming hath become known unto us thy Son, O Virgin; Him entreat also to save the souls of those who feelingly bless thee.

Ode 5. The Heirmos:

Thine enlightenment do send down unto us, O Lord, and free us from the mist of transgressions, O Good One, granting us Thy peace.

Whilst I am inflamed with the burning coals of wilderness and with the assaults of passions, do thou, O child of wilderness, bedew me with thine intercessions and keep me free from the noxious effects of the flame.

Under thy holy right hand, O all-blessed one, was baptized the Divine Right Hand of the Father that saveth us from the hand of the deceiver, through thy holy intercessions.

A refuge and mighty shelter and a great wall the whole world possesseth in thee, O precursor; do deliver us with thine intercessions from every oppression.   [*The Theotokion:*

God hath loved in thee, O youthful Virgin, the good qualities of Jacob, adorning through thee all that were darkened by the original trangression.

Ode 6. The Heirmos:

I have reached the depths of the sea and the storm of many sins hath submerged me, but as God do Thou, O Greatly-merciful, bring up my life from the deep.

Thou stoodest baptizing in the rapids the Master that taketh away the sins of all men; cease not, O precursor, to entreat Him to take compassion on our souls.

Thou wast manifested as the preacher of repentance; therein do thou, O precursor, preserve also my heart polluted with pernicious sins and having no recuperation.

Thou hast, O blessed one, proclaimed unto the souls in the impassable wilderness the Word that came down from above; wherefore every church with never-silent voices blesseth thee. [*The Theotokion*:

The types of the law were explained through thine awful bringing forth, O God's Bride, and their fulfilment now contemplating we worthily honour thee, O Sovereign-Lady. *The Contakion to be found in the Typicon. But if there be no Typicon, say the following Contakion. Tone* 8.

Unto thee who art truly greater of all the saints I, unworthy, sin much more than all the lawless ones, but nevertheless I bring unto thee a hymn, O John the precursor, and since thou possessest boldness before the Lord, I implore thee to free me from all misfortunes that I may call unto thee: Hail thou the proclaimer of grace. [*The Oikos*:

Whilst I begin an ode unto thee, O God-hymned, blessed John, I am full of joy and yet dread through the fear of thy remembrance and am frightened at not finding the words, O precursor. Strengthening me, do thou thyself grant me that I may worthily speak: Hail thou for whose sake the gladness came; hail thou for whose sake the curse was destroyed; hail thou, the teacher of the ends of the world; hail thou, the proclaimer of Christ's wonders; hail thou, the height of conscience that reacheth the heavens; hail thou, the breadth of purity that cleanseth all the earth; hail thou, since thou hast seen the Holy Trinity; hail thou, since thou hast despised the doubleness of the matter; hail thou, the star that sheweth the Sun; hail thou, the luminary that illuminateth all under the sun; hail thou, by whom Christ hath been proclaimed; hail thou, by whom Satan was hated; hail thou, the proclaimer of grace.

Ode 7. *The Heirmos*:

The youths of Abraham have once in Babylon trodden down the flame of the furnace, calling up in hymns : O God of our fathers, blessed art Thou.

Greater than all born didst thou appear, O prophet; with thy great intercession do thou deliver me so much sinning against God, from the great flame and everlasting darkness.

A barren fig-tree I have appeared and am afraid of being cut down; make me firm and fruitful with thine intercession, O precursor of the Saviour, that I may bless thee.

Lull asleep every storm of the enemy that is raised against those who in faith have recourse unto thee, O precursor John, with thy watchful entreaties unto the Deliverer of all.

The Theotokion: From the attacks of the deceiver and from wickedness and demons' thraldom do thou, O Virgin, deliver thy servants that with their souls and tongues ever glorify thee.

Ode 8. *The Heirmos*:

Thou, the Almighty Deliverer of all, having come down, didst bedew those that in the midst of the flame continued their piety, and hast taught them to sing : Bless the Lord, all ye the works and sing unto Him.

Whilst I am being held by the sleep of despair and darkened with the mist of malice, do thou, O precursor, restore me with thy bright intercession and grant that I may beseemingly walk as in the day of virtues.

The winter of temptations holdeth me and the storm of passions troubleth me; reach me thy hand, O precursor, which may lead up the ship of my soul unto the haven of penitence, through thine intercessions.

Him that taketh away the sins of the world, hast thou baptized in waters of the river; do thou dry up, O blessed John the precursor, with the streams of thine intercessions the abyss of my evil deeds.

Having seen the Holy Spirit, thou hast heard the voice of the Begetter testifying to Jesus Whom thou wast ineffably baptizing, O precursor; Him also entreat to save us. [*The Theotokion*:

As the source of our restoration, do thou entirely renew me broken through the attacks of the serpent, that I may in faith and with love bless thee, O Theotokos and all-spotless Virgin.

Ode 9. The Heirmos:

Whereas Eve by her failing of disobedience hath brought in the curse, thou, O Virgin Theotokos, through the sprouting of the fruit of thy womb, hast flowered forth the blessing unto the world, wherefore we all magnify Thee.

My strength and song is Christ the Lord; do thou, O blessed precursor, entreat Him to fortify me against passions and all the attacks of the demons, and to vouchsafe unto me the performance of the divine will, that I may ever and with love bless thee.

As a beautiful turtle-dove, as a swallow sweetly-spoken hast thou appeared, O divine precursor, announcing Christ—the Divine Spring; Him entreat to deliver me from the soul-corruptive winter and from the storm of sins, I implore thee.

Having leaped in thy mother's womb for joy, thou hast announced Him that shone forth from the Virgin; Him entreat to mortify the emotions of my flesh that are killing me, and to fill up with joy my heart, that I may hymn thee, O divine precursor. [*The Theotokion:*

Having given birth unto the Greatly-loving God; do thou, O greatly-loving Theotokos, entreat Him to deliver me from every evil and to make my heart solicitous for Him and averse to fleshly voluptuousness, that I may magnify thee in odes.

[*The Photagogicon:*

As a morning hast thou shone forth God beseemingly before the Sun of Glory, O blessed precursor, from the very old, barren one and an old priest; thou hast announced the Lord's birth from the Virgin for the redemption of mankind; wherefore we do lovingly hymn and adore, O baptist, thy most honoured (*name of the event.*) [*The Theotokion:*

The prophets have announced, apostles have taught, martyrs have clearly and God-wisely confessed thy Son, O most pure Theotokos, as the God of all, Who through thee hath delivered us from the ancient condemnation; together with those we magnify thee.

With the Lauds the Stichera. Tone 4:

Possessing boldness unto God and being the greatest of all men, do thou, O precursor, ever entreat Him for those that in faith call unto thee, to grant us invocation and cause for repentance that we ever being saved may hymn thee. *Twice:*

Thou, O precursor, wast called a prophet from the mother's womb, from the bosom a preacher and apostle; and whereas I am given over unto the demons and am a hard-working slave of sin, do thou deliver me from both, as a powerful warrior, that I may declare thy speedy intercession.

Being the fan of the Divine Spirit, do thou cast away from my heart the chaff-like inclinations, and the divine works as wheat do gather from me into the God's granary that I may become unto the Master an acceptable food, O blessed one, being enriched by thine intercession, O baptist of Christ.

[*Glory...Tone* 8.

Unto John becometh sweet smell, unto the baptist befitteth the beauty of hymns, for he hath announced the commencement of our salvation, when he leaped in the womb, and whilst crying in the wilderness: Repent ye; he—the Sovereign's warrior, the precursor of grace that proclaimeth the Lamb and entreateth the Saviour for our souls. [*Both now...The Theotokion:*

Do thou, O Sovereign-Lady, accept the prayers of thy servants and deliver us from every want and sorrow. *The Great Doxology. And the Dismission. At the Liturgy with the Beatitudes the 3rd, and 6th Odes of the Canon.*

CHAPTER VI.

THE GENERAL SERVICE OF THE HOLY FATHERS, IN REMEMBRANCE OF COUNCILS, *sung on the 7th Sunday after Easter, also on July 16th after the memory of the holy hieromartyr Athenogenos; and on October 11th after the memory of the holy apostle Philip. On Saturday at Vespers for O Lord, I have cried, the Stichera, Tone 6: Similar to:* The desperate...

Before all ages, without mother, wast Thou born from the

bosom of the Father, before the morning star, although Arius doth glorify Thee as a creature and not as God, audaciously commixing Thee—the Maker—unto the creatures and presumptuously usurping unto himself the substance of the eternal Fire, but the council that was held in Nicea, did proclaim Thee, O Lord, the Son of God, Co-throned unto the Father and the Spirit.

Who hath torn Thy raiment, O Saviour? Arius, didst say Thou, since he hath cut the equally honourable single origin of the Trinity into divisions. He rejected Thee being One of the Trinity; he taught also Nestorius not to say Theotokos; but the council that was held in Nicea, did proclaim Thee, O Lord, the Son of God, Co-throned unto the Father and the Spirit.

Detesting to see the light, Arius doth fall to the extremity of his sin and with the divine hook his bowels are torn: he has to give up his whole substance and the soul in the same manner as another Judas of his temper; but the council that was held in Nicea, did proclaim Thee, O Lord, the Son of God, Co-throned unto the Father and the Spirit.

Foolish Arius hath cut the one origin of the Holy Trinity into three independent and disunited substances; wherefore the God-bearing fathers having in their zeal come together and moved by the flame of the fervour, just as Elijah the Tishbite did cut down with a spiritual sword the blasphemer, as the Spirit hath directed. [*Glory...Tone* 6:

Let us this day praise the trumpets of the mysteries of the Spirit—the God-bearing fathers who melodized in the midst of the church the harmonious ode of theology—the One Trinity without distinction, both in substance and divinity,—who have overthrown Arius and vindicated the orthodox and are ever praying the Lord that our souls may be saved. *Both now...The Theotokion*: Who would not bless thee, O all-holy Virgin?... *The Entrance*: *The Prokeimenon of the day*...

The Reading from the Book of Genesis (14, 14-20).

When Abram heard that Lot his brother's son was taken captive, he armed his trained servants, born in his own house, three hundred and eighteen, and pursued them unto Dan. And he divided himself against them, he and his servants, by night, and smote them, and pursued them unto Hobah, which is on the left hand of Damascus. And he brought back all the goods, and also brought again his brother's son Lot, and his goods, and the women also, and the people. And the king of Sodom went out to meet him after his return from the slaughter of Chedorlaomer, and of the kings that were with him, at the valley of Shaveh, which is the king's dale. And Melchizedek king of Salem brought forth bread and wine; and he was the priest of the Most High God. And he blessed him and said: Blessed be Abram of the Most High God, Who created heaven and earth; and blessed be the Most High God, Who hath delivered thine enemies into thy hand.

The Reading from the Book of Deuteronomy (1, 8-11 *and* 15-17).

In those days spake Moses unto the sons of Israel saying: Behold, I have set the land before you: go in and possess the land which the Lord sware unto your fathers, Abraham, Isaac and Jacob, to give unto them and to their seed after them. And I spake unto you at that time saying: I am not able to bear you myself alone. The Lord your God hath multiplied you, and, behold, you are this day as the stars of heaven for multitude. The Lord God of your fathers make you a thousand times so many more as ye are and bless you, as He hath promised you! So I took from amongst you wise men and known and experienced, and made them heads over you, captains over thousands, and captains of hundreds, and captains over fifties, and captains over tens, and scribes unto your judges. And I charged your judges at that time, saying: Hear the causes between your brethren, and judge righteously between every man and his brother, and the stranger that is with him. Ye shall not respect persons in judgment, but ye shall hear the small as well as the great; ye shall not be afraid of the face of man; for the judgment is God's.

The Reading from Deuteronomy (10, 14-21).

In those days spake Moses unto the sons of Israel, saying: Behold, the heaven and the heaven of heavens is the Lord's thy

God, the earth also, with all that therein is. Only the Lord had a delight in thy fathers to love them, and He chose their seed after them, even you, above all people as it is this day. Circumcise therefore the foreskin of your heart, and be no more stiffnecked. For the Lord our God is God of gods, and Lord of lords, a great God, a mighty and a terrible, which regardeth not persons nor taketh reward; He doth execute the judgment of the fatherless and widow, and loveth the stranger, in giving him food and raiment. Love ye therefore the stranger; for ye were strangers in the land of Egypt. Thou shalt fear the Lord thy God; Him shalt thou serve, and to Him shalt thou cleave, and swear by His name. He is thy praise, and he is thy God that hath done for thee these great and terrible things, which thine eyes have seen.

For the Litany the Sticheron of the Temple. Glory...Tone 3.

Of the apostolic traditions ye, the holy fathers, were renowned preservers, for having in an orthodox manner declared the unity of substance of the Holy Trinity, overthrew in council the blasphemy of Arius, and together with him ye convicted Macedonius the pneumatomach and condemned Nestorius, Eutyches and Dioscorus, Sabellius and Severus the headless; we implore you to obtain that we may be delivered from their allurements and that our unpolluted life may be preserved in the faith.

Both now...The Theotokion: Without seed from the Divine...
For Versicles from the Octoechos. Glory...Tone 4.

Let us in faith and with pious veneration celebrate to-day, in the assembly of the faithful, the thanksgiving memory of the God-bearing fathers that from all the universe were gathered together in the bright city of Nicea, for they have in pious wisdom overthrown the godless teaching of the ferocious Arius and have ex cathedrâ driven him away from the catholic church; they have clearly taught all to confess the Son of God as of One and of Coëval Substance that existed before the ages, having piously and eminently expounded this in the symbol of the faith; wherefore we also, following their divine teaching and believing, do rightfully serve, together with the Father, the Son and All-holy Spirit in One Godhead, the Trinity of One

Substance. *Both now...The Theotokion*: Look down upon the supplications...*For the blessing of the loaves the Troparion*: Mother of God and Virgin, hail...*Twice. And of the Fathers, Tone* 8:

Most glorious art Thou, O Christ our God, since Thou hast firmly set our fathers as the luminaries on earth and through them instructed us all in the true faith. O Most merciful, glory to Thee. *Once.*

At Matins, for God is the Lord, the Troparion of the resurrection twice. Glory...of the Fathers. Both now...The Theotokion: Thou that wast for our sake born....*After the Stichologia, the Cathismata from the Octoechos: The Canon of the resurrection with the Heirmoi in* 4, *that of the Cross and resurrection in* 2, *of the Theotokos in* 2 *and of the Fathers in* 6. *The work of the holy and œcumenical Patriarch, Lord Germanus. Tone* 6:

Ode 1. *The Heirmos:*

Whilst travelling on foot along the depths of the sea as if upon dry land, Israel, seeing Pharaoh, their pursuer, drowned, cried out : Unto God let us sing an ode of victory.

With sacred words let those be honoured who from Nicea as if from some heaven have everywhere thundered the Word of the Living Father and shewn His enemies killed by thunder.

The evil spirit of the pneumatomachoi hath Christ through the Holy Spirit driven far away from His church, having united her by the deeds of the second council.

The enticement of the christomach hath driven away Nestorius, Cyril being the chief of the council and having clearly confessed Virgin Mary to be the pure Mother of God.

The Theotokion: Of the uncreated Trinity One Christ in two natures and desires dost thou, O pure one, bring forth, Who hath for thy sake brought about the union of men and angels.

Ode 3. *The Heirmos:*

There is none holy as Thou, O Lord my God, that hast, as Good One, exalted the horn of Thy believers and established us upon the rock of Thy confession.

Of creature the servant did the foolish Arius appear, and

Macedonius was also abominable, both equally are tormented in the fiery Gehenna together with the Hellens.

With the seven sacred councils of the holy fathers hast Thou, O Christ, illumined Thy church as with the light of seven lamps, having driven far away the darkness of enchantment.

Thy flock, O Word, was being ruined by the manifold rabble of heretics, but the shepherds of Thine intellectual sheep have by their teaching changed this. [*The Theotokion*:

To One of the Uncreated Trinity hast thou, O most pure one, given birth in two natures and desires; Whose venerated image we adore, being filled with grace.

The Contakion and the Oikos of the resurrection; thereupon the Cathisma of the Fathers, Tone 4.
Similar to: Speedily prevent...

As the brightest lamps of the truth of Christ unto the world have ye the God's instructed appeared on the earth, O truly most blessed fathers, since ye have dried up the blasphemous prattle of the heretics, and extinguished the fiery agitation of the infamous teachers; wherefore as hierarchs of Christ intercede that we may be saved.

Twice. Glory...Both now...The Theotokion: With thy divine birth hast thou, O pure one, renewed the mortal and corrupted by passions nature of the earth-born and raised all from death unto the life of incorruption; wherefore, as in duty bound, we all bless thee, O most glorious Virgin, as thou didst foretell.

Ode 4. The Heirmos:

Christ is my power, my God and Lord—the venerable church God-beseemingly singeth, thus calling out, with pure mind feasting in the Lord.

Thine enemies have made noise and those that hate Thee, O Saviour, raised their heads for a short while, but soon fell unable to stand the sound of the spiritual trumpets.

The suns of the Sun have doubly made clear the Son and the Spirit to be of the Father, Uncreated, Co-unoriginate; unto Both the Father alone is believed to be the sole cause.

Seven are the spirits that have descended upon Christ, according to the prophecy of Isaiah, and on the seven councils hath rested Christ with the Father and the Divine Spirit.

The Theotokion: God hast thou brought forth Who carried the flesh from thy pure blood, O pure Maiden; and Him in two substances and one hypostasis the fathers have proclaimed.

Ode 5. *The Heirmos:*

With Thy divine light, O Good One, do illumine, I pray Thee, the souls of those who lovingly watch early unto Thee, that they may know Thee, O Word of God, as the true God, recalling them out of the darkness of sin.

The divine grapes of Christ that were brought from Egypt, were first eaten up by the beasts of the dark, desperate destroyer; but with a sling from the holy fathers these were driven far away.

With the divine thrice-shining radiance having enlightened their minds, the venerable fathers have proclaimed Christ the Lord as One of the Venerated Trinity, double in natures and desires.   [*Of the Trinity:*

On earth, as among the seraphim, the church was made, O Trinity, by the wise fathers like unto heaven; ever singing unto Thee the trisagion hymn she doth unite into one Thy Triunal Godhead.   [*The Theotokion:*

Of thy Son wast thou, O pure one, both Mother and servant; for He that was of thee, was before thee as thy Maker, Who became known in two natures and united through hypostatic Word.

Ode 6. *The Heirmos:*

Beholding the sea of life swelling with the storm of temptation, and taking refuge in Thy calm haven, I cry unto Thee: Lead up my life from corruption, O Greatly-merciful One.

The God of gods hath spoken and called the earth from the rising of the sun unto the going down thereof,—sung once David, signifying the œcumenical councils of the fathers.

The wisdom of God hath fixed seven pillars—Thy church, O Master, by the sevenfold number of the councils of the holy fathers, which is being undeviatingly kept from all heresies.

Let shame cover the countenances of Eutyches and Dioscorus who invented the commingling in the nature of Christ, for it was not in appearance only, but in deification that He took the nature of the earth-born.   [*The Theotokion:*

Let Nestorius be taken into the dark assemblies of the

Hebrews and let his blasphemous tongue be cut off, for the Virgin Mary hath given birth unto God incarnate for us.

The Contakion, Tone 8. *Similar to:* As the first fruits...

The preaching of the apostles and the dogmas of the fathers have sealed for the church the one faith which, whilst it weareth the garment of truth woven by theology that is from above, setteth aright and glorifieth the great mystery of piety. [*The Oikos:*

Let us hearken unto the church of God crying in her sublime teaching: He that thirsteth, let him come unto me and drink of the cup that I hold; it is the cup of wisdom. This drink of truth I have drawn by the word and therefrom doth issue the water not of strife, but that of confession, drinking which the present Israel contemplateth God, Who saith: See ye, see that it is I Myself and that I change not; I am the first God, and I am also thereafter and there is none other; those that partake thereof shall be satisfied and will praise the great mystery of godliness.

Ode 7. *The Heirmos:*

Dew-yielding hath an angel made the furnace unto the pious youths, and God's injunction burning the Chaldeans hath inclined the tyrant to cry out: Blessed art Thou, O God of our fathers.

The Babylonian serpent was once shattered by Daniel, and the ferocious Egyptian serpent—Arius, who was destroying the flock of Christ, undoubtedly perished through the prayers of the fathers.

Moved by unforgivable wickedness, the wolf Macedonius hath revolted against the Spirit that deifieth men and through the bath of baptism doth bring all the faithful unto the whilom good estate.

Dioscorus, Eutyches and Severus—the Leviathan,—the three who have commingled and mixed the Christ's substance by spiritual medley, have daringly revolted against the Venerable Trinity. [*The Theotokion:*

Of Thy fleshly countenance the image, O Master, we kiss with veneration and of Thy Mother and of all saints the honour we hold in a right spirit that we may well pass over to the prototype.

Ode 8. The Heirmos:

Unto the pious hast Thou made dew out of the flame to flow and the sacrifice of a righteous man didst Thou consume with water, for everything makest Thou, O Christ, just as Thou willest; Thee we exalt unto all he ages.

As the sprouts of one single, God-planted root the Son and the Spirit have shone forth; for the Father is the One Cause, the Ever-existing unto the Ever-existing Hypostases being of equal honour.

From immaterial bosom wast Thou for ever shining forth, O Word of the same substance with the Father and the Spirit, but for our sake didst Thou tabernacle in the temporal maternal womb of the only Theotokos.

Arrows burning with the spiritual fire have pierced the cold hearts of the enemies—the heretics, and their death was brought about by the sevenfold and divine assemblies of the fathers. [*The Theotokion:*

Not in persons do we glorify one Christ, nor unite Him in the commingling of His substance, for one and the same is He in person and is divided in natures thy Son and Maker, O Virgin.

Ode 9. The Heirmos:

It is not possible for man to behold God on Whom the angelic orders dare not cast a glance; but through Thee, O all-pure one, was seen of men the Incarnate Word; Him magnifying with heavenly hosts we call thee blessed.

It behoveth not either to add or to omit anything of the sacred tradition of our orthodox faith, for unto it we were truly baptized, and as to perverters of this faith, they will as truly be given over unto the ban of anathema.

With joyful hearts let us exult in the union of the sacred councils of the fathers, for by their means we have seen the light of orthodoxy, since they appeared as lamps that instruct us all unto the right ways of finding the true teaching.

Let us entreat for the cleansing of our souls and let us strive to pass our lives in piety, that we may be participators with the holy fathers who have preserved the riches of the true dogmas unto us their children. [*The Theotokion:*

God hath shone forth out of thy side, O Mother of God, and

He hath deified the race of men, and vouchsafed unto them His own glory and made His heirs all those who always declare thee as the true Theotokos.

The Photagogicon. Similar to : Hearken O ye, women...

Celebrating to-day the memory of the divine fathers, through their entreaties we supplicate Thee, O All-Compassionate One; deliver Thy people, O Lord, from every form of heresies and vouchsafe that they all may glorify the Father, the Son and the Holy Ghost. [*The Theotokion...Similar to :*

Hail thou, divine mansion; hail thou, the mount overshadowed; hail thou, the unconsumed bush; hail thou, the throne of glory; hail thou, the divine table; hail thou, the handle of pure gold; hail thou, the lamp all-radiant; hail thou, the light-cloud, O Virgin Mother Mary.

With the Lauds the Stichera of the resurrection 4 and of the Fathers 4. Tone 6. Similar to : Having laid aside all...

Having gathered together all the spiritual art and having consulted together under the guidance of the Divine Spirit, the venerable fathers have divinely composed the blessed and venerable creed, in which they most clearly teach the Word to be Co-unoriginate with the Begetter and most truly of the same substance, manifestly following therein the teaching of the apostles and being illustrious, most endowed and God-wise indeed. *Twice.*

The Verse : Blessed art Thou, O Lord, the God of our fathers, and praised and glorified is Thy name unto the ages.

Having obtained all the intellectual light, the supernatural knowledge, of the Holy Spirit, the blessed fathers have, in a few words, full of meaning, made an inspired declaration, as preachers of Christ, as chief interpreters of the teaching of the Gospel and of the sacred traditions, the revelation of which they had clearly received from above, and being so enlightened they have expounded the God-inspired rule of the faith.

The Verse : Gather unto Him His righteous. Having gathered all the pastoral art and having put forth the anger, now most righteous, the divine pastors in taking vengeance drove away the dangerous and pernicious wolves, striking them with the sling of the spirit of the fulness of the church as those fallen unto death and incurably afflicted, and this they have done as the truest servants of Christ and the most sacred adepts of the divine teaching. [*Glory...Tone* 8. *George of Nicomedia:*

The choir of the holy fathers, gathered together from the ends of the universe, have taught of the Father, the Son and the Holy Spirit one substance and nature, and have clearly handed over unto the church the mystery of the Divinity. Praising them therefore, let us faithfully bless them saying: O divine band, the God-inspired weapon-bearers of the Lord's army, the many-lighted stars of the intellectual firmament, the unassailable pillars of the mystical Zion, the flowers of paradise smelling of myrrh, the most precious golden mouths of the Word, the glory of Nicea, the ornament of the universe, do assiduously entreat for our souls.

Both now...Most blessed art thou, O Theotokos Virgin....*The Great Doxology. After the Trisagion, the Troparion of the resurrection only. The Ectenes. And the Dismission. And the Catechetical discourse by Theodore of the Stadium. The Procession into the porch. Glory...Both now...The Sticheron of the Gospel... Thereupon the First Hour and the final Dismission. In the Hours the Troparion of the resurrection, Glory...of the Fathers. Both now...the Theotokion of the Hours. After our Father, the Contakion of the resurrection. At the Liturgy, for the Beatitudes from Octoechos, in 6 and of the Fathers Ode 3 in 4. After the Entrance Troparion of the resurrection and of the Fathers, thereupon Contakion of the resurrection, Glory...of the Fathers... Both now...either of the temple of the Theotokos or Defence of the Christians. The Prokeimenon of the Tone and the hymn of the Fathers, Tone* 4. Blessed art Thou, O Lord, the God of our fathers, and blessed and glorified is Thy name unto the ages. *The Apostle of the day and of the Fathers from the Epistle to the Hebrews* (10, 19-31). *Alleluia of the Tone, and of the Fathers Tone I.* The God of Gods, the Lord hath spoken. *The Verse:* Gather unto Him His righteous. *The Gospel of the day and of the Fathers, from St. John* (17, 1-13). *The Communion Verse:* Praise ye the Lord from the heavens, *and of the Fathers:* Let the righteous rejoice in the Lord...

CHAPTER VII.

THE GENERAL SERVICE TO A PROPHET.

At the Vespers, for O Lord, I have cried, the Stichera, Tone 4.
Similar to : Called from above...

Thou that hast in the purity of thy mind received the reflex of the God-emitted light and wast the herald of the divine words and seer and divine prophet, thou appearedst as the God-moved mouth of the Spirit, conveying that which was shewn by Him unto thee, O all-honoured (*mentioned by name*), and declaring unto all the peoples the salvation that was being granted and the Kingdom of Christ; do entreat Him to save and enlighten our souls.

Thou that dost worthily shine with the sight of God and prophetic contemplation and wast honoured with grace, O God-inspired (*mentioned by name*), and made worthy of the divine blessedness, being now possessed of boldness towards the Most gracious One and of sympathy to us, cease not to supplicate for those who in faith praise thee and honour thee as God-declaring, venerable and acceptable to God, that we may be delivered from dangers and that our souls may be saved.

Thy prophet (*mentioned by name*) hast thou, O Immortal One, shewn as a living cloud pouring out the water of life truly eternal, and in sending him, Thou hast richly endowed him with the All-holy Spirit, of one substance with Thee the Father Almighty, and with Thy Son that hath shone forth out of Thy substance; through him hast Thou foretold the saving manifestation of Christ, our God, and announced salvation unto all the peoples.   [*Glory...Both now...The Theotokion :*

Since I, miserable, have fallen into the depth of manifold transgressions, through my laziness, dejection and ignorance, and am now kept in the state of despair, be thou unto me, O

70 SERVICE TO A PROPHET.

most pure one, help, purification and salvation, granting me consolation in the good stead thereof; thee I implore, thee I supplicate, and falling down before thee in faith do I call unto thee that I may not be the joy for the evil one unto the end. *The Stavro-theotokion*: Bewail Me not, O Mother, beholding hung on the tree thy Son and God Who hath suspended the earth on the waters unrestrained and hath made all creation, for I shall rise again and be glorified, I shall lay low the kingdoms of the hades with mighty hand and shall destroy its power, freeing its captives from its villanies, as Compassionate One, and bringing them unto My Father, as Lover of man.

If there be Idiomelion, Glory...Tone 6.

O prophet, the herald of Christ, thou dost never part from the throne of glory, and art ever present with every sufferer; rendering service up on high, thou blessest the universe and art glorified everywhere; do thou supplicate for mercy unto our souls. *Both now...the Theotokion*: Let us, O ye faithful, like archangel, sing the heavenly chamber and the door truly sealed. Hail thou through whom unto us hath grown the Saviour of all, even Christ—the Giver of life and God. Do thou, O Sovereign-Lady, put down the tormentors, our wicked enemies, with thine arm, O most pure one, the hope of Christians. [*The Stavro-theotokion:*

Seeing Thee, O Christ, hanging on the cross, the one that gave Thee birth cried out: What a strange mystery do I see now, my Son? How is it that Thou, being hung in flesh on the tree, dieth, O Giver of life?

If the Celebration be with the Polyeleon, say the Theotokion of the resurrection, Tone 6: Who would not bless thee... *The Entrance ...The Prokeimenon of the day and the Paroimias. (See Appendix.) For Versicles the Stichera, Tone 2. Similar to*: When from the tree...

The Spiritual Star hath found the purity of thy mind, O prophet (*mentioned by name*), shining as clearly as a mirror, and hath illumined the world with the brightness of God's knowledge, resplendent of, and typifying, the images of the divine mysteries and of the grace that was to be granted unto all men, O most wonderful.

The Verse: Thou art a priest unto the ages, after the order of Melchisedek.

Being the mouth of God, thou hast openly reproved the evil doers, condemning them unto the inevitable judgment, O most opulent (*mentioned by name*), and following the righteous teaching and God's decrees; wherefore seeing thy most wise sayings fulfilled, we do worthily praise thee in hymns, O blessed one.

The Verse: Moses and Aaron are in the midst of His priests.

Standing before the throne of the Master and being sated with the ineffable and divine glory, seeing the things above this world and being filled with light, do thou, O God-inspired prophet (*mentioned by name*), remember all those that in faith honour thee, entreating for them, O God-favoured one, the salvation of their souls, and for all the remission of sins.

Glory... Tone 1.

The glorious and honourable prophets, through communion and grace, secondarily as a gift, become partakers of those first qualities and indications of substance wherewithal God is depicted, since the Lord enlighteneth those pleasing unto Him with His brightness.

Both now...the Theotokion of the resurrection: Behold, fulfilled is Isaiah's...

If it be not a Feast, say this Theotokion: The joy of the heavenly orders and on earth the strong protection of men, do save, O all pure Virgin, us who have recourse unto thee, for after God in thee we have put our trust. *The Stavro-theotokion:*

A sword did pierce, O my Son,—said the Virgin, seeing Thee hanging on the tree,—my heart is being pierced, O Master, as Simeon hath of old foretold; but rise and glorify, O Immortal One, Thy Mother and servant, I entreat Thee.

The Troparion from the Typikon; but if there be no Typikon, say the following Troparion, Tone 2:

Of Thy prophet (*mentioned by name*), O Lord, the memory now celebrating, through him we supplicate Thee: Save our souls.

Glory...Both now...the Theotokion, according to the Tone of the Troparion.

SERVICE TO A PROPHET.

At the Matins, for God is the Lord, the same Troparion. After the first Stichologia the Cathisma, Tone 3. Similar to: Unto the beauty of virginity...

The incarnation of the Word hast thou announced beforehand, being enlightened by the Divine Spirit, O great one among the divine prophets, God-inspired *(mentioned by name)*; wherefore we glorify thee as a prophet and solemnize to-day thy memory, harmoniously vociferating unto thee, O wise one: Entreat Christ to save our souls.   [*Twice.*

Glory...Both now...the Theotokion: Inconceivable and incomprehensible is the awful, divine mystery that hath taken place in thee, O God-gladdened Sovereign-Lady, for having conceived, thou hast brought forth the Boundless One clothed with the flesh of thy most pure blood; do, O pure one, always entreat Him as thy Son that our souls may be saved.

After the 2nd Stichologia, the Cathisma, Tone 6. Similar to: Of the divine faith...

As the divine organ of the Comforter, ever and clearly prompted by His grace, wast thou, O blessed one, a prophet; for thou doth declare beforehand the manifestation of things unknown and illumineth those that in faith have recourse to thee, O glorious *(mentioned by name)*; do entreat Christ the God to grant unto us a great mercy.   [*Twice.*

Glory...Both now...the Theotokion: The prophets have predicted, apostles taught, martyrs confessed, and we do believe thee to be the true Theotokos; wherefore we also magnify thine ineffable bringing forth.

After Praise ye the name of the Lord, the Refrain:

We magnify thee, O prophet of God *(mentioned by name)*, and honour thy holy memory, for thou dost entreat for us Christ our God.

The selected Psalm: Blessed is the man that feareth the Lord...
After the Polyeleon the Cathisma, Tone 6. Similar to:
The gate of commiseration...

Having cleared thy mind O all-wise one from filth, thou

SERVICE TO A PROPHET.

hast made it into a divine mirror, receptive of the rays of the Divine Spirit, and now art thou joyfully gone unto the source of illumination, O prophet (*mentioned by name*). *Twice.* *Glory* ...*Both now*...*the Theotokion:*

The Son and the Word of God, that was before the ages born of the Father without a mother, hast thou at the end of days brought forth incarnate of thy pure blood without a husband, O God's parent; Him entreat that unto us may be granted the remission of sins before the end. *The Graduals,* 1*st Antiphon, Tone* 4.

The Prokeimenon: Thou art a priest for ever after the order of Melchisedek. *The Verse:* The Lord said unto my Lord: Sit Thou at My right hand. Every breath...*Thereupon the Gospel* (*Matthew* 23, 29-39).

After the 50*th Psalm, Glory*... At the intercessions of the prophet, O Merciful One, blot out the multitude of our sins. *Both now*...At the intercessions of the Theotokos...*Thereupon:* Have mercy on me, O God...*The Sticheron, Tone* 6: O prophet, the herald of Christ...*See Glory*...*for O Lord I have cried*...

The Canon. Tone 6. *Ode* 1. *The Heirmos:*

Whilst travelling on foot along the depths of the sea as if upon dry land, Israel, seeing Pharaoh, their pursuer, drowned, cried out: Unto God, let us sing an ode of victory.

We beseech thee, O prophet, standing before the throne of God, assiduously to supplicate that enlightenment may be granted unto us, who in faith hymn thy honourable memory.

As a divine organ-depository of the illuminations and gifts of the Divine Spirit—wast thou manifested, O most wise (*mentioned by name*); wherefore joyfully do we the faithful glorify thee.

Before God the Saviour standing as a prophet, do now with boldness entreat that with lustrous rays may be enlightend in the faith those who under God's inspiration glorify thee.

The Theotokion: The Sun that hath shone forth from thy holy womb, O Sovereign-Lady, illumineth all the earth with the brightest auroras; therewith enlightened, we honour thee as the Mother of God.

74   SERVICE TO A PROPHET.

Ode 3. *The Heirmos:*

There is none holy as Thou, O Lord my God, that hast, as Good One, exalted the horn of Thy believers, and established us upon the rock of Thy confession.

He that doth see everything as God, God-beseemingly and clearly manifesteth unto thee, O blissful and wonderful one, the knowledge of the future and the cognisance of events that are going to take place.

With pious boldness having fixed thy mind, thou hast, O glorious one, submitted thyself unto the Divine Spirit, and becamest receptive of the divine inspirations thereof.

As a stream of the mysterious waters flowing from an abyss wast thou God's herald of the gifts of the Spirit.

The Theotokion: Behold, all generations in faith call thee blessed, since the Ever-existing Word thou hast in time brought forth in the flesh supernaturally and hast still remained Virgin.

The Cathisma, Tone 6. Similar to : The gate of commiseration...

Having cleared thy mind, O all-wise one, from filth, thou hast made it into a divine mirror, receptive of the rays of the Divine Spirit, and now art thou joyfully gone unto the source of illumination, O prophet *(mentioned by name)*.

Glory...Both now...The Theotokion: The most glorious Mother of God, who is greatly holier than the holy angels, let us unceasingly hymn with our hearts and mouths, confessing her as the Theotokos, since she hath truly borne God Incarnate and is continually praying for our souls.   *The Stavro-Theotokion:*

O come, let us all hymn the One Who was crucified for us, for Him Mary saw on the tree and said : Although Thou dost suffer even crucifixion, yet art Thou my Son and my God.

Ode 4. *The Heirmos:*

Christ is my power, my God and Lord—the venerable church God-beseemingly singeth, thus calling out, with pure mind feasting in the Lord.

The Lord of all hath appeared unto us, according to thy prophecy, O glorious one, calling all unto His intimate knowledge and hath freed us from thraldom.

Enlightened by the grace, thou hast proclaimed saying: Unto those that follow the faith and serve the Lord, it behoveth to put the neck under one yoke and to work.

Being a prophet, ever enlightened with the brilliancy of the light-giving auroras, do thou, O glorious one, enlighten us lovingly hymning thee. [*The Theotokion:*

O Mary, the all-purest! do away with the agitation of my thoughts through passions and with the whirlwind of temptation—thou, O Mother and Virgin, who hast given birth unto the Source of impassiveness.

Ode 5. *The Heirmos:*

With Thy divine light, O Good-one, do illumine, I pray Thee, the souls of those who lovingly watch early unto Thee, that they may know Thee, O Word of God, as the true God, recalling them out of the darkness of sin.

From unrighteousness to virtue and from the thraldom of passions turn me, O blessed one, through thy supplications, O glorious prophet, and direct me unto the light of the works of piety.

Having illumined with excellent deeds of virtue thy soul, thou hast shewn it to be receptive of the brightness of the Divine Spirit, from Whom wast thou also enriched with the grace of prophecy.

Thou wast a divine prophet, hast led a pure life and wast a receptacle for the Holy Spirit; therefore wast thou made worthy to contemplate Him Who is comprehended invisibly.

The Theotokion: The prophetic utterances herald thy birth, O most pure one, in various types, and we, seeing now their fulfilment, proclaim thee as the true Theotokos.

Ode 6. *The Heirmos:*

Beholding the sea of life swelling with the storm of temptations, and taking refuge in Thy calm haven, I cry unto Thee: Lead up my life from corruption, O Greatly merciful One.

Having received illumination from the Spirit, thou hast, O glorious one, reflected before the world as clearly as in a mirror the divinely shining prophecies, foretelling the future as current events.

Thy King is come—rejoice, O Zion, and exult at the sight— and He hath enlightened the world with the brightness of His Divinity, putting to shame the deceit of the demons.

By the power of the Divine Spirit hast thou, O prophet, foreseen the future with the lucidity of thy soul as in a mirror receiving the impressions of the divine phenomena.

The Theotokion: He that is the Only-begotten of the Father, in thy womb became united unto the perishable flesh, one coming out of the two without corruption and having preserved unhurt thy pure virginity, O all-hymned one.

The Contakion to be taken from the Typicon: in the absence of the latter say the following Contakion, Tone 4.
Similar to: Thou hast appeared to-day...

Illumined of the Spirit thy pure heart became a receptacle for the illustrious prophecy, for thou dost see as the present the events afar off; wherefore we honour thee, O glorious prophet, blissful *(mentioned by name.)* [*The Oikos:*

Enriched with the grace of prophesying, unto the comprehension of the future events wast thou, O God-inspired *(mentioned by name)*, God-beseemingly taught of the Spirit, and foretelleth unto all the coming of Christ and the most abundant call of the Gentiles; wherefore we celebrate thy honoured memory and lovingly hymn thee, glorifying thee in faith and calling unto thee, O glorious one: do unceasingly supplicate Christ the God for us all.

Ode 7. The Heirmos:

Dew-yielding hath an angel made the furnace unto the pious youths, and God's injunction burning the Chaldeans hath inclined the tyrant to cry out: Blessed art Thou, O God of our fathers.

Thy memory, O prophet, hath shone forth unto the world as the sun, illumining with thy grace of prophecy all those who in faith harmoniously sing: Blessed art Thou, O God of our fathers.

Having appeared as the most abundant cloud thou, O blissful one, hast showered unto us a whole cloud of God's knowledge from the saving sources, wherewithal we are enlightened to vociferate: Blessed art thou, O God of our fathers.

Enlightened of God, the prophets foreherald the meaning of the future, they God-wisely proclaim the Word that hath been from the beginning, unto Whom we sing: Blessed art Thou, O God of our fathers. [*The Theotokion:*

The Word of old giving unto all their being, having, with the divine desire, wished to recall man, did come, O pure one, down into thy womb to reside, O blessed one, that gavest birth unto God in the flesh.

Ode 8. *The Heirmos*:

Unto the pious hast Thou made dew out of the flame to flow, and the sacrifice of a righteous man didst Thou consume with water, for everything makest Thou, O Christ, just as Thou willest; Thee we exalt unto all the ages.

Having given thyself entirely unto the Almighty, thou hast mystically learned the ways of providence and hast taught the economy to the Gentiles, wherefore we hymn Thee, O prophet, God-spoken.

Supplicatory melody do thou, O blessed one of God, bring unto God for those that hymn thee, and put down the agitation of temptations, that we may hymn thee, O prophet, God-spoken.

As the fire before those sitting in darkness hast thou appeared unto all, God-wisely illumining with the divine light those that in faith hymn the Lord unto the ages.   [*The Theotokion*:

Having given birth unto God and Lord—the Life-giver, thou, O all-holy one, hast put an end to the destruction of death that was unrestrainably putting all to death; wherefore we hymn thee unto all the ages.

Ode 9. *The Heirmos*:

It is not possible for men to behold God on Whom the angelic orders dare not cast a glance; but through thee, O all-pure one, was seen of men the Incarnate Word; Him magnifying, with heavenly hosts we call thee blessed.

In the land of the benign art thou dwelling wherein thou dost see the angelic sereneness, O all-wise God's prophet (*mentioned by name*), having been benign whilst shining with the grace; therefore we the faithful glorify thee joyously.

Of thy predictions, O all-glorious one, clearly seeing the fulfilment in the past, we wonder at the grace that was given unto thee, and are amazed at the purity of thy mind and of thy soul the clear sight of God.

Wherein are the angelic orders, of the prophets and patriarchs the choirs and the limpidities of the holy ones,—therein,

O prophet (*mentioned by name*), hast thou found a habitation; and now joyfully exulting with them, supplicate the Lord for us that those may be saved who in faith praise thee.

The Theotokion: As thou, there never was from ancient generations granted another one, O all spotless Mother of God; for thou alone of all possessedst holiness and purity incomparable; wherefore thou hast received God, in thee incarnate.

The Photagogicon: All the prophets are rejoicing and are exulting in thy joyful day, O Godly-wise one, whilst participating of thy gladness and of the divine glory; do supplicate together with them and save those who hymn thee.

The Theotokion: With the sprinkling of thy compassions, O pure one, wash off the filth of my soul, and grant, O Maiden, that I may unceasingly pour the drops of tears which should dry up the streams of my passions.

With the Lauds the Stichera, Tone 8. Similar to: O most glorious wonder.

The Divine Spirit hath been poured out, as thou, O honourable (*mentioned by name*), moved of Him, didst in thy prophesying say, upon us the believers and He doth reveal the manifestation of the divine mysteries, and those who have received His operation prophesy, being illumined both by the divine light and the divine grace. [*Twice.*

The wonderful (*mentioned by name*), filled with godly messages, cometh forth from Thy house, O Master, as a source giving drink to the souls, and he hath trickled for us sweetness which doth sweeten the thoughts, since he was great in his whole spirit and was carried by his virtues unto the divine height.

Through thy prophetic boldness and intellectual nearness to God, on account of which thou, O (*mentioned by name*), dost see the heavenly sights, do make Him merciful unto us that in faith celebrate thy memory, entreating of Him, O glorious one, remission of transgressions, participation of the divine delights and great mercy.

Glory...Tone 4. Rejoicing in the Lord God and thy Saviour and exulting, O God-spoken and glorious one, since thou hast received the luminous light of the Existing One and art mentally illumined with the light proceeding from God, do thou deliver us that are in faith celebrating thine all-festal memory, from temptations and afflictions through thine intercessions.

Both now...The Theotokion: Deliver us from our wants, O Mother of Christ the God, who gavest birth unto the Maker of all, that we all may call unto thee: Hail thou, the sole intercession for our souls.

The Stavro-theotokion. Similar to: As a virtuous...

Seeing Christ being put to death and destroying the deceiver, the all-pure Sovereign-Lady, lamenting Him as Master Who came out of her womb, hymned Him and wondering at His long-suffering, cried out: O my most beloved Child, do not forget Thy servant, tarry not, O Lover of man, with my consolation.

CHAPTER VIII.

THE GENERAL SERVICE TO AN APOSTLE. *At the Vespers, for O Lord, I have cried, the Stichera, Tone* 8. *Similar to:* What shall we call ye...

What shall we name thee, O apostle? heaven, since thou hast confessed the glory of God? or a stream, since thou dost mystically give drink unto the creation? or a star, that illumineth the church? or a cup pouring out the holy drink? or Christ's nearest friend and of the bodiless ones equal? Do supplicate for our souls.

O glorious God-seeing apostle! Beautiful have become thy feet treading well along the paths of preaching and making narrow the way of the enemy by the width of the divine knowledge of the Word that hath appeared in the coarseness of the flesh and thee as a most glorious disciple hath selected, O blissful one. Him supplicate that our souls may be saved.

Truly wast thou, O God-spoken apostle, sent from Christ as a luminous arrow wounding the enemies and unto the wounded souls manifestly granting cure; wherefore we, as in duty bound, glorify thee and celebrate to-day thy holy feast. Do supplicate that our souls may be saved. [*Glory...Both now...the Theotokion:*

Thousands of times, O all-pure one, have I promised to make penitence for my transgressions, but the beloved habit of my evil deeds does not forsake me; wherefore unto thee I cry and fall down before thee with the supplication: Do thou, O Sovereign-Lady, release me from this tyranny, instructing me unto the better ways, nearest to salvation.

The Stavro-theotokion: Thee, the Lamb and Shepherd, seeing on the tree, the lamb that bare Thee was bewailing and as a Mother thus spake to Thee: O most beloved Son, how is it, O Long-suffering, that Thou art hung on the tree of the cross? how is it that Thy hands and Thy feet, O Word, are nailed down by the wicked and Thou hast shed Thy blood, O Master?

If there be Idiomelion, Glory...Tone 6.

The grace was poured out through thy lips, O glorious apostle (*mentioned by name*), and thou wast the lamp of the church of Christ, teaching the intellectual sheep to believe in the Trinity Consubstantial, in the One Godhead.

Both now...The Theotokion: No one who fleeth for refuge unto thee, ever leaveth thee ashamed, O most pure Theotokos-Virgin, but asking for grace, he receiveth the grant of his profitable petition. [*The Stavro-theotokion:*

The all-pure one seeing Thee hung on the cross with motherly tears cried out unto Thee: O my Son and my God, my sweetest Child, how is it that Thou sufferest the ignominious death?

If the Celebration be with the Polyeleon, say the Theotokion of the resurrection: Who would not bless thee...*The Entrance. The Prokeimenon of the day. Thereupon three Paroimias of Apostles* (see *Appendix*).

For Versicles, the Stichera, Tone 4. Similar to: Thou hast given a token...

Thou hast obtained, O apostle, an invincible authority over demons, and the power in the name of Christ to drive away their princes of darkness; thou hast passed through the earth enlightening as the sun, and hast instructed all the lands, preaching, O glorious one, Christ's first and saving coming.

The Verse: Through all the earth is gone out their sound and their words to the end of the world.
Resembling the first grace and the natural and most divine life, wast thou (*mentioned by name*) a good man in very deed, and wast called son of the divine grace, whilst on account of goodness of thy character and of the purity of thy mind thou didst appear to be a sincere disciple of Christ.

The Verse: The heavens declare the glory of God, and the firmament sheweth His handiwork. An instrument well constructed, through the divine leading hast thou, O apostle (*mentioned by name*), devoted thyself unto the calling in of the Gentiles, instructing them, by word and deed, in the knowledge of Christ, and hast enlightened all to confess the true Godhead of Jesus, the Saviour of our souls. *Glory...Tone* 2. Leaving the earthly cares, thou hast followed Christ and having been sealed with the breath of the Holy Spirit was sent by Him unto the lost nations to turn men unto the light of the knowledge of God, O apostle (*mentioned by name*); thereupon, having ended the exploits of thy divine passion and of various tortures, hast thou given up thy soul unto Christ; Him supplicate, O all-blissful one, to grant us great mercy. *If there be a Festival, say the Theotokion of the resurrection:* O new wonder—the greatest of all the ancient wonders!...*But if there be no Celebration, say the following Theotokion:* As a fertile olive-tree the Virgin hath brought forth Thee, the Fruit of life to fructify unto the world great and abundant mercy. [*The Stavro-theotokion:*

Seeing Thee, O Jesus, nailed to the tree of the cross, the innocent of marital life said in tears: O my sweetest Child, why hast Thou left alone me that bare Thee, O Unapproachable Light of the Unoriginate Father? Make an effort and glorify Thyself that the divine glory may be obtained by those who glorify Thy divine passion. *The Troparion from the Typicon. If there be no Typicon, say the following Troparion, Tone* 3. O holy apostle (*mentioned by name*), entreat the Merciful God that He may grant the remission of sins to our souls. *Glory...Both now...the Theotokion, according to the Tone of the Troparion.*

At the Matins, for God is the Lord, the same Troparion. After the 1st Stichologia, the Cathisma, Tone 2: Having caught the nations, the glorious apostle hath taught the ends of the earth to adore Thee, O Christ the God, together with the Father and the Spirit; for his sake do Thou stablish Thy church and send down unto the faithful Thy blessing, O Only-merciful One and Lover of man. *Twice.*

Glory...Both now...the Theotokion: Of the divine nature we have become partakers through thee, O Theotokos and Ever-Virgin; for thou hast brought forth unto us the God Incarnate; wherefore as in duty bound we all piously magnify thee.

After the 2nd Stichologia, the Cathisma, Tone 4: Since the Sun of righteousness—Christ—hath emitted thee, O glorious apostle (*mentioned by name*), as a ray to enlighten all the earth, thou dost illumine with thine intercessions and enlighten with the divine, never-setting Light all those that in faith celebrate thy holy memory. *Twice. Glory...Both now...the Theotokion:*

A hope which can never be put to shame, of those that trust in thee—the only one who, above nature, broughtest forth in the flesh Christ our God, Him do thou with the holy apostles supplicate to grant unto the universe cleansing of transgressions and unto us all, before the end, amendment of our lives.

The Refrain: We magnify thee, O holy apostle (*mentioned by name*), and honour thy sufferings and pains with which thou hast laboured in the preaching of the Gospel of Christ.

The selected Psalm: The heavens declare the glory of God...

After the Polyeleon, the Cathisma, Tone 8. *Similar to:* Of the wisdom...

Having with the net of divine words caught the intellectual fishes, thou hast brought them as firstlings unto our God, and, being desirous to put on Christ's wounds, thou didst appear resemblable to Him in His passion; wherefore being gathered together we dutifully honour thine, O glorious apostle, all-festive memory and harmoniously vociferate unto thee: Supplicate Christ the God that He may grant remission of sins unto those who lovingly venerate thy holy memory. *Twice.*

Glory...Both now...the Theotokion: Let us hymn the heavenly gate and ark, the all-holy mountain and the light cloud, the bush unconsumed, intellectual paradise, the recall of Eve, of all the universe the great treasure, since in her was brought about the salvation of the world and the remission of the ancient transgressions. Wherefore let us vociferate unto her: Supplicate thy Son to grant the remission of sins unto those who piously adore thine all-holy bringing forth. *The Graduals. The 1st Antiphon of the 4th Tone. The Prokeimenon:* Through all the earth is gone out their sound... *The Verse:* The heavens declare the glory of God... Let every breath... *Thereupon the Gospel* (*Matth.* 9, 36-38; 10, 1. 5-8).

After the 50th Psalm, the Sticheron, Tone 6: Having manifestly received the grace of the Divine Spirit, thou (*mentioned by name*) wast a member of the sacred choir of apostles; wherefore thou hast also inhaled the fiery breath that was once carried down from heaven in the shape of tongues of fire, and hast burned up the thorny godlessness of heathens. Do thou, O preacher, supplicate Christ the God that our souls may be saved.

The Canon, Tone 8. *Ode* 1. *The Heirmos:*

Let us, O people, send up a melody unto our marvellous God Who hath liberated Israel from bondage, singing unto Him an ode of victory and vociferating : We sing unto Thee, the only Master.

Standing on high before the Master Who hath glorified thee, O wondrous apostle (*mentioned by name*), and hath manifestly shewn thee His disciple, do enlighten my soul that I may hymn thy divine memory.

Having granted unto thee every abundance of good things, as the uppermost of divine gifts Christ, righteous in His judgment, hath shewn thee, O God-manifested apostle, being Himself the Only-righteous.

Having received the all-spiritual light that came down from heaven upon thee, O apostle, thou wast fire-inspired and burning all the deceit of polytheism. [*The Theotokion:*

My mortal and corrupt substance hast Thou, O Saviour, shewn as immortal and incorrupt, having dwelt in the womb of the holy, all-pure Virgin, innocent of marital life, and having taken up the nature of man.

Ode 3. *The Heirmos:*

There is none holy as the Lord, and none righteous as our God, Whom the whole creation thus hymneth : There is no one righteous except Thee, O Lord.

The divine mystery of incarnation hast thou, O God-acceptable apostle, truly learned, having received from the Saviour Himself the illumination from above.

The Word Unoriginate and Ever-existing hath thee, O wondrous apostle—His minister, abundantly illumined with the lustrous brightness of the divine grace.

Kindled with the aurora and spiritual working as a God-seen arrow wast thou, O most glorious apostle, sent from Christ, and thou hast, O blissful one, enlightened the world with thy teaching. [*The Theotokion:*

As a golden candlestick hath the prophet foreshadowed thee, carrying the never-setting Light— Christ our God Who enlighteneth the world with the rays of divinity.

The Cathisma, Tone 3. Similar to: Of the divine...

With the illumination of the Divine Spirit thou hast dispersed the darkness of polytheism and hast enlightened the hearts of the faithful, having loudly proclaimed the saving commandments, O all-wise apostle (*mentioned by name*); supplicate Christ the God to grant us great mercy. *Glory...Both now... the Theotokion:* Every one hath rightfully the recourse thither where he obtaineth salvation, and what can other such refuge be that sheltereth our souls, beside thee, O Theotokos?

The Stavro-Theotokion: Having acquired as a staff of strength the cross of thy Son, O Theotokos, therewith we put down the rage of the enemies and unceasingly and lovingly magnify thee.

Ode 4. *The Heirmos:*

Thee, O Word, desiring to become incarnate of the overshadowed mount— the only Theotokos, the prophet hath with Godly-sight perceived and with awe doxologized Thy might.

Being the treasury of all the gifts of the gospel, thou, O all-blissful (*mentioned by name*), wast full of grace, light of the world and salt of the universe.

From things of shameful aspect hast thou, O wondrous one,

turned away and wast made worthy to see the immaterial light of Divinity that hath assumed the form of a human thing.

As a disciple of the incorruptible Life, do thou slay the sin that liveth within us, with the life-bearing power of the Lifegiver Whose energy hast thou received. [*The Theotokion:*

Being equal unto Thy Father in substance, Thou wast equal unto men in nature, having taken, O Master, our flesh of the all-pure Virgin.

Ode 5. The Heirmos:

Having enlightened with the knowledge of God the ends of the world that was in the night of darkness, do Thou, O Lord, illumine me with the morning of Thy love to man.

Thy tongue, O God-seer, became mingled with the spiritual fire which thou lovingly receivedst sitting in the upper chamber.

Being high as living in the uppermost dwellings, thou, O (*mentioned by name*), hast brought unto us high and great teachings.

Having thy pure mind towards God in His serenity, thou hast acquired a heart as pure and hast seen the God Incarnate, incomprehensible for the intellect. [*The Theotokion :*

With thy bringing forth, O Virgin, the first law ceased, and the grace blossomed, truth shone forth.

Ode 6. The Heirmos:

A bright garment do grant me Thou that puttest on light as a garment, O Multi-merciful Christ, our God.

As a disciple and friend of Christ hast thou, O glorious apostle, zealously worked for the Lord God Almighty.

The Saviour hath shewn thee as self-worker of divine wonders, having given thee the power through the operation of His graciousness.

Adorned with the divine grace of teaching, thou, O most laudable apostle of Christ (*mentioned by name*), dost announce unto the world the general salvation of God Who is over all.

The Theotokion: Let the mouths of the wicked that do not philosophize thee, O all-spotless one, as Theotokos, be closed, and let their faces be clothed with shame.

The Contakion to be found in the Typicon; in the absence of the latter, say the following Contakion, Tone 4. *Similar to:* Thou hast appeared... As a most bright star the church hath for ever acquired thee, O apostle (*mentioned by name*), being enlightened with the grant of a multitude of thy miracles: wherefore we call unto Christ: Save, O Greatly-merciful, those who in faith honour the memory of Thine apostle.

The Oikos: A stream of speech grant me, O Lord, Who hast made the nature of water, and strengthen my heart, O Compassionate One, Who hath firmly set the earth with Thy Word, enlighten also my thoughts Thou that puttest on light as a garment, that I may speak and sing such things as are worthy of the veneration of Thine apostle, O Greatly-merciful One.

Ode 7. *The Heirmos:*

The Hebrew youths in the furnace have boldly trodden upon the flame and have changed the fire into dew, vociferating: Blessed art Thou, O Lord God, unto the ages.

Possessing wonderful zeal, thou, O (*mentioned by name*), standest now before the throne of the Master; as servant of Christ wast thou crowned, O God's teacher, that criedst out: Blessed art Thou, O Lord God, unto the ages.

Exulting together with the Word and having been His companion, thou wast made co-partaker of the Kingdom of the Most High, calling out: Blessed art Thou, O Lord God, unto the ages.

Full of wisdom, enlightened by the grace, adorned with the serene beauty, thou, O God-spoken holy apostle, dost cry out: Blessed art Thou, O Lord God, unto the ages. [*The Theotokion:*

Through the flattering idea of a better destiny, the serpent did of old drive away the forefathers, and thou, O Mother of God, hast recalled them; blessed is the Fruit of thy womb, O most pure one.

Ode 8. *The Heirmos:*

Whilst the musical instruments gave out harmonious sounds and people innumerable were adoring the image on Dura, three youths disobeying orders hymned the Lord and doxologized Him unto all the ages.

As thy feet appeared beautiful, so stately was also thy speech that proclaimed the glory of Christ and taught us to call: Hymn the Lord and exalt Him unto all the ages.

Adorned with brilliant-rayed virtues and emitting lights of miracles, thou becamest known unto the people as a blessed seed persuading us to call out: Hymn the Lord and exalt Him unto all the ages.

A holy disciple, well versed in the heavenly mysteries, thou hast passed throughout the universe, teaching openly the word of the faith in Christ, O apostle, and confessing the ineffable grace, whilst vociferating: Hymn the Lord and exalt Him unto all the ages. [*The Theotokion*:

The mind cannot explain thy bringing forth, O God's Mother, and is too feeble to express it in words; for having conceived, thou, O Virgin, didst give birth unto God, Whom we exalt unto all the ages.

Ode 9. The Heirmos:

As truly Theotokos we confess thee, being saved by thee, O pure Virgin, and together with the bodiless choirs magnify thee.

Unto the ends wast thou manifested, O apostle, shining with the divine light, and having received the spiritual fire, thou appearedst, O (*mentioned by name*), resplendent with light; wherefore we magnify thee.

Given up entirely unto God, unto Him thou becamest thoroughly mingled; Him do now, O God-manifested one, supplicate for us who in faith and with love are praising thee.

Celebrating thy memory, O most blissful one, we entreat thee that we ever may be freed from great agitation through the intercession of thy boldness, which as apostle of Christ thou dost possess, O all-honourable God-seer.

The Theotokion: We magnify in hymns the mediatrix of the salvation of all that appeared unto men and illumined the world with the lustre of the God-like purity.

The Photagogicon. Similar to: By the Spirit foreseeing...

The progress of thy beautiful feet, O apostle (*mentioned by name*), having been arrested, thou hast joyfully ascended for the heavenly progress, and standing before the Trinity thou dost see in the Father—the Son and the Divine Spirit; wherefore we do in faith celebrate thy most sacred and divine memory.

The Theotokion: Of the dreadful trial I recall to myself the hour, the multitude of my wicked deeds horrifieth and frighteneth me; but take compassion on me, O most pure one, in thy warm supplication and vouchsafe unto me salvation; for what thou willest do thou canst.

With the Lauds, the Stichera, Tone 4. *Similar to:*
As a virtuous...

With the staff of grace hast thou, O wondrous one, snatched men out of the depth of vanities, having thyself obeyed, O (*mentioned by name*), the beck of thy Teacher, Who hath in everything enlightened thine understanding and hath shewn thee, O all-blissful one, apostle and honourable God's herald of the incomprehensible Divinity. *Twice.*

Enlightenment of the Spirit came down upon thee in the shape of fire and hath made thee, O blissful one, into a divine receptacle, that swiftly drivest away the mist of godlessness and enlightenest the world with the lustre of thy most wise speech, O expounder of mysteries, ornament of apostles, blessed eye-witness of Christ.

With the lightnings of thy preaching hast thou, O glorious one, shewn those that were sitting in the darkness of ignorance, sons of the Master and God for the sake of their faith; His passion and death hast thou emulated and becamest the heir of His glory, as a wise one and God-spoken, as the disciple of truth.

Glory...Tone 2.

Having given up the earthly things, thou hast followed Christ and having been sealed with the breath of the Holy Spirit, wast thou sent by Him unto the lost nations to turn men unto the light of the knowledge of God, O apostle (*mentioned by name*); having thereupon ended the exploits of thy divine passion and of various torments, thou hast given up to Christ thy soul; Him supplicate, O all-blessed one, to grant us great mercy.

Both now...The Theotokion: All my trust I place in thee, O Mother of God, do thou preserve me under thy shelter.

The Stavro-theotokion: When the undefiled lamb saw her

offspring being dragged as a man to the willing slaughter, she thus spake with sobs : Dost Thou strive now, O Christ, to make me childless who gave Thee birth? Wherefore hast Thou done this, O Deliverer of all? Howbeit, I hymn and glorify Thine extreme goodness, O Lover of man, which is above the mind and speech.

CHAPTER IX.

THE SERVICE COMMON TO TWO OR MANY APOSTLES.

At the Vespers, for O Lord I have cried, the Stichera, Tone 4.
Similar to : As a virtuous...

As personally knowing and eye-witnesses of the incarnation of the Word, ye—the most fortunate disciples—are being blessed, for as brilliant lightnings have ye made your appearance in the world, and as intellectual mountains you let fall the sweet things; and as the ever running parted rivers of paradise you give unto the churches of the Gentiles the divine waters to drink.

As the rays resplendent with the brightness of the Spirit, were ye sent into the whole world, and you have wrought an abundance of miracles; ye were the ministers of the mysteries of Christ and God-written tablets of the divine grace inscribed with the God-taught law, O ye sacred adepts abounding in mysteries.

The calamus of the fishermen hath put in order the waverings of philosophers and current of orators, having clearly expounded in the gospel the God-wise teachings, the doctrines of grace and of the beneficent mysteries, as well as the participation of the eternal food, the delight of angels and ever-abiding glory.

Glory...Both now...The Theotokion : Hail thou, O luminous sun—the bearer of the never-setting Sun, that hast beamed forth the Incomprehensible Sun ; hail thou, O mind, that flashes forth the divine lights; hail thou, O ray of light that illuminest the ends of the earth, and art truly of golden light, perfectly beautiful and most unblemished, that hast flashed unto the faithful the never-ending Light.   [*The Stavro-theotokion:*

Seeing Christ the Lover of man, hung and being pierced through His side with a spear, the most pure one did bewail crying out: What is this, O my Son? What have the ungrateful people rewarded Thee with for all the good Thou hast done unto them? and Thou most lovingly takest care of my childlessness. I wonder at Thy voluntary crucifixion, O Compassionate One.

Should there be Idiomelion: Glory...Tone 8. Enlightening the creation among whom ye, the disciples of the Saviour, have moved, and burning the deceitful idols as dry sticks with your teaching, ye have brought the nations from the depths of ignorance unto the divine understanding and saved them, and now do supplicate Christ that He may be merciful unto us in the day of judgment.   [*Both now...the Theotokion:*

O most pure Virgin—Theotokos, do receive the voices of thine entreaters and supplicate the Lord unceasingly to grant us the remission of sins.   [*The Stavro-theotokion:*

O Lord, when the sun saw Thee—the Sun of righteousness—hung up on the tree, it hath hidden its rays and the moon hath changed light into darkness, whilst the all-spotless one, Thy Mother, was sorely wounded in her innermost soul.

If the Celebration be with the Polyeleon, say the Theotokion of the resurrection: The King of the heavens. *The Entrance... The Prokeimenon of the day...The Readings of the Apostles* (see Appendix). *For the Versicles, the Stichera, Tone* 6. *Similar to:* Risen on the third day...Ye, the disciples of God—theologians and God-seers—were the ministers of the great mysteries of God, and having received the grace of healing, ye cure the maladies of all men. *The Verse: Through all the earth is gone out their sound and their words to the end of the world:* A great refuge and shelter for our souls and the driving away of the evil spirits ye are, O apostles of the Lord and God-seers; wherefore we always honour you. *The Verse: The heavens declare the glory of God, and the firmament sheweth His handiwork.* O ye, blessed apostles of God, do deliver those that praise you in faith, from every attack and injury of the demons, from transgressions and from captivity of the evil one. [*Glory...Tone* 4:

Organs well appointed by the divine nursing, ye, apostles, were entrusted with the call of the Gentiles, instructing them both by word and deed in the knowledge of Christ, and you have enlightened all to confess the true divinity of Christ, the Saviour of our souls. *If there be Celebration, say the Theotokion of the resurrection:* Look down upon the entreaties of thy servants...*But in case of no Celebration, say this Theotokion:*

Possessing in thee, O Theotokos, the hope and protection, we are not afraid of the assaults of the enemy, for thou dost save our souls. [*The Stavro-theotokion:*

A sword, as Simeon hath said, did pierce thy heart, O all-holy Theotokos, when thou sawest the ineffable Word, Who shone forth from thee, condemned by the lawless, lifted up on the cross, partaking of vinegar and gall, whilst His side was pierced and His hands and feet were nailed; with bitter wailing hast thou cried, vociferating as a Mother. What is this new mystery, O my sweet Child? [*The Troparion, Tone* 3:

O holy apostles, entreat the Merciful God that He may grant forgiveness of sins to our souls.

Glory...Both now...the Theotokion according to the Tone of the Troparion.

At the Matins, for God is the Lord, the same Troparion. After the 1st Stichologia, the Cathisma, Tone 1. *Similar to: Thy sepulchre O Saviour...*

The spiritual choir of apostles of the Most High God have been mysteriously sent and appeared as physicians of those suffering in thraldom, invoking only the Three-hypostatic One; they have wisely described the divine incarnation of Emanuel the Lord. [*Twice. Glory...Both now...the Theotokion:*

As the bush which Moses saw unconsumed, as God's mountain, holy cloud, undefiled tabernacle, God-acceptable table, palace of the Great King, all-luminous and impassable door,—we hymn thee, O Virgin.

After the 2nd Stichologia, the Cathisma, Tone 4. Similar to:
Thou hast appeared to-day...

As the stars, ye apostles, illumine the ends of the earth with resplendent beams—with the instructions of your holy preaching, O heavenly adepts of the Lord.

Twice. Glory...Both now...the Theotokion: As ardent protection of those in need, our help and turn God-wards, for whose sake we have been freed from corruption, let us, O ye faithful, bless the Theotokos.

After Praise ye the name of the Lord...the Refrain: We magnify you, O holy apostles, since you have enlightened the whole world with your teaching and have brought unto Christ all the ends.

The selected Psalm: The heavens declare the glory of God...

After the Polyeleon, the Cathisma, Tone 3. Similar to:
The Divine...

Ye, divine trumpets of the Comforter, emitting the breath of the words of salvation, do proclaim it unto the world, and awakening those that are sleeping in the darkness of deceit, do bring unto the light of the knowledge of God, O apostles of the Divine Light, supplicating Christ the God that our souls may be saved.   [*Twice. Glory...Both now...the Theotokion:*

Without divesting Himself of His divine nature, God became flesh in thy womb, but the Incarnate did remain God, and hath, after the birth, preserved all-spotless thee, His Mother and Virgin, just as before the birth, being One and the same Lord; Him do assiduously supplicate to grant unto us great mercy.

The Graduals, the 1st Antiphon of the 4th Tone. The Prokeimenon: Through all the earth is gone out their sound. *The Verse:* The heavens declare the glory of God...Let every breath...*Thereupon the Gospel unto one apostle (Matth. 9, 36-38; 10, 1. 5-8)....After the 50th Psalm the Sticheron, Tone 6:*

The all-honourable festival of the apostles hath come unto the church of Christ intercessory of salvation for us all; wherefore in secretly applauding let us call unto them: Hail, O ye lamps, shedding forth the beams of intellectual Sun unto those in darkness; hail, O ye apostles—the immoveable foundations of the divine doctrines, friends of Christ, honourable vessels; come invisibly into our midst and vouchsafe the immaterial gifts unto those that praise in songs your festival.

The Canon. Tone 4. Ode 1. The Heirmos:

The red abyss of the sea with unmoistened steps having crossed on foot, the Israel of old hath, through the cruciform arms of Moses, obtained victory in the wilderness over the forces of Amalek.

Unto me desirous to melodize the choir of apostles, through their intercessions, grant, O Christ, as God, a ray of the All-holy Spirit and the light of Thy wisdom.

Strengthened with Thy might and grace, O Christ, Thy honourable apostles, the God-seers, have broken down the power of the opposing enemies by their constant watching for Thee.

Accomplishing healings in Thy name, O Master, the glorious apostles have caught entire heathen nations unto the knowledge of Thee and enlightened with Thy light.

Having learned the heavenly wisdom, the most glorious and wise apostles have clearly made foolish the verbosity of the impious by the conciseness of their preaching.

The Theotokion: One of the most divine Trinity hast Thou, O most pure one, brought forth—Him that appeared from thee, O Virgin and Mother, in our flesh, by the goodwill of the Begetter and by the working of the Most Holy Spirit.

Ode 3. The Heirmos:

Delighted on Thine account is Thy church, O Christ, calling unto Thee: Thou art my strength, O Lord, both refuge and support.

The preachers of Christ, having proclaimed on earth the divine and honourable dogmas, and having had them confirmed by the tongues of fire, delivered them over unto us.

Thou, O Master, hast shewn Thy disciples to be the intellectual heavens that declare Thy glory unto all the ends of the world.

Written in the heavens and appearing as co-dwellers with Christ, do ye, O most wise ones, preserve now us who lovingly venerate you. [*The Theotokion:*

He that dwelleth on high, O most pure one, hath found His abode in us, for having without seed taken the flesh of thee, He did appear.

The Cathisma, Tone 8. Similar to: Of Wisdom...

With the net of divine words having caught the intellectual fishes, you have brought these as firstlings unto our God, and having desired to put Christ's wounds, you have appeared like unto Him in His passion; wherefore, having come together, we dutifully honour your, O glorious apostles, all-festive memory, and harmoniously vociferate unto you: Supplicate Christ the God that He may grant remission of sins unto those who lovingly venerate your holy memory.

Glory...Both now...the Theotokion:

As Virgin and one amongst women that, without seed, hast brought forth God in the flesh, we—all generations of men—call thee blessed, for the fire of the Divinity hath tabernacled in thee and, as an infant, dost thou suckle the Maker and the Lord. Wherefore, both the angels and the mankind, we do worthily glorify thine all-holy bringing forth, and harmoniously vociferate unto thee. Supplicate Christ the God that He may grant the remission of sins unto those who in faith adore thine all-holy bringing forth.   [*The Stavro-theotokion:*

Seeing the Lamb, the Shepherd and the Redeemer upon the cross, the lamb exclaimed in tears, and loudly lamenting, thus vociferated: The world indeed rejoiceth receiving through Thee the deliverance, but my innermost is consumed at the sight of Thy crucifixion which Thou dost endure on account of the mercifulness of Thy compassion. O Longsuffering Lord, abyss of mercy and a source inexhaustible, take compassion and grant the remission of transgressions unto those who in faith hymn Thy divine passion.

Ode 4. The Heirmos:

Elevated on the cross seeing Thee, the Sun of righteousness, the church stood up in her order worthily calling out: Glory to Thy power, O Lord.

The utterance of divine words of the apostles, fire-like hath passed through the entire universe, consuming the matter of deceit and enlightening with grace the nations of the pious.

The disciples of the Lord, having appeared as God's bright light, have enlightened the world that became black through the darkness of godlessness, with the beams of grace and the brightness of their preaching.

Illumined with the sacred rays of the intellecual Sun, ye, O most famous, shine in the world as the sun and drive away the mist of deceit with the divine light.

In Thy cross possessing the staff of strength, Thine eye-witnesses have divided in two the salty sea of life, disturbing, as horses, the waters of polytheism. [*The Theotokion:*

Adorned with the variegated illumination, the animated heaven of Thee, O Christ, the King of kings, the most pure Virgin is now glorified as the Theotokos.

Ode 5. *The Heirmos:*

Thou, my God, didst come into the world as light, as a holy light that bringeth out of the darkness of ignorance those who in faith hymn Thee.

Thy divine and most wise servants hast Thou shewn in the world as a light that announceth unto all Thee—the never-setting Light.

Ye, apostles, who have manifestly practiced every virtue, do now destroy the various plots of the malice of the demons.

Uttering in tongues of fire, the apostles made clear unto us the Trinity shining in the Unity of the Godhead.

The Theotokion: We offer thee as an invincible weapon against our enemies; in thee, O God's Bride, we have acquired the anchor and the hope of our salvation.

Ode 6. *The Heirmos:*

I will sacrifice unto Thee, O Lord, with the voice of praise—crieth out unto Thee the church having been cleansed of the demons' blood with the blood that mercifully ran out of Thy side.

Having fortified Thy disciples, O Saviour, with wisdom and miracles, Thou hast made them stronger than the hellenic charlatans, and they overthrew the deceitful doctrines of these.

The divine rivers of wisdom have filled with the waters of salvation all the valleys of the church, having enriched them with the streams from the sources of salvation.

Having appeared as living stars, O most highly praised ones, ye have dispersed all the dark deceitfulness by the brilliant beams, and have shone forth the light of the knowledge of God. [*The Theotokion*:

Having found in thee a dove entirely perfect and beautiful, bright lily and flower of the valley, the intellectual Bridegroom hath tabernacled in thee. *The Contakion from the Typicon. If there be no Typicon, say the following Contakion, Tone* 4: Ye, the wise ones, have appeared as the branches of the vine of Christ, bearing clusters of virtues and making the wine of salvation to flow unto us; drinking of which and filled with gladness, we celebrate your honoured memory; whereon, O apostles of the Lord, do supplicate that great mercy may be granted unto us and remission of sins. [*The Oikos*:

As disciples of the Master of all, with the net of your prayers, O God-seers, do snatch out of the depth of transgressions my humble soul which hath been caught with the nets of the wiles of demons, that passing well the rest of my life I may lovingly hymn you and glorify your spotless life which ye have led on earth, enlightening those in extreme darkness and teaching to divinely honour the Trinity, O apostles of the Lord.

Ode 7. *The Heirmos*:

In the Persian furnace the youths, descendants of Abraham, burning rather with love of piety than with the flame of fire, have called out: Blessed art Thou in the temple of Thy glory, O Lord.

Thou that wast before God by nature and hast made sons of Thy disciples, O Most Gracious One, hast shewn them heirs of Thy Father's patrimony and hast deigned them to go about with you as God and Master.

Having granted unto Thy divine disciples the outpouring of wisdom, the largeness of heart and well-spoken tongue, Thou hast, O Word, sent them to preach the Gospel of the Kingdom unto all the ends.

Having appeared as clouds of the divine light, the apostles are raining unto all the life-effecting water, calling: Blessed art Thou in the temple of Thy glory, O Lord. [*The Theotokion*:

Adorned with the divine glory hast thou appeared, O most pure one, since thou wast the only one, O Mother and Virgin, that ever conceived the Word of God. Blessed art thou among women, O all-spotless Sovereign-Lady.

Ode 8. The Heirmos:

Having spread his hands, Daniel did close the jaws of the lions in their den; and the force of the fire was deadened by the zealously pious youths who girded themselves with virtue and called out: Bless the Lord, all ye the works of the Lord.

The divine and most wise choir of the apostles of Christ with the fire of the Spirit have burned as the tares the multi-formous temples of the demons, and have illumined the hearts of the faithful, calling out: Bless the Lord, all ye the works of the Lord.

Let us harmoniously honour the apostles as divine disciples of Christ who have loudly proclaimed unto us the divine dogmas, as refuges of the faithful, as common benefactors of the whole human race and as servants of the Saviour.

Let us honour the all-venerable and capacious vessels of virtues, the firstlings of men, the trumpets of preaching, the streams of the life of incorruption, the God-bearing lightnings, the sources of healings and the beautiful feet of the Gospel. [*The Theotokion:*

The Full One emptieth Himself for our sake that we may partake of His fulness; for He, the Immeasurable One, having entered thy most pure womb, without leaving His Father's bosom, hath become incarnate; wherefore we all bless thee, O Mary, God's Bride.

Ode 9. The Heirmos:

A stone cut out without hands from an untouched mountain—from thee, O Virgin, was separated—that corner stone, even Christ, Who hath joined together the distant natures; rejoicing thereat we magnify thee, O Theotokos.

Having received from the Master the power to loose the bonds of transgressions, do ye, O God-seers, mercifully cleanse the sins of those who hymn you, and make worthy of salvation.

Ye all, O glorious apostles, have received the whole light of the Spirit that in substance appeared unto you, and in the upper room ye have learned the sublime teaching and dogmas, and now ye are worthily being blessed.

Unto you His friends that are gone to rest, Christ doth grant now the unfading crowns and filleth you with the contemplation of God; do supplicate Him now to save all the churches.

The Theotokion: Having desired to come down in flesh He Who hath adorned everything with His word, made His abode in thee, having found thee to be the holiest of all, and hath shewn thee as the true Theotokos, O Mother and Virgin.

The Photagogicon: O come, ye people! Let us melodize in divine hymns the apostles of Christ, the preachers of faith, as those who supplicate Christ for our souls.   [*The Theotokion:*
O all-holy, pure Sovereign-Lady, the only one who had no marital experience, our salvation and hope, do thou supplicate our God that was born of thee to save the world from deceit, calamities and afflictions.

With the Lauds...the Stichera, Tone 8. Similar to:
O Lord, although before the judgment seat.

O Lord, Thou hast illumined Thine apostles with the auroras of the Comforter and hast set them as lights for the strengthening of faith, through the mental enlightenment of Thine understanding, O Master; wherefore we adore Thine unspeakable love to mankind. *Twice.*

O Lord, through the intercessions of Thine apostles Thou hast fenced in this Thy flock, preserving it unhurt from the temptations of the enemies, for Thou hast bought it with Thy precious blood from the thraldom of the adversary, as Compassionate One and Lover of man.

Ye have appeared together in the foundation of the church, as good stones, clearly emitting unto the universe in a bright light the knowledge of God, O divine apostles that are standing before the Trinity and supplicating for our souls.

Glory...Tone 4: As winged eagles ye have traversed the whole earth, spreading the venerable dogmas, and tearing up the tares of deceit by the grace and producing multy-eared fruit, O all-famed ones, of which ye also keep the intellectual granaries for ever, preserving it in all richness unto the Immortal Worker.

Both now...The Theotokion: Possessing in thee, O Theotokos, our hope and defence, we are not afraid of the assaults of the enemy, for thou dost save our souls.

The Stavro-theotokion. Similar to: As virtuous...

Seeing Christ-Lover of man crucified and with a lance pierced in His side, the most pure one bewailed crying out: What is this, O my Son? What have the ungrateful people rendered unto Thee for all the good Thou hast done unto them, and Thou dost most lovingly take care of my childlessness? I wonder, O Compassionate One, at Thy voluntary crucifixion.

CHAPTER X.

THE GENERAL SERVICE TO ONE HIERARCH. *At the Vespers, for O Lord, I have cried, the Stichera, Tone* 6. *Similar to:* Having put off all...

Wholly consecrated, thou hast appeared as God-bearer, holy chrism of God, clothed with the Holy Spirit; and dost always enter serenely into the holy of holies, art illumined with the splendour proceeding from God, and partaketh of the holy mysteries of grace, as the true and most glorious hierarch, with boldness supplicating for our souls.

Thy life hath become resplendent with the rays of virtues, and thou hast both illumined the faithful and dispersed the darkness of deceit, for thou didst truly appear as a bright sun, O most blessed hierarch (*mentioned by name*); and now having become, by the grace of the Holy Spirit, a son of day, thou hast found thine abode wherein the Never-setting Light doth shine; wherefore, honourably celebrating thy divine and light-bearing memory, we lovingly venerate thee, O ever-memorable one.

Thy mind, O God-wise one, directed unto God and nourished by faith, hath become clear, O all-glorious, and having in the mortal and corrupt body learned incorruption, O all-wise one, thou hast acquired the serenity of the bodiless ones, and remaining passionless thou hast adorned thyself with impassivity, O hierarch, most wise father (*mentioned by name*), bright light and intercessor for those who lovingly honour thy memory.

Glory...Both now...The Theotokion:

Hail thou, the fulfilment of the law; hail thou, the temple of the Holy Trinity, the uncorrupted Bride; hail thou, the divine bearer of the King of all; hail thou, the immaterial fire, as tongs carrying in thine arms the coal, the new paradise, the shut up garden, the most bright, divine table, the uncorrupted dove;—the throne of the Most High, the intellectual, divine bed, which, O Maiden, the Holy Spirit hath overshadowed.

The Stavro-theotokion: As the undefiled lamb of old and spotless Sovereign-Lady saw her Lamb lifted up on the cross, she did motherly exclaim and in astonishment vociferated: What is this new and most glorious sight, O my sweet Child? how the graceless people give Thee over unto the Pilate's judgment and condemn unto death the Life of all? But I hymn, O Word, Thine ineffable condescension.

If there be Idiomelion, Glory...Tone 8:

The fruit of thy virtues, O venerable father, hath enlightened the hearts of the faithful; for who hearing of thine immeasurable humility would not wonder at thy patience, at thy gentleness towards the needy, at thy consolation of the sorrowing? Thou hast God-beseemingly instructed all, O hierarch (*mentioned by name*), and now art adorned with the never-fading crown; do supplicate for our souls. [*Both now...the Theotokion:*

Thy shelter, O Theotokos and Virgin, is the spiritual cure, fleeing unto which we get delivered from the infirmities of the soul.

The Stavro-theotokion. Similar to: O most glorious wonder... I cannot endure, O my Child, the sight of Thee dying on the tree, whereas Thou grantest vigour unto all. O that Thou mayest vouchsafe the divine and saving vigour unto those also who through the fruit of the ancient transgression have already fallen into the sleep of perdition,—spake in tears the Virgin, whom we magnify. *But if the Celebration be with the Polyeleon, say the Theotokion of the resurrection:* The King of the heavens.

The Entrance. The Prokeimenon of the day. The readings, three, of the Hierarchs (see Appendix). For the Versicles, the Stichera, Tone 8:

O hierarch (*mentioned by name*), aurora of the intellectual light, light of the church, ornament of hierarchs and of the monks' life of fasting the true rule, thou hast appeared unto us a defender delivering our souls from the destructive enemy. *The Verse: Precious in the sight of the Lord is the death of His saints.* O hierarch (*mentioned by name*), thou hast received from God a great power, thou hast driven off with thy prayer a multitude of the evil demons with their attacks from all those that in faith have recourse unto thee. *The Verse: What shall I render unto the Lord for all His benefits toward me?* How can we worthily hymn the great hierarch (*mentioned by name*), the venerable mind, the light God-illumined that enlighteneth us and granteth the divine understanding, the confessor of the profound mysteries. Let us harmoniously say: Hail thou, O (*mentioned by name*), the father of fathers.   [*Glory... Tone* 8:

Thou art a good shepherd and fervent teacher, O hierarch (*mentioned by name*), and ever praising thee we vociferate: God hath made of thee an ornament of His church and hath shewn unto His people as incorrupt thy body which for many years remained hidden in the earth; wherefore cease not supplicating Him for those that praise thee and honour thy memory, entreat also for the remission of sins and for the salvation of our souls.   [*Both now...*

The Theotokion of the resurrection: O Virgin innocent of marital...

But if there be no Celebration, say this Theotokion: O Sovereign-Lady, accept the prayers of thy servants and deliver us from every want and woe.   [*The Stavro-theotokion:*

Seeing Thee nailed to the cross, O Jesus, and voluntarily accepting the passion, the Virgin, Thy Mother, O Master, cried out: Woe unto me, O my sweet Child! how dost Thou endure the unrighteous wounds, O Physician, that hast healed the infirmity of mankind and hast delivered all from corruption through Thy compassion? [*The Troparion from the Typicon; but if there be no Typicon, say the following Troparion, Tone* 4:

As a rule of faith and model of tenderness, and teacher of abstinence hath the reality shewn thee unto thy flock; therewithal hast thou acquired by humility greatness, by poverty—riches; O father hierarch (*mentioned by name*), intercede before Christ the God that our souls may be saved.

At the Matins, for God is the Lord, the same Troparion. After the 1st *Stichologia the Cathisma, Tone* 1. *Similar to:* Whilst Thy sepulchre...

Being the servant of Christ, the Master of all, thou hast taught the people and illumined them with the divine baptism, having instructed them in the understanding thereof, O hierarch; wherefore we all call thee preacher of truth, hierarch and favourite of Christ. [*Twice.* Glory...*Both now...the Theotokion:*

O unmarried, pure Theotokos and Virgin—the only intercessor and protector of the faithful, do deliver from calamities and woes and from all violent attacks, those that put their trust in thee, O Maiden, and save thou our souls with thy divine supplications.

After the 2nd *Stichologia, the Cathisma, Tone* 4.

From youth having taken up thy cross, thou hast piously followed Christ, keeping down the subtleties of the flesh by abstemiousness; wherefore when thou didst sit on the hierarchical throne, thou hast magnified, O hierarch, the Master and His most pure Mother, Who have adorned with various gifts thy shrine, O God-blessed (*mentioned by name*). [*Twice.*

Glory...Both now...the Theotokion: O Virgin all-spotless that gavest birth unto the Ever-existing God, do, with the hierarch, unceasingly supplicate Him to grant us remission of sins and improvement of life before we reach our end, since we dutifully hymn thee in faith and with love, O only all-hymned one.

After Praise ye the name of the Lord, this Refrain:

We magnify thee, O hierarch, father (*mentioned by name*), and honour thy holy memory; for thou dost supplicate for us Christ our God. *The selected Psalm:* Hearken unto this all ye nations...

After the Polyeleon the Cathisma, Tone 8. *Similar to:* Of the wisdom...

Having ruled over the passions of the flesh, thou didst appear as a God-like hierarch and thy flock hast thou most gloriously tended, O holy one; thou hast also enlightened with baptism and hast enjoined to glorify One God in three Hypostases; wherefore even after thy departure thou sheddest healings unto those that come to the holy church of God and approach the shrine of thy relics, O hierarch (*mentioned by name*); supplicate Christ the God to grant the remission of sins unto those that lovingly honour thy holy memory. [*Twice.*

Glory ... Both now ... the Theotokion: Let us hymn the heavenly door and ark, all-holy mountain, light cloud, unconsumed bush, intellectual paradise, Eve's deliverance, great treasury of the whole universe, since therein was effected the salvation of the world and the remission of the ancient sins; wherefore we also vociferate unto her: Supplicate Christ the God to grant remission of transgressions unto those that piously adore thine all-holy child-birth.

The Graduals, 1st Antiphon of the 4th Tone. The Prokeimenon: My mouth shall speak of wisdom, and the meditation of my heart shall be of understanding. *The Verse:* The mouth of the righteous speaketh wisdom. Let every breath. *The Gospel of a hierarch (John 10, 9-16). After the 50th Psalm, the Sticheron, Tone 6:*

O God's inheritor, associate of Christ, servant of the Lord, holy (*mentioned by name*), in perfect accord with thine appellation was thy life, for together with grey hairs there shone forth wisdom, the serenity of thy countenance testified to the gentleness of thy soul and thy benignness was manifested in the calmness of thy speech. Thy life was glorious and thy repose is with the saints; do thou supplicate for our souls.

The Canon, Tone 6. Ode 1. The Heirmos:

Whilst travelling on foot along the depths of the sea as if upon dry land, Israel, seeing Pharaoh, their pursuer, drowned, cried out: Unto God let us sing an ode of victory.

Numbered with the highest choirs, as a hierarch, and as a servant of God standing before Him, do assiduously supplicate for us, that we may obtain eternal good things through thine intercessions.

Having been elected of the Lord to serve unto the precious

gospel, thou, O blessed father (*mentioned by name*), with thy wise instructions hast brought up thy people in wisdom.

Enriched with God's understanding, thou hast made the living-word to flow from thy heart and gave it to drink unto the souls frozen up by passions, O most wise hierarch of God, God-blessed (*mentioned by name*).

The Theotokion: The sacred choir of prophets hath, from afar, shewn thee, O pure one, as one that was to become a true Parent of God, higher than the cherubim and all things created.

Ode 3. *The Heirmos:*

There is none holy as Thou, O Lord my God, that hast, as Good One, exalted the horn of Thy believers and established us upon the rock of Thy confession.

Shedding the divine sweetness from thy lips, O father, thou hast dried up the drops of bitter godlessness by giving to drink the drink of the pious,—that of God's understanding, O blessed one.

Having been fore-elected by God's judgment, thou didst appear a hierarch offering the bloodless sacrifices unto God that offered up Himself for our sake, O father hierarch (*mentioned by name*).

The sepulchre, wherein lieth thy precious body, doth shed perfume as God's paradise, filling the faithful with sweet smell, O most glorious and all-honoured hierarch (*mentioned by name*). [*The Theotokion:*

To understand the unspeakable depths of thy bringing forth, O pure one, the mind of man is incapable, for God having humbled Himself for the sake of compassion, hath entirely renewed me in thy womb.

The Cathisma, Tone 4. *Similar to:* Thou hast appeared to-day...

Orthodoxly hast thou, O holy one, tended the church of Christ and having driven off the heretical bitter tares, dost find now, O blessed one, thine abode on high. [*Glory...Both now...the Theotokion:*

We have learned to know the Word of the Father, Christ our God that was incarnate of thee, O Theotokos-Virgin—the only pure, the only blessed one; wherefore in unceasing hymns we magnify thee. [*The Stavro-theotokion*:

Seeing thy Son hung on the cross and being lacerated in thy motherly bosom, thou, O most pure one, hast pityingly vociferated: Woe unto me! How art Thou gone down, O my Light, Ever-shining?

Ode 4. *The Heirmos*:

Christ is my power, my God and my Lord—the venerable church God-beseemingly singeth, thus calling out, with pure mind feasting in the Lord.

Filled with the Holy Spirit, O sacred father (*mentioned by name*), thou hast driven away the evil spirits from men and these made faithful with thy spiritual instructions.

Thou hast taught of God as of an Unity uncreated and divided into three Persons, but not to be cut up or mingled, thus enlightening the pious with thy sacred theology.

Having first mortified the subtleties of the flesh by abstemiousness and labours, thou hast appeared a divine hierarch and all-sacred intercessor before the Trinity. [*The Theotokion*:

The great grandmother's curse hath been done away with by thee, O Mother of God; for thou, O most pure one, hast brought forth unto us the Source of holiness—the Ever-abiding Life.

Ode 5. *The Heirmos*:

With Thy divine light, O Good One, do illumine, I pray Thee, the souls of those who lovingly watch early unto Thee, that they may know Thee, O Word of God, as the true God, recalling them out of the darkness of sin.

Performing divine acts in a divine way and with the most pure mind approaching the holy things, thou hast appeared blameless, serving God as God's most sacred hierarch.

Those who were addicted to idols have become favourites of God through thy precious instructions, and in recalling them from their unworthy ways thou hast become a worthy servant of the God Almighty.

Having been called by grace, thou hast abolished the lawlessness of the idol-worship by the downpour of thy words, O holy one, and hast made, by the grace of God, the frozen hearts fruitful. [*The Theotokion*:

After thy strange bringing forth thou hast remained Virgin as before, for it was God Who was born and Who changeth everything as He willeth, O husbandless Mary, God's Bride.

Ode 6. The Heirmos:

Beholding the sea of life swelling with the storm of temptations, and taking refuge in Thy calm haven, I cry unto Thee: Lead up my life from corruption, O Greatly-merciful One.

Thy tongue being sharpened by the Spirit in intelligence, thou hast written with it, as with a calamus of the copyist, in the hearts of the pious the words of grace, at the bidding of God, O all-sacred father.

Learning the things divine, as one entering into the intellectual holy of holies, thou, O sacred father, dost perfect in spirit the faithful by the light of the Trinity, thyself being the most perfect, O *(mentioned by name)*.

With the streams of thine injunctions having barred up the turbid commands of the wicked, thou hast appeared as a placid river watering with piety the communities of the faithful, O all-honoured hierarch.

The Theotokion: The Word hath found, without seed, His abode in thy womb and there appeared a perfect man, renewing God-beseemingly the nature as He only Himself alone knoweth, O all-spotless Maiden favoured of God.

The Contakion from the Typicon; but if there be no Typicon, say the following Contakion. Tone 2. Similar to: Of the highest...

O divine thunder, spiritual trumpet, planter of faith and cutter off of heresies, great favourite of the Trinity, hierarch *(mentioned by name)*, standing with the angels before God do ever and unceasingly pray for us all. [*The Oikos:*

Through laziness have I, wretched one, fallen off, and am in sleep unto death, but thou, a good shepherd, raise me up, O father, and appease the passions which so wickedly torment me, that on arising I may in a pure spirit hymn thy bright festival, which the Master of the universe hath worthily glorified as that of the most faithful servant and the most wise teacher, the friend and adept and minister of His traditions, which thou hast well preserved; O, unpolluted unction, most wise (*mentioned by name*), do thou unceasingly pray for us all.

Ode 7. *The Heirmos:*

Dew-yielding hath an angel made the furnace unto the pious youths, and God's injunction burning the Chaldeans hath inclined the tyrant to cry out : Blessed art Thou, O God of our fathers.

Illumined by the grace of the Spirit unto the penetration of the Divine commands, thou wast a light-giving star enlightening those that wisely sing: Blessed art Thou, the God of our fathers.

Thou wast the holiest of the church, shining with virtuous deeds, and hadst abiding in thee, O sacred one, the Uncreated Trinity, and sangst: Blessed art Thou, O God of our fathers.

Repelling somnolency from thine eyes, with divine vigour hast thou received the divine light from the Angel of Light, Who hath made thee a pillar and support of the faithful, a true hierarch. [*The Theotokion:*

He that sitteth in the bosom of the Begetter uncircumscribed, is now sitting in thy womb, O most pure one, circumscribed, invested with thine image, having been circumscribed for the sake of saving Adam.

Ode 8. *The Heirmos:*

Unto the pious hast Thou made dew out of the flame to flow and the sacrifice of a righteous man didst Thou consume with water, for everything makest Thou, O Christ, just as Thou willest; Thee we exalt unto all the ages.

The proud serpent hast thou, O blessed one, humbled with thy humility, being elevated unto God by thy pure thoughts; wherefore we honour thee, exalting Christ unto the ages.

The Incarnate Word hast thou preached and saved the people from thraldom to deceit, driving away the wickedness of idolatry, O hierarch, father (*mentioned by name*), most wise and God-bearing.

Having thy life like unto that of the Master, thou hast also thy speech like unto thy life; thy spiritual days having been fulfilled, thou, O father, didst go over into the highest regions for repose. [*The Theotokion:*

Having been freed from the first curse by thy bringing forth,

O most blessed, God-greeted Maiden, we send up unto thee the greeting of Gabriel: Hail thou—the cause of the salvation of all.

Ode 9. *The Heirmos:*

It is not possible for men to behold God on Whom the angelic orders dare not cast a glance; but through thee, O all-pure one, was seen of men the Incarnate Word; Him magnifying, with heavenly hosts we call thee blessed.

In the land of the benign hast thou found thine abode, having been benign and meek, and art now in the company of the highest hosts, being adorned with virtues as bright ornaments and invested with the light thereof.

Thou dost behold the brightness of God and of angels, of patriarchs, martyrs and of apostles the lustre, with them supplicating the Lover of man to grant the remission of sins and improvement of life unto us that are praising thee, O holy one.

Manifestly hast thou firstly adorned with thy lustre the throne of all other cities; having lived therein as an angel, and having adorned the city with thy prelacy, thou hast hallowed her with thine unction and perfected therein the Godly-wise people. [*The Theotokion:*

As a heavenly drop, into thy womb, O Virgin, rain came down and hast dried up the streams of deceit; it showered incorruption unto all men and the redemption hath been granted by thee, O God-greeted one.

The Photagogicon. Similar to: Thou hast visited us...

Gloriously is to-day displayed the light-bearing festival; standing in the light of the glory of the countenance of God, do thou, O hierarch (*mentioned by name*), remember us who laud thy memory. [*The Theotokion:*

With God, in thee do we put our trust, O most pure one, being co-crucified unto Christ that hath come out of thee. With thine entreaties unto Him do preserve us unhurt even to the end.

With the Lauds, the Stichera, Tone 8. Similar to: O most glorious wonder...

O holy father (*mentioned by name*)! Having reached the top

of the ladder of divine understanding and approaching God as one who hath obtained the gift of adoption, thou dost heal incurable diseases and drivest away the unclean spirits; therefore with joyful hearts we celebrate thy memory, magnifying Christ Who hath exalted His favourite. *Twice.*

O marvellous father (*mentioned by name*)! Brightly illumined with thy clear-sighted mind, thou hast pacified the multi-billowed sea of passions, and, flying in thine impassiveness with clean wings, thou hast reached the height of the ineffable and incomprehensible goodness, ever supplicating for us who laud thee.

O father of fathers (*mentioned by name*)! Thou wast the rule of priesthood, model of charity, stronghold of monks, strengthening of the church, lamp of love, throne of compassion, source of miracles, tongue of fire, sweet-spoken mouth, vessel of the Divine Spirit and intellectual paradise, O God-blessed one. [*Glory...Tone* 6.

O holy one, thrice blessed, holiest father, good shepherd, disciple of Christ—the chief shepherd—and one that hast laid thy life for thy flock! Do thou now also, O most praised hierarch (*mentioned by name*), importune Him with thine entreaties to grant us great mercy.

Both now...the Theotokion: The God that was incarnate of thee, O Theotokos-Virgin, we have learned to know; Him supplicate for the salvation of our souls.

The Stavro-theotokion: Standing at the cross and seeing her Son voluntarily suffering, the Virgin-Mother did magnify Him.

CHAPTER XI.

THE SERVICE COMMON TO TWO OR MANY HIERARCHS.

At the Vespers, for O Lord, I have cried, the Stichera, Tone 4. Similar to: As virtuous...

As ever-shining stars of the intellectual firmament, O most glorious ones, ye have adorned the world, O most honourable, and enlighten the universe with the dogmas of the right faith and drive away the darkness of heresies, O hierarchs. Do supplicate that may be delivered from corruption and dangers those who in faith celebrate your all-honoured memory.

Having with the brightness of the Spirit enlightened the world, ye have appeared as light-giving suns; spreading into all the ends the dogmas as rays, ye enlighten the hearts of the faithful, O most blessed ones, and drive away the darkness of heretics, O God-bearers, by the power of Him Who hath shone forth from the Virgin.

Ye, O most blessed ones, have driven away from the church of Christ the intellectual wolves with the staff of your dogmas, and have made an intellectual wall round about her, presenting her whole and unassailable unto Christ; Him supplicate that may be delivered from corruption and dangers those who in faith celebrate your all-honoured memory.

Glory...Both now...The Thetokion: O most holy God's Bride! From condemnation and wicked transgressions deliver my humble soul and turn away from death through thy supplications; grant that in the day of trial I may obtain justification which assemblies of saints have met with, and before the end show me cleansed with repentance and effusion of tears.

The Stavro-theotokion: Seeing Christ the Lover of man hung and pierced through His side with a spear, the most pure one did bewail, crying out: What is this, O my Son? What have the ungrateful people rewarded Thee with for all the good Thou hast done unto them, and Thou most lovingly takest care of my childlessness? I wonder, O compassionate One, at Thy voluntary crucifixion.

If there be Idiomelon. Glory...Tone 6:

O ye men of God and faithful servants, ministers of the Lord, men wished for, select vessels, pillars and supports of the church, heirs of the kingdom,—never cease to vociferate unto the Lord for us. [*Both now...the Theotokion:*

The God that was incarnate of thee, O Theotokos-Virgin, we have learned to know; Him supplicate for the salvation of our souls. [*The Stavro-theotokion:*

Seen Thee crucified, O Christ, she who hath given Thee birth, vociferated: What a strange mystery do I see now, my Son? How being hung in the flesh dost Thou die on the tree, O Giver of life?

If the Celebration be with the Polyeleon, say the Theotokion of the resurrection: Who would not bless thee...*Entrance. The Prokeimenon of the day. The Readings for hierarchs (see Appendix).*

For the Versicles the Stichera, Tone 1. Similar to...All praised martyrs...

Let us worthily praise to-day both adepts of the Spirit and intellectual trumpets of God, divine mirrors, hierarchs divine and flame-inspired who are shedding unto us the golden streams of instruction. Pray ye unto Christ that He may grant unto our souls peace and great mercy.

The Verse: Precious in the sight of the Lord is the death of His saints. Let us worthily melodize in hymns the intelligent power of the divine and holy faith, the rivers golden-streamed, the all-bright lamps, the champions of the Trinity, the receptacles of the grace of the Holy Spirit, the immoveable pillars and supports of the church.

The Verse: Let Thy priests be clothed with righteousness, and let Thy saints shout for joy. O ye, spiritual organs of thunder and of divine signs, lightenings of preaching, golden candlesticks—bright and carrying the light of God, most blessed hierarchs!—do supplicate for us, honouring you, that Christ may grant unto our souls peace and great mercy.

Glory...Tone 6 : Let us to-day praise the mysterious trumpets of the Spirit—the God-bearing fathers who in the midst of the church have sung the hypostatical hymn of theology, the Trinity immutably One both in substance and divinity,—the exterminators of heresies and champions of the orthodox, who ever pray God that our souls may be saved.

Both now...the Theotokion: O Theotokos, thou art the true vine that did bring forth for me the fruit of life, of thee we supplicate: Pray, O Sovereign-Lady, with the hierarchs, that mercy may be shewn to our souls. [*The Stavro-theotokion :*

Standing once before the tree, during the crucifixion, with the chaste-disciple, the Virgin cried out, bewailing: O woe unto me! How dost Thou, O Christ, suffer being Thyself impassiveness unto all? *The Troparion from the Typicon, but if there be no Typicon, say this Troparion, Tone* 4 : O God of our fathers, that ever dealest by us according to Thy kindness, do not withdraw from us Thy mercy, but at their intercessions direct our lives in peace. *Glory...Both now...the Theotokion or the Stavro-theotokion.*

At the Matins, for God is the Lord, the same Troparion. After the 1st *Stichologia, the Cathisma, Tone* 5. *Similar to :* The Co-unoriginate Word...

As royal adornment of the church let us praise the hierarchs of the Lord—the inexhaustible treasury of dogmas, for through these He Himself hath instructed us to honour the Holy Trinity, united in substance and divided hypostatically. [*Twice.*

Glory...Both now...the Theotokion: O most holy Virgin, have mercy upon us who in faith flee unto thee, O compassionate one, and beg for thy warm protection, for thou canst, as a tender-hearted one and the Mother of the Most High God, save all, ever embracing in thy motherly supplications, O God-greeted one.

After the 2nd *Stichologia, the Cathisma, Tone* 3. *Similar to :* Of the divine...

O God-worded hierarchs! ye have appeared as the pillars of the church and the inalienable riches of piety, your life ye have made illustrious through impassiveness and have expounded the dogmas of the Trinity. O holy fathers! Supplicate Christ the God for the salvation of our souls. [*Twice.*

Glory...Both now...the Theotokion: Without divesting Himself of His divine nature, God became flesh in thy womb; but the Incarnate did remain God and hath, after the birth, preserved all-spotless thee, His mother and Virgin, just as before the birth, being One and the same Lord. Him assiduously supplicate to grant unto us great mercy.

After: Praise ye the name of the Lord...*the Refrain:* We magnify you, the great hierarchs, and honour your holy memory, for ye supplicate for us Christ, our God.

The selected Psalm: Hearken unto this, all ye nations...
After the Polyeleon, the Cathisma, Tone 4:

Let the most wise teachers of the universe, who have glorified God with their deeds and words on earth, be magnified to-day as the mediators of salvation unto us. [*Twice.*

Glory...Both now...the Theotokion: O invincible defender of the assaulted and fervent protectress of those that trust in thee, deliver me from dangers, for thou art help unto all.

The Graduals, 1*st Antiphon of the* 4*th Tone. The Prokeimenon:* Precious in the sight of the Lord is the death of His saints. *The Verse:* What shall I render unto the Lord for all His benefits towards me? Let every breath...*The Gospel of the hierarchs* (Matt. 5, 14-19.)

After the 50*th Psalm, the Sticheron, Tone* 6:

O holy fathers! Through all the earth is gone forth the sound of your exertions, wherefore ye have found in heaven the reward of your labours; ye have annihilated the armies of the demons and have reached the orders of angels, whom ye have blamelessly emulated in your lives. Possessing boldness before the Lord, do obtain peace for our souls.

The Canon, Tone 8. *Ode* 1. *The Heirmos:*

Let us sing unto the Lord Who hath led His people through the Red sea, for He alone hath triumphed gloriously.

As the most wise hierarchs have ye shone forth in the world, resplendent with the divine dogmas of the King that reigneth over all; wherefore let us hymn Christ, for He hath triumphed.

As those who shone forth in the world with the light of piety and dispersed the darkness of wickedness, let us, O faithful, honour the hierarchs, great and all-honourable.

As standing with the angels before the Unapproachable King, supplicate, O ye sacred preachers and God-bearing, that cleansing of sins may be granted unto us who celebrate your memory.

The Theotokion: As one that hast conceived the Ever-existing and Unoriginate Word of the Father, and hast above word brought Him forth in the flesh, do thou, O most holy one, pray assiduously that we may be delivered from dangers.

Ode 3. The Heirmos:

Thou that hast in the beginning stablished the heavens in wisdom and the earth founded upon the waters, do Thou, O Christ, stablish me upon the rock of Thy commandments, for there is none holy but Thou, O only Lover of man.

With true abstemiousness and steadfast prayer ye have ascended the upper city of virtues, O holy and God-bearing ones, wherein ye are in constant enjoyment of the stream of divine food.

As possessing boldness before God, do, O holy hierarchs, supplicate for us, in faith hymning your memory, that we may be saved.

As teachers of the pious dogmas and true proclaimers of the most wise words, ye, O holy ones, have obtained victory over heresies. [*The Theotokion:*

As the heaven and throne of God we all hymn thee, O God's Parent, pure Virgin, for from thee hath appeared Jesus Christ—the Truth for our salvation. [*The Cathisma, Tone 3:*

Precious vessels of abstemiousness and inviolable riches of piety have ye, O blessed ones, truly appeared, having illumined your lives with impassiveness and enriched with mercy those asking for it; O holy fathers, supplicate Christ the God to grant unto us great mercy.

Glory...Both now...The Theotokion:

Every one hath rightfully the recourse thither where he

obtaineth salvation, and what can other such refuge be that sheltereth our souls, beside thee, O Theotokos?

The Stavro-theotokion: Having acquired as a staff of strength the cross of thy Son, O Theotokos, therewith we put down the rage of the enemies, and unceasingly and lovingly magnify thee.

Ode 4. The Heirmos:

I have hearkened, O Lord, unto the mystery of Thine economy, comprehended Thy works, and glorified Thy Godhead.

Let us all praise in hymns the most wise hierarchs, saying: O God-bearing fathers! do assiduously supplicate that we may be saved.

Possessing in you, O truly God-blessed ones, expounders and planters of the pious dogmas, and most wise teachers and hierarchs, we praise you in hymns and odes.

Your sacred memory, O holy hierarchs of the Lord—the instructors and nourishers—we, the faithful, celebrate in hymns and odes. [*The Theotokion:*

O unmarried Bride, pure Mother of Christ the God, that had no marital experience! Him unceasingly supplicate to save the souls of those that hymn thee.

Ode 5. The Heirmos:

Watching early we cry out unto Thee: O Lord save us, for Thou art our God, beside Thee we know none other.

Ye have, O God-wise ones, as shepherds anointed yourselves with the ointment of piety, wherefore, as hierarchs, we all honour you, O God-bearers.

As emulators of the apostles in labours and vigilance, ye, O God-wise and glorious, have presided over the people of the church.

Having emulated Isaiah the zealous and Moses the God-seer, ye have, O God-seeing fathers, put to shame the heresiarchs

The Theotokion: O come all ye faithful, let us, together with the angels, bless the God-blessed one, as the Queen that gave birth unto the King of all.

Ode 6. The Heirmos:

A bright garment do grant me Thou that puttest on light as a garment, O Multimerciful Christ, our God.

The glory of the church have ye adorned, O blessed fathers, with your divine dogmas, and extirpated heresies with their roots.

As lights of piety ye have shone unto all creation, O glorious teachers, with the beauty of dogmas, having darkened the heresies with God's word.

Making use of the tongue and the word, instead of the weapon, ye have, O holy ones, cut off all the strange teachings and have clearly expounded the Trinity unto all.

The Theotokion: Having been born of the Virgin, Thou hast, O Christ the God, enlightened the world; do Thou deliver me also from transgressions, as Lover of man, and set straight my life, I implore Thee.

The Contakion from the Typicon; but if there be no Typicon, say this Contakion, Tone 8. Similar to: As the first fruits...

As the teachers of virtues and ornaments of hierarchs doth the church glorify you, thus melodizing: Through your intercessions grant as invincible ones unto those who lovingly honour you, improvement in virtues and deliverance from temptations. *[The Oikos:*

Ye have appeared, O divine hierarchs, as rivers of piety that have filled all the earth with the streams of your dogmas, ye have also, with the clouds of miracles, washed away all the filth and have worthily inherited the nourishing stream; wherefore, being gathered together, we piously honour you to-day with hymns, and in faith cry out unto you: Supplicate unceasingly for us all Christ the God, as invincible ones.

Ode 7. *The Heirmos:*

Thou that hast in the beginning founded the earth and made firm the heavens with Thy word, blessed art Thou unto the ages, O Lord God of our fathers.

Thou that hast shewn the true hierarchs shepherds of Thy flock, blessed art Thou, O God of our fathers.

Ye have extinguished the flame of passions and have divinely bedewed the souls of the pious that are now crying out: Blessed art Thou, O God of our fathers.

Ye, O hierarchs, have laboured in abstinence, vigilance and true faith; do remember us all. [*The Theotokion*:

Thou that for our sake wast born of the Virgin and hast delivered the world from the enemy,—blessed art Thou, O God of our fathers.

Ode 8. *The Heirmos*:

Him that was glorified on the holy mountain and in the bush through the fire unto Moses hath shewn the mystery of the Ever-virgin, hymn the Lord and exalt unto all the ages.

Like unto Moses, the fathers have ascended the cloudy mountain of impassiveness and obtained as hierarchs the intellectual law of grace; wherefore we hymn Christ unto the ages.

Ye, O holy ones, have well tended the people of Christ, have escaped the Egyptian bondage, eluded the passions of Babylon, and in Zion above have found an abode unto all the ages.

With words and deeds of piety anointed as if with myrrh, ye, O divine hierarchs, are performing sacred and divine acts; wherefore the Trinity in one substance ye hymn unto all the ages. [*The Theotokion*:

Him that hath dwelt in the womb of the holy Virgin and therein hath, in an awful and ineffable manner, restored Adam,—hymn the Lord and exalt unto all the ages.

Ode 9. *The Heirmos*:

In unceasing hymns we magnify the bringing forth of the Ever-virgin unto the salvation of us faithful, which was manifested unto the law-giver in the fire and the bush on the mountain.

O ye, the most wise hierarchs, that in impassiveness and faith, in hope and love, have shewn unto us the words of the life eternal, supplicate that our souls may be saved.

Ye, the hierarchs all-honoured, have well tended the people with the staff of the Holy Spirit, and have driven away from the church of God the heresies of God's enemies; wherefore we praise you in hymns.

In hymns and odes we all unceasingly honour you, O

hierarchs, as the lights of the church, and worthily magnify the shrine of your relics, O blessed fathers. [*The Theotokion*:

Hail thou, the ever-living source of incorruption; hail thou, the all-bright cloud of the sun; hail thou, the chariot of the entire Godhead; hail thou, the ark of sanctification.

The Photagogicon: Let us praise the God-bearing fathers as the brightly-shining, much clearer than the rays of the sun, lamps of the Origin of light—the Trinity and of the three-rayed Unity supernaturally commingled. [*The Theotokion*:

We bless in unceasing hymns thee, O Virgin, that having conceived in thy womb, O Theotokos, One of the Trinity, thou hast in thy divine arms carried the Ever-existing Word, unchangeable and immutable.

With the Lauds, the Stichera, Tone 6. Similar to:
Of three days...

The grace hath overcome, the faith is strengthened, everything is filled with the knowledge of God and we are enriched with the salvation, through the apostles and hierarchs. *Twice.*

Thou, O Lord, hast made Thy hierarchs wonderful through the heavenly mysteries and human teaching—a combination of graces with corrections that must overcome every heretical invention.

Let the most wise teachers of the universe, that have glorified God by word and deed on earth, be magnified to-day as the presenters of salvation unto us all. [*Glory...Tone* 6:

Ye were good and faithful servants, assiduous workers of the vineyard of Christ, who have well endured the burthen of your day's work, have increased the talent given you and borne no grudge unto those that came after you; wherefore the gate of heaven was open unto you; having then entered into the joy of Christ, the Master, do supplicate for us, O holy hierarchs.

Both now...The Theotokion: O Theotokos, thou art the
true vine...

The Stavro-theotokion: Seeing Thee hung on the cross, the most pure one cried out, motherly bewailing: O my Son and my God, my sweetest Child, how dost Thou endure the horrible passion?

CHAPTER XII.

THE GENERAL SERVICE TO A MONK.

At the Vespers, for O Lord, I have cried, the Stichera, Tone 8.
Similar to: The martyrs of the Lord...

A divine and light-bearing lamp that is holy and precious, never remaineth hidden under the bushel of the thick covering of life, but the Lover of man placeth him on the summit of high miracles; through his intercessions grant, O Christ, unto Thy people great mercy.

Thou, all-honoured one, hast set thyself to the plough with the work of thy hands, and ever working the things divine, thou didst not turn to look back, but wast directed into the Kingdom of Christ, the Incarnate God, unto the salvation of our souls.

Carried in a light boat of the body by the gentle breezes of thy gentle spirit, thou, O wise one, hast easily passed across the abyss of life, and having disposed of thy possessions for the priceless Pearl and obtained it, thou hast kept It unto thyself, finding thy bliss in the divine virtues thereof.

Glory...Both now...the Theotokion:

My thoughts are unclean, my lips flattering, and my deeds are all defiled. What then can I do? How can I meet the Judge? O Sovereign-Lady Virgin, supplicate unto thy Son and Maker and the Lord that He may receive my spirit in contrition, as the only Compassionate One.

The Stavro-theotokion: The undefiled youthful Maiden seeing the Youth voluntarily nailed on the tree, piteously bewailing, called out unto Him: Woe unto me, O my most beloved Child! What hath the graceless assembly of the Hebrews rendered unto Thee? They are bent on depriving me of Thee, O All-beloved One.

If Idiomelion be appointed. Glory...Tone 6:

Having preserved unhurt that which is in the image, and

having through fasting made thy mind master over the perilous passions, thou hast ascended as far as possible unto that which is in the likeness; for, having manfully constrained thy nature, thou hast taken pains to subdue the inferior unto the higher, and to make the flesh a slave unto the spirit, wherefore thou, O hermit, hast appeared an instructor of the monks, teacher of good life, most certain rule of virtue. And now, in the heavens, when mirrors do no longer intervene, thou, our father (*mentioned by name*), dost clearly see the Holy Trinity and supplicate immediately for those that in faith and love honour thee.

Both now...the Theotokion: O Theotokos, thou art the true vine...

The Stavro-theotokion: Seeing Thee crucified, O Christ, she who hath given Thee birth, vociferated: What a strange mystery do I see now, my Son? How, being hung in the flesh, dost Thou die on the tree, O Giver of life?

If the Celebration be with the Polyeleon, say the Theotokion of the resurrection: Who would not bless thee...*Entrance...The Prokeimenon of the day. The Readings of the Religious. (See Appendix).*

For the Versicles, the Stichera, Tone 1. *Similar to:*
Of the heavenly orders...

Thy festival, O God-bearer, brighter than the sun hath come; it illumineth those that in faith have recourse unto thee, filleth with the sweet smell of immortality and sheddeth healings unto the souls, O holy father, intercessor for our souls.

The Versicle: Precious in the sight of the Lord is the death of His saints. Through the furrows of abstinence having obtained victory over the sensual passions of the body, and having shewn on earth the zeal of the bodiless, thou hast subdued unto the spirit all desires of the flesh, O wonder-worker, (*mentioned by name*); wherefore, dwelling now in the heavenly habitations, do supplicate for our souls.

The Versicle: Blessed is the man that feareth the Lord, that delighteth greatly in His commandments.

O blissful (*mentioned by name*)! Having laid the foundation of virtue, thou didst put off the ancient man with his hosts, and hast truly put on Christ; wherefore hast thou, O holy one, put to shame many armies of the enemy and wast instructor of the monks. Supplicate that our souls may be saved. [*Glory...Tone* 8.

We honour in thee, O (*mentioned by name*) our father, the teacher of the multitude of monks, for we have truly learned to walk straight in thy path. Blessed art thou that hast laboured for Christ and hast laid bare the might of the enemy ; O friend of angels and companion of the holy and just ones, with them do supplicate unto the Lord that our souls may be saved.

Both now...the Theotokion of the resurrection : O Virgin unmarried
  ...But if there be no Celebration, say this Theotokion :

O pure virgin, gate of the Word, Mother of our God, supplicate that we may be saved. [*The Stavro-theotokion:*

I cannot endure, O my Child, the sight of Thee dying on the tree, whereas Thou grantest vigour unto all, O that Thou mayest vouchsafe the divine and saving vigour unto those also who, through the fruit of the ancient transgression, have already fallen into the sleep of perdition,—spake in tears the Virgin, whom we magnify.

The Troparion from the Typicon, but if there be no Typicon,
  say this Troparion, Tone 8 *:*

In thee, O father, was manifestly preserved what is in the image of God, for having taken up thy cross, thou didst follow Christ, and by thine own example hast taught that the flesh is to be despised as transient, but that particular care should be bestowed on the soul, as a thing immortal ; wherefore, together with the angels, rejoiceth also thine, O holy (*mentioned by name*) spirit. [*Glory. Both now...the Theotokion or the Stavro-theotokion.*

At the Matins, for God is the Lord, the same Troparion. After the 1*st Stichologia, the Cathisma, Tone* 4. *Similar to :* Speedily prevent.

Unto the call of thy Lord hast thou, O all-blessed (*mentioned by name*), followed, when thou hadst forsaken the world and everything there is beautiful in the world, with fervour didst thou endure the hardships of the eremitical life and manfully repulsed the armies of the demons; wherefore in faith we also constantly praise in hymns thy memory. *Twice.*

Glory...Both now...the Theotokion: Thou, O pure one, hast renewed, with thy divine bringing forth, the mortal nature of the earth-born ruined by passions, and hast raised all from death unto the life of incorruption; wherefore we all dutifully bless thee, O most glorious Virgin, as thou hast foretold.

After the 2nd Stichologia, the Cathisma, Tone 5. Similar to:
The Co-unoriginate...

Let us honour with hymns the ascetic of the Lord as one that, by true abstemiousness and enduring patience, hath exterminated all the assaults of passions, and hath put to great shame the opposing enemy with all his pride, and is now supplicating the Lord that our souls may be saved. *Twice.*

Glory...Both now...the Theotokion: The awful miracle of conception and unspeakable manner of giving birth that became known in thee, O pure Ever-virgin, frighten my mind and excite wonder in my thoughts; thy glory, O Theotokos, hath reached everywhere unto the salvation of our souls.

After Praise ye the name of the Lord...the Refrain: We bless thee, O religious father (*mentioned by name*), and honour thy holy memory, O preceptor of monks and associate of angels. *The selected Psalm:* I waited patiently for the Lord...*After the Polyeleon, the Cathisma, Tone 1. Similar to:* Thy sepulchre, O Saviour...

Through mortification of the flesh thou, O sacred father, hast buried all the risings of passions, and after thy decease thou hast obtained unending life; wherefore the church of Christ doth celebrate to-day thy wonder-worthy memory, the ornament of the ascetics. [*Twice. Glory...Both now...the Theotokion:*

Do set in the way of repentance us, who constantly deviate into the evil libertinism, and anger the Most kind Lord, O most blessed Mary, that hadst no marital experience and art the refuge of despairing men and God's dwelling place.

The Graduals. The 1st Antiphon of the 4th Tone. The Prokeimenon: Precious in the sight of the Lord is the death of His saints. *The Verse:* What shall I render unto the Lord for all

His benefits towards me? Let every breath. *The Gospel of the religious (Matth.* 11, 27-30). *After the* 50*th Psalm, the Sticheron, Tone* 6:

O holy father, through all the earth is gone forth the sound of thine exertions, wherefore hast thou found in heaven the reward of thy labours; thou hast destroyed the armies of demons and hast reached the orders of angels, whom thou hast irreproachably emulated in thy life. Possessing boldness before Christ the God, do obtain peace for our souls.

The Canon. Tone 8. *Ode* 1. *The Heirmos:*

Having crossed the water as if it were dry land, and having escaped the evils of Egypt, the Israelites cried out: Let us sing unto our Deliverer and our God.

Adorned with good moral qualities, from thine youth thou didst cleave unto Christ, and passions of thy flesh mortifiedst with abstemiousness and art gone over unto the Life, O holy one.

Having been the performer of the divine sayings and laws, thou hast become, O most wise father, filled with divine gifts and miracles, and hast unto all richly emitted thy rays.

Helped by the strength of Christ, thou hast, O father, put down the power and might of the enemy, and honours for thy victory hast thou, O holy one, received in the brilliancy of miracles.

Thou didst possess a good conscience, and the eye of thy heart was directed to God; wherefore, in answer to thy prayer, O most wise one, He counted thee with the just. [*The Theotokion*:

The passions of my flesh and evil insinuations of my mind do appease, I implore thee, O most pure Virgin, and set me with my strayed mind into the right path.

Ode 3. *The Heirmos:*

Thou art the stablishing of those that flee unto Thee, O Lord; Thou art the light unto those in darkness and my spirit hymneth Thee.

Being entirely devoted unto the Almighty, thou hast, O most wise holy father, escaped all the malice of the demons.

Adorned with the height of humility, thou hast, with thine excellent works, hurled down to the ground the great boaster.

Whilst still in the flesh, thou hast, O most wise father, humbled the high-borne neck of the wicked one with the humility of thy words.

Having as thy help God's power, thou dost, O most wise and wonderful one, shed miracles and drivest away diseases.

The Theotokion: In becoming incarnate, the Maker hath found abode in thy womb, O all-spotless one, unto the benefit of those who in faith hymn thee.

The Cathisma, Tone 4. Similar to: Speedily prevent...

Thou hast vanquished the fleshly subtlety of passions, and having subdued the worst unto the best, thou didst, O most glorious father (*mentioned by name*), by fasting destroy the wily scheming of the demons, and shonest forth in the world as a ray of the sun in the brilliant lustre of thy virtues; wherefore we hymn thee. [*Glory...Both now...the Theotokion:*

An unassailable wall unto us Christians art thou, O Theotokos-Virgin, for fleeing unto thee for shelter we remain unhurt, and when we sin afresh, we possess in thee a supplicant; wherefore, in giving thanks, we vociferate unto thee: Hail thou, full of grace, the Lord is with thee. [*The Stavro-theotokion:*

O all-spotless Virgin, Mother of Christ the God, a sword hath pierced thy most holy soul when thou beheldest thy Son and God voluntarily crucified; Him do not cease to supplicate, O most blessed one, to grant us the remission of our transgressions.

Ode 4. The Heirmos:

I have hearkened, O Lord, unto the mystery of Thine economy, comprehended Thy works and glorified Thy Godhead.

Having made thy soul into a temple of the Holy Spirit, thou didst become, together with the highest hosts, heir of the Kingdom on high.

Thou ever dost relieve from sufferings through manifold diseases those that have recourse unto thee; for thou, O holy one, hast obtained from the Lord the grace to work wonders and miracles.

In the house of God hast thou, O father, vegetated up as the best sprout, being adorned with virtues and filled with the sweet smell of a wonderful fruit. [*The Theotokion:*

A spiritual field art thou, O Ever-virgin, since out of a furrow thou hast brought forth an ear that feedeth the whole creation—the God of all.

Ode 5. The Heirmos:

Watching early we cry out unto Thee : O Lord, save us, for Thou art our God, beside Thee we know none other.

With thy purified mind, O all-glorious one, dost thou behold the ineffable goodness of Christ, the God of all.

Like unto Elijah in the chariot, thou, O father, hast ascended into heaven on thy virtues, being helped by the Spirit.

Having contracted thy body with abstemiousness and purity, unto the breadth of the upper habitations hast thou reached, O father. [*The Theotokion:*

Heal the blindness of my diseased mind, having given birth unto the Physician, even Christ, O all-spotless Sovereign-Lady.

Ode 6. The Heirmos:

Unto the Lord will I pour my prayer and to Him will I make known my sorrows, for my soul is become full of afflictions and my life hath come nigh unto the hades, and I will pray as Jonah : O God, raise me up from corruption.

With thy sacred prayers, O God-blissful one, is slain the cunning serpent and therewithal is destroyed the malice of those who demanded of thee a sign, for thou art God's favourite, beaming with light, proved in thy faithfulness.

With assiduous ploughing having renewed thy soul, thou hast, O sacred father, most wisely thrown therein multifruitful seeds of virtues, and hast gathered in rich ears of multifarious healings.

Helped by the strength of the Spirit, thou hast, O father, put down the power and might of the enemy, and honours for thy victory hast thou, O holy one, received in the brilliancy of miracles. [*The Theotokion:*

The Lord is with thee, O most pure one ! As it hath pleased Him, He was with thee, O Maiden, and through thine intercession hath delivered us all from the dominion of the deceitful one; wherefore now we dutifully from generation to generation call thee blessed.

The Contakion from the Typicon; but if there be no Typicon, say this Contakion, Tone 2. Similar to : Seeking the highest...

Having divinely armed thyself with the purity of thy soul

and unceasing prayers firmly grasping as a spear, thou, our father (*mentioned by name*), hast pierced the armies of the demon; supplicate unceasingly for us all. [*The Oikos:*

Having conceived a loving attachment to the divine commandments of Christ, and a hatred for the delights of this world, thou hast with diligence achieved thine end and wast a lamp that did enlighten the ends with the spiritual lustre. Wherefore falling down before thee I implore thee: Enlighten my spiritual eyes to hymn thine exploits of fasting, watchfulness, shedding tears, labours and maceration of the body, for the sake of the blissful future life, of which thou art now in the enjoyment. Supplicate unceasingly for us!

Ode 7. *The Heirmos:*

From Judea coming the youths did once in Babylon tread down the flame of the furnace by their faith in the Trinity, singing: O God of our fathers, blessed art Thou.

Having strong-mindedly gone through thine exploits of fasting, thou hast, O father, humbled the proudest mind with the divine humility, singing: Blessed art Thou, O God of our fathers.

In the house of God hast thou, O father, vegetated up as the best sprout, being adorned with virtues and filled with the sweet smell of a wonderful fruit.

Having enlightened thy heart, thou, O father, wast the superior of the sacred assembly, giving directions, teaching and bringing all under the will of God, singing: O God of our fathers, blessed art Thou. [*The Theotokion:*

Having given birth unto a new Youth—the Unoriginate Word, thou, O Virgin, hast renewed us grown old through sin, and made us strong to sing: O God of our fathers, blessed art Thou.

Ode 8. *The Heirmos:*

The God-spoken youths, whilst treading down in the furnace the flame with the fire, sung: Bless the Lord, ye the works of the Lord.

The heir of the divine habitations, thou didst, O father, live as an angel; wherefore with the angels doth thy spirit rejoice.

Having undeviatingly proceeded, O most wise and marvellous father, along the divine paths leading to heaven, thou hast unto the end avoided those that lead to evil.

Through the grace which hath found abode in thy soul, O father, are driven away the unclean spirits that cunningly find their abode in men. [*The Theotokion*:

Thou art, O Virgin, an inexhaustible source of water, drinking of which all become filled with the grace, being cleansed both in soul and body.

Ode 9. The Heirmos.

Every one became terrified at hearing of the ineffable God's condescension, that the Most High did voluntarily come down even unto the flesh itself, having become man in the Virgin's womb ; wherefore we the faithful magnify the most pure Theotokos.

Thy honoured shrine by the Holy Spirit richly sheddeth healings, cureth long standing diseases of those that have recourse unto thee, O father; it driveth away the cunning, ferocious spirits and raiseth up the faithful to the praising of thine illustrious deeds.

As a great sun that hast shone forth unto us in the greatness of thy deeds, O most wise one; thou hast enlightened the ends of the earth, and in thy death thou art gone from a light unto a brilliant light; wherefore we vociferate unto thee: Enlighten our thoughts, O holy father (*mentioned by name*).

Thine enduring body bound with chains, O blessed one, doth heal by a touch incurable diseases, since God and Saviour hath greatly glorified thee, O most wise and wonderworthy father (*mentioned by name*); for thou hast made thyself famous with thy good works, O holy one.

In the dales of fasting hast thou, O most praised father, blossomed as a wild sweet-smelling rose, and as a lily hast thou filled the consciences of the faithful with perfume of thy virtues and miracles; wherefore, O holy one, drive away from us the malodorous passions. [*The Theotokion*:

Enlighten, O pure Virgin, my heart ever grieving for transgressions and on account of manifold worldly resorts, do not leave me a joy unto mine enemies, that I may glorify and lovingly hymn thee, O most hymned one.

The Photagogicon. Similar to: Hearken, O ye women...

Thou hast flourished as David's palm, O father, and hast appeared an abode of the Holy Spirit, Who hath made thee famous in the universe, do unceasingly pray for us that in faith honour thy most honoured memory, O holy (*mentioned by name*). [*The Theotokion:*

We bless in unceasing odes thee, O Virgin, for unto One of the Trinity hast thou, O Theotokos, given birth and dost bear in thy divine arms the most abundant Word, unchangeable and immutable.

With the Lauds, the Idiomelic Stichera, Tone 6:

O God-bearer, most blessed (*mentioned by name*)! All the subtleties of thy flesh hast thou subjugated unto thy spirit, having strengthened thyself with the pains of fasting, and assayed as gold in the forge, hast thou appeared shining and wast a receptacle of the Most Holy Spirit. Having gathered multitudes of monks, thou hast with thine instructions, as with a ladder leading into heaven, brought them up unto the height of virtues. Remember us, honouring thy sacred memory, and supplicate that our souls may be saved. [*Twice.*

To-day doth shine forth thy most illustrious and all-festive memory, O most glorious (*mentioned by name*), calling together multitudinous assemblies of the fasting and choirs of the religious, both truly angels and men, unto the praise of Christ, our God adored in the Trinity. Wherefore, coming up unto the sacred shrine of thy relics, we abundantly receive the gifts of healing and glorify Christ, the Saviour of our souls, Who hath crowned thee.

O God-bearer, most blessed father (*mentioned by name*)! As the prophet of old, hast thou covered the earth with thy tears and never gave sleep unto thine eyes nor allowed dozing unto thine eyelids in manifesting the yearning of thy heart after Christ, Whom thou didst love; wherefore, wast thou a model unto monks and hast improved the manifestation of every virtue; wherefore, we also bless thee, magnifying Him Who hath glorified thee. [*Glory...Tone* 2.

O holy father! Having from childhood assiduously studied virtue, thou wast an organ of the Holy Spirit, and having obtained from Him the working of miracles, thou hast admonished the people to shun the sweets of life. Being now most clearly illumined with the divine light, enlighten also our thoughts, O our father (*mentioned by name*). [*Both now...the Theotokion:* All my trust I place in thee, O Mother of God, do preserve me under thy shelter.

The Stavro-theotokion. Similar to: When from the tree... Many humiliations hast thou endured; seeing the Maker of all things lifted up on the cross, thou, O most pure one, with moaning didst say: O Most Holy Lord, my Son and my God! How is it that when Thou desirest to honour Thy creation, O Master, Thou dost suffer dishonour in the flesh? Glory unto Thy great mercy and Thy condescension, O Lover of man.

CHAPTER XIII.

THE SERVICE COMMON TO TWO OR MORE MONKS.

At the Vespers, for O Lord, I have cried, the Stichera, Tone 8.
Similar to: O most glorious wonder...

O God-wise, holy fathers! Ye give light to the blind, unto the sick—cure, and to the lame—health, mercifully inclining unto those that in faith come to your temple and implore your help, for we all that praise you, have found in you sure protectors and intercessors.

O all-honoured, holy fathers! Entering the chariot with your virtues, ye have ascended up to God to receive the honours of your victory, and as a favour to us ye have left, O fathers, your bodies placed in the graves, to shed healings and to drive away the evil spirits; wherefore we bless you, O most praised ones.

Unto the choirs of ascetics were ye united, having been adorned with the life of fasting, and now, O blessed ones, ye joyfully reside in the heavenly habitations where angels exult, and are being truly deified with the divine light. Remember those who lovingly bless you on earth and celebrate your holy festival. [*Glory...Both now...the Theotokion:*

My thoughts are unclean, my lips flattering, and my deeds are all defiled. What then can I do? How can I meet the Judge? O Sovereign-Lady Virgin, supplicate unto thy Son and Maker and the Lord that He may receive my spirit in contrition, as the only Compassionate One. [*The Stavro-theotokion:*

The undefiled youthful Maiden seeing the Youth voluntarily nailed on the tree, piteously bewailing, called out unto Him: Woe unto me, O my most beloved Child! What hath the graceless assembly of the Hebrews rendered unto Thee? They are bent on depriving me of Thee, O All-beloved One.

If Idiomelion be appointed, Glory...Tone 6:

O holy fathers! Through all the earth is gone forth the sound of your exertions; wherefore have you found in heaven the reward of your labours; ye have destroyed the armies of the demons and have reached the orders of angels whom you have irreproachably emulated in your life. Possessing boldness before Christ the God, do obtain peace for our souls.

Both now...the Theotokion: O Theotokos, pure Virgin, supplicate the Lord that through thine intercessions He may grant unto our souls the remission of sins, peace and great mercy.

The Stavro-theotokion: Beholding our Life hanging on the tree, thou, O all-spotless Theotokos, motherly bewailing, hast cried out: O my Son and my God, do save those who lovingly hymn Thee.

If the Celebration be with the Polyeleon, say the Theotokion of the resurrection: Who would not praise thee...*The Entrance...The Prokeimenon of the day and the Readings of the religious.* (*See Appendix.*)

For the Versicles the Stichera, Tone 4. Similar to:
As a virtuous...

Having put on Christ, ye have God-wisely pulled off the corrupt man; thereupon, being ever illumined with the spiritual grace, ye have shone unto the world as lustrous stars, supplicating that may be delivered from corruption and dangers those who constantly celebrate in faith your honourable memory.

The Versicle: Precious in the sight of the Lord is the death of His saints.

Now that ye are enjoying the food, surrounded with the light and inheriting the life eternal, do deliver those who have recourse unto you, from dangers, various temptations, and from every affliction, making use of the boldness unto God of which God-wisely ye are in possession, and shewing love truly like unto that of Christ Himself.

The Versicle: Blessed is the man that feareth the Lord, that delighteth greatly in His commandments.

O all-wondrous God-bearers, champions of the Trinity! Having equipped yourselves for the struggle against the prince of this world with manly wisdom, ye have put him down with firmly united front and obtained the crowns of victory; wherefore we, illumined by the grace, celebrate your divine and illustrious memory. [*Glory...Tone* 8:

O holy fathers! Having conceived detestation unto the beauties and the food of this world and a greater love to the monastic life, ye have become associates of angels, and as multi-lighted lamps ye shine unto the universe with your miracles as a second sun; but do remember us who celebrate your sacred memory, for we are your children and the sheep of your pastoral teaching; we call you to our aid, imploring that through you we may obtain peace and great mercy.

Both now...the Theotokion of the resurrection: O Virgin unmarried...

But if there be no Celebration, say the following Theotokion:

O holy Virgin-Theotokos! I flee up unto thy shelter and know that through thee I shall find the salvation, for thou, O pure one, art able to help me. [*The Stavro-theotokion:*

Beholding Thee, O Jesus, nailed on the cross and voluntarily accepting the passion, O Master, Thy Mother, the Virgin, cried out: Woe unto me, O my sweet Child! How dost unjustly endure the wounds Thou, O Physician, that hast healed the infirmity of man and hast delivered all from corruption through Thy compassion.

The Troparion from the Typicon; but if there be no Typicon, say this Troparion, Tone 4:

O God of our fathers that ever dealest by us according to Thy kindness, do not withdraw from us Thy mercy, but at their intercessions direct our lives in peace.

Glory...Both now...The Theotokion or the Stavro-theotokion.

At the Matins, for God is the Lord, the same Troparion. After the 1st Stichologia, the Cathisma, Tone 4. Similar to: Speedily prevent...

Being the brightest lamps of the truth of Christ, ye have, O God-spoken fathers, enlightened the world with your teaching; having demolished the heresies of the wicked blasphemers, ye have extinguished the flaming agitation of the blasphemers; wherefore ye enlighten all as the favourites of Christ. [*Twice.*

Glory...Both now...the Theotokion:

O Virgin all-spotless, that gavest birth unto the Ever-existing God, do, with the religious, unceasingly supplicate Him to grant us remission of sins and improvement of life before we reach our end, since we dutifully hymn thee in faith and with love, O only all-hymned one.

After the 2nd Stichologia, the Cathisma, Tone 8:

For Christ's sake ye have renounced flesh and have appeared the spiritual leaders of men, having hearkened unto the words of the mystic teaching; unto the monks ye have appeared the rule of uprightness, having subdued by force all the passions; wherefore, having also destroyed unto the end the wiles of the demons, do, O God-bearing fathers, fervently pray unto God that the remission of sins may be granted unto those who lovingly honour your holy memory. [*Twice.*

Glory...Both now...the Theotokion:

Behold the generations after generations glorify thee, as thou hast foretold, O Maiden, for thou wast a palace of the Maker of all and a divine temple in which the Most High hath dwelled and put on the flesh that He might save us.

After Praise ye the name of the Lord, the Refrain:
We bless ye, O religious fathers, and honour your holy memory, preceptors of monks and associates of angels. *The selected Psalm:* I waited patiently for the Lord...
After the Polyeleon, the Cathisma, Tone 8. *Similar to:* Of the wisdom...
When ye, O blessed ones, have concentrated your minds on the desire of God, you have discarded all the dragging down sophistries, and having found your abode in wilderness, you have flourished therein with your good deeds as beautiful lilies, extirpated the thorns and planted the fruits of your labours. Having therefore gathered in an inalienable and rich harvest in heaven, supplicate Christ the God, O holy fathers, to grant remission of sins unto those who in faith honour your holy memory.
Twice. Glory...Both now...the Theotokion:
In thee, O full of grace, rejoiceth all the creation, the body of angels and the race of men; O thou hallowed temple and rational paradise, glory of virgins, of whom God was incarnate and became a little Child, our God that is before the ages; for thy womb He made into a throne and thy belly He rendered wider than the heavens. In thee, O full of grace, rejoiceth all the creation, glory to thee.
The Graduals, the 1st *Antiphon of the* 4th *Tone. The Prokeimenon:* Precious in the sight of the Lord is the death of His saints. *The Verse:* What shall I render unto the Lord for all His benefits toward me? Let every breath...*The Verse:* Praise God in His saints...*The Gospel of the religious.* (*St. Matth.* 11, 27-30.)
After the 50th *Psalm, the Sticheron, Tone* 6:
Let us honour the great fathers that are on earth angels and in heaven men of God, fine ornament of the world, adornment of kind nourishers, praise of monks and superiors; for, planted in the house of the Lord, ye have flourished in righteousness, and as cedars ye have multiplied in the wilderness the flock of Christ's reasonable sheep in holiness and righteousness.
The Canon, Tone 2. *Ode* 1. *The Heirmos:*
Come, O ye people, let us sing an ode unto Christ the God that hath divided the sea and instructed the people whom He brought out of the Egyptian bondage, for He is glorified.

Illumined with the brightness of the Three Suns of the Godhead, ye have appeared, O most wise ones, as lights, and unfailingly enlighten those that honour your bright memory.

Having given yourselves up entirely unto the Creator, all your spiritual desires have ye poured out before Him, wherefore you have obtained the spiritual grace.

Illumined with the light of grace, do, O holy ones, illumine those that in faith celebrate your memory and deliver them with your prayers from the darkness of sin. [*The Theotokos:*

Having in the flesh given birth unto the Bodiless One, do, O most pure God's Parent, cleanse with the drops of your divine prayer the impurities of our bodies and souls.

Ode 3. The Heirmos:

Fix us firmly unto Thee, O Lord, that hast slain sin on the tree, and plant Thy fear in the hearts of us that hymn Thee.

Having filled your souls with the streams of tears, ye have made them, O holy ones, fruitful, productive of every virtue and exhibitory of most glorious miracles.

Your divine temple worketh healing, driveth away diseases of men and strengtheneth the devices of these to praise your labours, O all-honoured ones.

Having of old striven against the enemy with abstemiousness and having now placed against him as stronghold the victory which ye have manfully obtained, ye have, O holy ones, put down the rage of the demons.

The Theotokion: Out of thy womb, O Virgin, hath most gloriously shone forth the great Sun that, having enlightened the earth, received the choir of the holy ones.

The Cathisma, Tone 4. Similar to: Thou hast appeared to-day...

Having passed the sea of life in abstemiousness without difficulty, ye have reached the reasonable haven of impassiveness, O holy and God-wise fathers.

Glory...Both now...the Theotokion: Virginity and child-birth, above nature and speech, have in thee, O Theotokos, met together, for thou gavest birth unto the Incarnate God, Saviour of our souls. [*The Stavro-theotokion:*

Seeing thy Son hung on the cross and being lacerated in thy

motherly bosom, thou, O most pure one, hast cried out: Woe unto me! Whither art Thou gone down, O my Light Ever-shining.

Ode 4. *The Heirmos:*

I have hearkened unto Thy glorious economy and glorified Thy incomprehensible might, O Lover of man.

As those who loved Christ's humility, ye have been exalted by impassiveness and have humbled the pride of demons.

Shining forth as the sun from the east, with the rays of miracles, ye enlightened, O holy ones, every thing under the sun.

As a censer full of sweet odour, ye, O holy ones, have brought your prayers unto the All-seeing; having smelled and accepted thereof, He ordaineth the celebration of asceticism.[*The Theotokion:*

The choir of the holy ones and the soul of every faithful one bless thee, O most pure one, for, above mind and understanding, thou didst give birth unto the Divine Word.

Ode 5. *The Heirmos:*

O Granter of light and Creator of ages! Do Thou, O Lord, lead us in the light of Thine injunctions, for beside Thee we know no other God.

Having given yourselves up entirely unto the love of Christ and assiduously endeavoured to perform the divine commandments, ye have obtained the grace of many miracles, O most glorious ones.

Meek and mild, ye have frustrated all the malice of the enemy and have remained gracious to the end, and from the Only Merciful One obtained the true and saving grace.

Ye have always endured in law, prayer and fasting, and have put on impassivity, having humbled fleshly intellect with the strength of the Holy Spirit. [*The Theotokion:*

Sing unto the Lord a new song, sing unto the name of Him Who God-beseemingly hath shone forth from the womb of one inexperienced in marital life, and hath shewn her unto the faithful—a firm hope and praise.

Ode 6. *The Heirmos:*

Wallowing in the abyss of sin I call unto Thine unfathomable abyss of mercy: Bring me up, O God, from corruption.

With the shedding of your great exploits, ye, O fathers, have obtained victory over the countenances of demons, making yourselves, O holy ones, pleasing unto the Lord Who was crucified for our sake.

Having acquired benign dispositions, ye, O fathers, have in abundance received gifts from the Benefactor-God and these ye dispense, O holy ones, unto those requiring them.

Having been filled with spiritual gifts, ye, O fathers, have subjugated the inimical spirits, and as reasonable and wise have always kept near God. [*The Theotokion*:

Heal the passions of my soul, since thou wast the source of impassivity and hast enlightened the choirs of the holy fathers with thy child-birth.

The Contakion from the Typicon; but, if there be no Typicon, say this Contakion, Tone 2. Similar to: Seeking the highest...

Passing unmoistened through a multitude of waves, in the streams of your tears ye have deeply immersed your bodiless enemies, O God-wise and holy ones, and have received the gift of miracles; do incessantly pray for us all. [*The Oikos*:

As a beautiful garden, having been filled with the greatest multitude of your virtues, ye have, O holy ones, flourished as if coming out of paradise with your fasting and prayer, filling all with the sweet odour of your many labours, deeds and toils, amidst which ye have skilfully passed unto the sorrowless life and were covered with the crowns of victory; do incessantly pray for us all.

Ode 7. *The Heirmos:*

Whilst a golden image in the flames of Dura was being worshipped, Thy three youths have not taken heed of the godless command, and thrown into the midst of the fire, but bedewed, they sung: Blessed art Thou, O God of our fathers.

With the weapon of your prayers, ye have, O holy ones, vanquished the evil spirits and from heaven obtained the grace to heal the diseases of, and to drive away the evil spirits from, those that call out: Blessed art Thou, O God of our fathers.

Your bodies ye have, O wise fathers, subjugated unto the spirit by abstinence of every kind; having lived the life of good works, ye had clear conscience, O most praised ones, and attained the life in heaven, singing: Blessed art Thou, O God of our fathers.

Entering by the right way into the divine rest, ye, O blessed ones, have escaped the assaults of demons, being protected by the divine grace and crying out: Blessed art Thou, O God of our fathers.

The Theotokion: The flaming sword, which of old held the gates of Eden, doth now, O pure Virgin, serve as an elevator unto all those who through fasting have put down the great enemy and are ever calling out: Blessed art Thou, O God of our fathers.

Ode 8. The Heirmos:

Him that once in the bush, on the Sinai mountain, typified unto Moses the miracle of the Virgin, do ye hymn, bless and extol Him unto all the ages.

The drops of your tears have quenched the fire of sin and have shewn unto us all a whole stream of miracles that drowneth all sufferings of those who have recourse unto you, O most glorious fathers.

You professed, O fathers, an indestructible faith and hope, true love and gracious assiduity, kindly patience and instruction of spiritual words, humbleness and perfect meekness.

Ye have laboured well until you obtained victory over all the workings of the enemy, and at the end of days you were crowned, O wise-ones, and numbered unto all the holy ones, with whom we honour you, and extol Christ unto the ages. [*The Theotokion:*

Save me, O Mother of God, that appearedst at the beginning of salvation unto the world, by delivering me from the agitation of unclean passions and from every affliction of the enemy, that I may glorify thee unto all the ages.

Ode 9. The Heirmos:

The Word of God that in unspeakable wisdom came down from God to renew Adam, who hath deeply fallen into corruption through eating, and became for our sake ineffably incarnate of the holy Virgin—Him let us, O faithful, with one mind magnify in hymns.

Behold the kingdom of heaven is open unto you, O fathers, who have finished your good course; ye see what the angels of God behold, and the reward of your labours God that honoureth you, granteth you in honours; wherefore, O holy fathers, we bless you.

Having pleased God with your contrite hearts, ye have wrecked the snares of demons and ye have, O God-bearers, restored those wrecked by them, wherefore, we bless you, adoring in faith the shrine of your relics, O God-blessed ones.

Having had your thoughts directed God-ward, on high, ye, God-bearing, holy fathers, left earthly things and received the heavenly for the sake of your labours and unremitted abstemiousness, wherefore we honour you.   [*The Theotokion*:

Spare me, O Lord, spare me, when Thou willest judge me, and condemn me not unto the fire, nor rebuke me in Thine indignation; Thee do entreat, O Christ, the Virgin that bare Thee, the choirs of angels and the assemblies of the holy ones.

The Photagogicon. Similar to: Thou hast visited us...

Ye have flourished as David's palms, O fathers, and have appeared the abodes of the Holy Spirit, becoming famous throughout the universe. Do unceasingly pray for us that in faith honour your most honoured memory, O holy ones.

The Theotokion: We bless in unceasing odes thee, O Virgin, for unto One of the Holy Trinity hast thou, O Theotokos, given birth and dost carry in thy divine arms the most abundant Word, unchangeable and immutable.

With the Lauds, the Stichera, Tone 4. Similar to: Thou hast given a sign...

Shining forth brighter than the sun, your all-festive memory, O holy ones, is resplendent of the rays of your virtuous deeds, and illumineth the senses of the faithful with the light of your miracles, O blessed ones; celebrating it therefore, we joyfully praise you and in faith bless your all-festive memory.

Twice. Like unto the other angels ye have lived your earthly life, keeping down your bodies by abstemiousness, yet by vigilance and remembrance of death, with assiduous consideration thereof, growing up and making great strides in ascending unto the highest desire; wherefore, O holy fathers, ye have truly reached the very corner stone—Christ.

The passions of the body ye have tired out with abstemiousness, and with the streams of tears in your assiduous prayers ye have strangled the flattering serpent, O holy fathers, and became more pleasing unto God than others, O wonder-worthy; wherefore Jesus, the Lover of man and the Saviour of our souls, hath adorned you with heavenly gifts.

Glory...Tone 8. Having meditated on the law of the Lord day and night, ye have, O holy fathers, been accounted worthy to be planted together with the tree of life, and the fruit of your suffering hath flowered forth crowns; possessing boldness unto the Agonothete—the God—entreat also for us purification and great mercy. *Both now...the Theotokion:* O Sovereign-Lady, accept the prayers of thy servants and deliver us from every want and woe. [*The Stavro-theotokion:*

When the most pure one saw Thee in the flesh hanging on the cross, her heart being broken she hath vociferated in tears: O Word, whither art Thou gone, my most beloved Jesu, my Son, my Lord? Do not leave, O Christ, me alone that gave birth unto Thee!

CHAPTER XIV.

THE GENERAL SERVICE TO ONE MARTYR.

At the Vespers, for O Lord, I have cried, the Sticheras, Tone 1.
Similar to: O all-praised martyrs...

Having, O all-honoured one, with the uprightness of thy heart comprehended the Boundless God, thou hast, O blessed one, believed in Him indubitably; having strictly followed His ineffable, saving injunctions, O most wise one, and having patiently endured the sufferings, thou hast attained the Kingdom immovable.

With thy honoured blood hast thou consecrated the earth and hast abrogated the defiled blood offered lawlessly unto demons, and received an incorruptible crown upon thy brow, O all-honoured one; wherefore, supplicate that unto our souls may be granted peace and great mercy.

Glorifying thy sacred struggles and exploits we also become consecrated, O all-honoured martyr (*mentioned by name*), thereby thou hast become associate of angels and companion of all the martyrs; supplicate together with them that unto our souls may be granted peace and great mercy.

Glory...Both now...the Theotokion: Woe unto me! What will become of me whose mind and soul and the body are defiled with transgressions? What can I do? How can I escape the unendurable flame, the unbreakable and eternal chains? But, O all spotless one, before the end supplicate thy Son to grant me the remission. [*The Stavro-theotokion:*

Beholding her Lamb without form or comeliness on the cross, the Maiden-lamb and all-spotless Sovereign-Lady said bewailing: Woe unto me! Whither is Thy comeliness gone, O my sweetest Child? Whither the stateliness? Whither the sparkling grace of Thine eye, O mine all-beloved Son?

If Idiomelion be appointed, Glory, Tone 6: To-day all the universe is illumined with the rays of the passion-bearer, and the church of God, decorated with flowers, vociferateth unto thee, O martyr (*mentioned by name*); O favourite of Christ and the most fervent intercessor, cease not to pray for thy servants.

The Theotokion: We have comprehended the God incarnate of thee, O Theotokos-Virgin; Him supplicate for the salvation of our souls.

The Stavro-theotokion, Similar to: Having laid all aside...

Seeing her Lamb lifted up on the cross, the Maiden-lamb undefiled of old and spotless Sovereign-Lady Motherly exclaimed and in astonishment cried out: What is this new and most glorious sight, O my sweet Child? How is it that the graceless people give Thee over unto the judgment of Pilate and condemn unto the death the Life of all? But I hymn Thine unspeakable condescension, O Word!

THE SERVICE TO A MARTYR. 141

If the Celebration be with the Polyeleon, say the Theotokion of the resurrection: Who would not bless thee?...*The Entrance. The Prokeimenon of the day. The Reading of the martyrs (see Appendix).*

With the Versicles the Stichera, Tone 4. Similar to: As a virtuous...

Although the cruel tyrant gave thee over to be subjected to the most painful tortures, and thy much-suffering and much-enduring body did undergo multifarious torments, thou, O God-mindful *(mentioned by name)*, didst not renounce Christ, neither didst thou sacrifice unto idols, but hast endured all as if it were somebody else who suffered, awaiting future reward and undying theology.

The Versicle: The righteous shall flourish like the palm tree; he shall grow like a cedar in Lebanon.

Raised up and pared, shot at with stones, wounded with iron and finished off with a sword, thou didst remain inflexible, having fixed thy soul on the reasonable Rock, and therefore wast thou numbered unto the choirs of angels, being accounted worthy of the never-setting Light.

The Versicle: Those that be planted in the house of the Lord shall flourish in the courts of our God.

Thy relics, O glorious *(mentioned by name)*, shed unto those that desire it, the healing of faculties, drown passions and diseases and disperse crowds of the evil demons; they give drink unto the hearts of the faithful that grow the divine fruits of virtues and the understanding of piety.   [*Glory...Tone* 6:

O come all ye, philo-martyrs, let us piously glorify the famous martyr of Christ *(mentioned by name),* who hath finished his course, for he hath bruised the head of the serpent, with his blood consecrated the earth, and is gone over from those living here unto the everlasting habitations; having obtained honours for his exploits from the hand of the Almighty, he doth implore unto our souls cleansing and great mercy.

Both now...the Theotokion: O Theotokos, thou art the true vine...

The Stavro-theotokion: The most pure one seeing Thee hung

on the cross, with motherly tears cried out unto Thee: O my God, my sweetest Child! How is it that Thou sufferest the ignominious death?

The Troparion from the Typicon; but if there be no Typicon, say this Troparion, Tone 4:

Thy martyr, O Lord (*mentioned by name*), through his suffering, an incorruptible crown did obtain from Thee, our God; for, rejoicing in Thy strength, he laid low his tormentors and did beat off impotent affronts of the demons also; at his intercessions save our souls.

Glory...Both now...the Theotokion or the Stavro-theotokion.

At the Matins, for God is the Lord, the same Troparion. After the 1st Stichologia, the Cathisma, Tone 1. Similar to:
The choir of angels...

Having held in detestation the military forces of the earth, thou, O martyr, didst desire the glory of heaven and hast endured pains and the necessary death; wherefore to-day we celebrate thine all-holy memory, offering praise unto Christ, O most blessed (*mentioned by name*). [*Twice.*

Glory...Both now...the Theotokion: As truly the Mother of God and Virgin we all supplicate thee, calling upon thy compassions and fleeing lovingly unto thy goodness, for in thee we, sinners, possess protection, and have acquired in thee salvation in afflictions, O only most pure one.

After the 2nd Stichologia, the Cathisma, Tone 4. Similar to:
Thou hast appeared to-day...

Having finished thy true course, thou hast vanquished all the might of thy tormentors, hast obtained the crown from the hand of the Almighty, O all-honoured (*mentioned by name*), and hast appeared as associate of angels. [*Twice.*

Glory...Both now...the Theotokion: The Word of the Father, Christ, our God, that was incarnate of thee, we have come to know, O Theotokos Virgin, the only pure, the only blessed one; wherefore, incessantly hymning thee, we magnify thee.

THE SERVICE TO A MARTYR. 143

After Praise ye the name of the Lord, the Refrain:

We magnify thee, O holy martyr (*mentioned by name*), and honour thy precious sufferings which thou didst endure for Christ's sake. *The selected Psalm:* God is our refuge and strength...

After the Polyeleon, the Cathisma, Tone 4:

As Christ's invincible warrior, great vanquisher of the enemy, shining forth in great miracles, let us all in faith laud the martyr (*mentioned by name*), for he doth shed healings unto those that come to him in faith, appeaseth great pains and intercedeth for those that are afflicted. [*Twice.*

Glory...Both now...the Theotokion:

A wall unassailable art thou for us christians, O Theotokos-Virgin, for, having recourse unto thee, we remain unhurt and, when we sin afresh, we have in thee our intercessor; wherefore rendering thee thanks, we vociferate unto thee! Hail thou, full of grace, the Lord is with thee!

The Graduals, the 1st Antiphon of the 4th Tone. The Prokeimenon: The righteous shall flourish like the palm tree; he shall grow like a cedar in Lebanon. *The Verse:* Those that be planted in the house of the Lord, shall flourish in the courts of our God. Let every breath...*The Gospel, St. Luke,* 12, 2-12.

After the 50th Psalm the Sticheron, Tone 6: To-day all the universe (*given in the Vespers*).
The Canon, Tone 5, *Ode* 1. *The Heirmos:*

Both horse and horseman hath Christ overthrown into the Red Sea destroying the hosts with His exalted arm, but He saved Israel who sung the hymn of victory.

Standing before the throne of God with boldness, as an invincible martyr, do thou, O God-blessed one, preserve with thine intercessions those who lovingly celebrate thy holy passion.

Having in thy soul an abiding supply of the living water, thou hast, O holy and all-glorious one, dried up the turbid streams of evil, being strengthened by the grace of the Saviour, O God-blessed one.

144 SERVICE TO A MARTYR.

Being strengthened with the power of God, thou, O God-blessed one, wast enabled to break down the pride of the enemy, and becamest a great vanquisher and a citizen of the city on high. [*The Theotokion*:

Do manifest on me, wretched, thy compassion, O most pure Lady, assiduously supplicating thy Son, O most holy one, that we may escape eternal fire through thine intercession.

Ode 3. The Heirmos:

Thou that hast set up the earth upon nothing with Thy command and suspended it freely hanging, do Thou, O Christ, stablish Thy church on the immoveable rock of Thy commandments, O only Good One and Lover of man.

Drawing away from the dung of passions and nearing God with divine purity, thou hast, O worthy of glory, obtained illumination from God, which sheweth thee to be the son of light, as one who does the work of light.

The military calling and great earthly glory hast thou accounted as nothing; wherefore hast thou enlisted as a soldier of Christ and was numbered among the companies of martyrs, rejoicing thereat, O blessed martyr (*mentioned by name*), the God-bearer.

The paths of thy progress, O wondrous one, being directed in the way of peace, thou didst, O glorious one, enter the Kingdom of God, the midst of paradise and eternal rest. [*The Theotokion*:

Having given birth unto the Master and Maker of the whole creation, thou hast appeared, O pure Sovereign-Lady, more honourable than the cherubim and seraphim, wherefore we—all the generations—dutifully bless thee.

The Cathisma, Tone 5. Similar to: The Co-unoriginate Word...

Illumined with the brilliancy of virtues and adorned with the halo of martyrdom, thou, O most wise one, dost steadily shine more than the sun, and enlighteneth truly those who faithfully keep thy light-bearing memory. O all-glorious martyr (*mentioned by name*), save those that adore thy relics.

Glory...Both now...The Theotokion: The awful miracle of conception and ineffable manner of child-birth were manifested in thee, O pure Ever-virgin. My mind is terrified and my reason bewildered thereat, and thy glory, O Theotokos, hath reached us all unto the salvation of our souls.

The Stavro-theotokion: By the cross of thy Son, O full of God's grace, the enchantment of idols hath been done away with and the might of demons vanquished. Wherefore we, the faithful, dutifully ever hymn and bless thee, and confessing thee as truly the Theotokos, we magnify thee.

Ode 4. The Heirmos:

Thine, O Christ, divine-emptying having perspicaciously penetrated, Habbakuk in his terror cried out unto Thee : For the salvation of Thy people, to save Thine anointed art Thou come.

Adorned with the love and trust in God, O most wise one, thou hast shone forth as a martyr, O most blessed one, and unto the angels co-citizen hast thou become, O most glorious one.

Immovable and inflexible didst thou remain, living in exile and deprived of thine own, for the sake of the Master—God of all, O God-blessed and most wise one.

Having laboured well and being adorned with the virtues of a martyr, thou didst go over unto the unseen good things, reaping the honours of thy labours.   [*The Theotokion :*

He that is known to be on high with the Father, for our sake becometh incarnate below of thee, O all-spotless Sovereign-Lady, through the abundance of compassion, the only Good One and Lover of man.

Ode 5. The Heirmos:

Unto Thee that arrayest Thyself with light as with a garment, do I watch and to Thee I call : Enlighten, O Christ, my darkened soul, as the only Compassionate One.

Strengthened by the laws of the Almighty, thou hast repelled the advices of the lawless, and having suffered in accordance with the laws, thou hast, O martyr, obtained the crown of incorruption.

The coals of seduction, hast thou, O most wise one, extinguished in the streams of thy blood, and now, pouring the waters of healing, dost thou drive away by God's grace the flame of disease.

Enabled wast thou, O martyr, in the infirmity of thy flesh to bring to ruin the resourceful in snares serpent, and by grace hast thou, O wise one, rejected his manifold allurements.

The Theotokion: Mortify, O most spotless Virgin, I implore thee, the soul corrupting passions of my body, having given birth in the flesh unto the source of impassivity, Christ the God.

Ode 6. *The Heirmos.*

Do tranquillize, O Master, Christ, the sea of passions infuriated by the soul-destructive tempest and bring me out of corruption, as Compassionate One.

Before the judgment of the law breakers didst thou stand, O martyr of Christ (*mentioned by name*), and hast uprooted all the deceit; thou wast judged for Christ's sake and in thy manly wisdom didst confute the accusation.

Thou wast adorned, O most wise martyr of Christ, in thy passion with divine virtues; wherefore wast thou enlightened by Christ and didst remain in incorruption.

With thy blood hast thou consecrated the earth and with thy consecrated soul hast thou, O most blessed one, illumined heaven and filled with joy the choirs of martyrs. [*The Theotokion :*

Taught of the Spirit, the prophet foresaw in thee a door through which God hath passed on becoming incarnate, leaving it again sealed, O most spotless one.

The Contakion from the Typicon; but if there be no Typicon, say this Contakion, Tone 2. Similar to: Seeking the highest...

Thou hast appeared as a bright star, uninviting for the world, but a sun announcing Christ with thy rays, O martyr (*mentioned by name*); all the enchantment hast thou extinguished and grantest unto us light, supplicating incessantly for us all. [*The Oikos :*

Grant me melody, O my God, to hymn and recite and honour the exploits of Thy passion—endurer and martyr, that I may harmoniously laud the great in suffering (*mentioned by name*), who ever was the vanquisher of passions, great in piety and is now shining forth in the midst of the choir of martyrs, with whom and a multitude of angels, he doth incessantly hymn Christ, receiving from above divine illumination and praying unceasingly for us all.

Ode 7. The Heirmos:

The most exalted Lord of the fathers hath subdued the flame and bedewed the youths who were harmoniously singing: O God, blessed art Thou.

Translating thy martyred body, the people loving to honour thee, O great sufferer and wise one, gratefully cried out: Blessed is the God of our fathers.

By the grace of God thou hast destroyed the offerings of the Hellens, and having loosed thyself from the bodily ties, by martyrdom hast thou, O blessed one, ended thy days for Christ's sake, having suffered according to law.

As if in a chariot didst thou sit on thy blood, O martyr worthy of praise, and with joy didst go up into the abodes of rest beyond this world. [*The Theotokion:*

Glory unto all art thou, O pure one, and strengthening unto those that confess thee, O all spotless one, to be the Mother of God Who hath above nature passed out of thy womb.

Ode 8. The Heirmos.

Unto Thee, the Maker of all things, the youths in the furnace, having formed an exquisite choir, sung: Hymn the Lord, all ye the works, and exalt Him unto all the ages.

Of Jerusalem above wast thou the heir and hast died in exile, O most wise one, singing incessantly: Hymn the Lord, all ye the works, and exalt Him unto all the ages.

Thou hast partaken of many woes, O blessed one, and now sorrowless life hast thou obtained, wherefrom dost thou call out: Hymn the Lord, all ye the works, and exalt Him unto all the ages.

Enabled wast thou by the all-accomplishing God's power to destroy the enchantments of the Hellens and their all-wily sophistries and to receive from the Master of all the crown of incorruption, O martyr. [*The Theotokion:*

The All-compassionate Word out of thee, O pure one, hath taken the flesh and united Himself unto men. Him, O all-holy one, supplicate to mortify the urging of my flesh and to save my soul.

Ode 9. The Heirmos:

Isaiah, exult! The Virgin had in the belly and bare a Son, Emmanuel, both God and man, Orient is His name: Him magnifying, we glorify the Virgin.

O come ye faithful gathered together, let us to-day celebrate the sacred solemnity of the most blessed and sacred martyr of Christ *(mentioned by name)*; for in his martyrdom he hath by divine power, vanquished all the multitude of enemies.

Adorned wast thou, O glorious one, with the divine qualities of martyrdom and on thy blood as in a chariot of fire hast thou joyfully ascended and reached the heavens to behold the ineffable goodness of our Saviour.

A select warrior of Christ the God and great-sufferer hast thou appeared; wherefore now dost thou dwell in the Kingdom on high, being gloriously adorned with the crown of a victor, O all-praised martyr.

The Theotokion: Having given birth unto the enlightenment of those in darkness, even Christ, do thou, O all-holy one, illumine my blinded soul and grant that I may proceed along the paths that lead unto the life, O instructress of all hymning thee. [*The Photagogicon:*

As a light-bearing sun with wondrous rays dost thou instruct all creation, O most glorious martyr *(mentioned by name)*; wherefore celebrating thy memory we entreat Him Who rose from the grave to deliver all from dangers. [*The Theotokion:*

With thy mighty protection do, O pure one, ever preserve unhurt by the assaults of the enemy us, thy servants; for in thee alone we have acquired a shelter from dangers.

With the Lauds, the Stichera, Tone 4. Similar to:
Called from above...

In psalms as well as in odes the people laud thy glorious memory, O *(mentioned by name)*, for it hath shone forth magnificently and brilliantly, adorned with glory and grace. Wherefore, to-day exult the orders of angels, the martyrs together with apostles praise, O martyr, thy sufferings at thy martyrdom, and hymn the Saviour-Christ, our God, that hath glorified thee; Him supplicate that He may save and enlighten our souls. [*Twice*.

Thou wast found, O (*mentioned by name*), equipped with a complete armament of Christ by those who did not look for thee; for being for Christ's sake burned with fire and treating with scorn the godless fury of the vain gods, thou didst then call out unto the lawless ones: I wage war for my King, Christ; neither beasts, nor wheels, nor any other torment can ever separate me from the love to my Christ. Him supplicate to save and enlighten our souls.

Having contemned both manifold vessels and various tortures together with the fearful instruments, thou hast, O crown-bearer (*mentioned by name*), ended thy pious course in martyrdom; wherefore we crown thy most illustrious memory with the flowers of hymns and in faith kiss thy precious relics; but since thou dost stand before the throne of the Master, Christ our God, cease not to supplicate that He may save and enlighten our souls. [*Glory...Tone* 1:

O glory of the martyrs (*mentioned by name*)! Having set against the deceit thine illustrious victories, thou dost, through thy diligence, carry everywhere the bodily glory benignly as victor, and now do raise up from falling into sin those who in faith honour thy memory. [*Both now...the Theotokion:*

Hail thou, O Theotokos-Virgin, since thou gavest birth unto the King of heaven, the Saviour and Illuminer of our souls.

The Stavro-theotokion. Similar to: O all-famous martyrs...

Beholding her Lamb without either form or comeliness, on the cross, the Maiden-lamb and all-spotless Sovereign-Lady, said bewailing: Woe unto me! Whither is Thy comeliness gone, O my sweetest Child? Whither the stateliness? Whither the sparkling grace of Thine eye, O mine All-beloved Son?

CHAPTER XV.

THE GENERAL SERVICE TO TWO OR MANY MARTYRS.

At the Vespers, for O Lord, I have cried, the Stichera, Tone 4.
Similar to: As a virtuous...

Having been enlightened by the Holy Spirit, ye, O most laudable ones, have taken up arms against the prince of this world and have obtained victory over his snares, with God's help; wherefore celebrating to-day your most illustrious memory, we dutifully honour with praises your sufferings.

Having been given over unto wounds and tortures, ye, O holy ones, did remain inflexible in your wisdom, as lamps attaining the highest heat from the spiritual warmth, ye have enlightened the hearts of the faithful with the grace; wherefore people of every station and age make a feast of your holy memory, glorifying the Lord in odes.

With the brightness of your miracles ye, O martyrs, have enlightened the whole creation, having driven away the mist of passions and woes from those who have recourse unto you and in faith seek your protection, O valiant sufferers of the Saviour; wherefore in faith we keep your holy and light-bearing commemoration.

Glory...Both now...the Theotokion:

Bent by assaults of the demons and thrown into the cave of ruin, do thou, O Sovereign-Lady, take compassion on me and establish me upon the rock of virtues, and having destroyed the incitements of the enemy, make me worthy to perform the commandments of thy Son and our God, that I may obtain pardon in the day of judgment.

The Stavro-theotokion: Seeing Christ the Lover of man crucified and pierced in His side with the spear, the most holy one wept vociferating: What is this, O my Son? What have the ungrateful people rewarded Thee with for all the good Thou hast done unto them? And thou most lovingly takest care of my childlessness! I wonder, O Compassionate One, at thy voluntary crucifixion.

If Idiomelion be appointed, Glory...Tone 3:

Behold how good and beautiful is the brotherly love of the martyrs one for another, O Christ the God! For although birth after the flesh hath not made them brethren, yet the brother-loving faith hath taught them to be of that mind even unto the blood; through their intercessions, O Christ the God, save our souls.

Both now...the Theotokion: O Theotokos the protection of all, invoking thee, through thee we become bold, by thee we boast, and in thee is all our trust, supplicate Him unto Whom thou didst give birth, for thine unprofitable servants.

The Stavro-theotokion. Similar to: Great of Thy cross...

Seeing Him Who was born of thee, hung on the tree, the all-spotless one exclaimed in loud lamentation: O my most desired Child? Where is gone down the light-bearing goodness of Thee Who hast improved the human race?

If the Celebration be with the Polyeleon, Both now...the Theotokion of the resurrection: How can we help wondering? *The Entrance. The Prokeimenon of the day. The three Readings of the martyrs (see Appendix).*

With the Versicles the Stichera, Tone 4. Similar to: As a virtuous...

As resplendent stars, ye, O most famous martyrs, illumine the ends of the universe with the divine brightness, delivering them from the darkening of the demons, from pernicious passions and dangers; wherefore being to-day gathered together we praise your bright, light-bearing and holy commemoration.

The Verse: The righteous have cried, and the Lord hath heard them. Let the wondrous, divine and the most wise martyrs be honoured with sacred odes; for having justly preached before the enemies the Uncreated Trinity, they have extinguished with the outpouring of their blood the enchantment of polytheism and have received the never-fading glory.

GENERAL SERVICE TO THE MARTYRS.

The Verse: Many are the afflictions of the righteous, and from them all will the Lord deliver them.

The lawless king, unlawfully commanding to bow down before, and to do honour unto, the mute and soulless gods, ye, O blessed and greatly renowned martyrs, have put to shame with your wisdom, and having suffered enduringly and lawfully, ye have plaited the crowns of victory and are interceding for the world. [*Glory...Tone* 6 :

O come, ye lovers of martyrs, and having in spirit performed the all-sacred memory of the now manifested and crowned of God company of martyrs—the unblemished offering zealously immolated for Christ, the sacredly-selected army, let us vociferate unto them : Do break the fury of the godless Agarenes and deliver from every affliction the piously minded people with your intercessions. [*Both now...the Theotokion:*

We have come to know God that was incarnate of thee, O Theotokos-Virgin ; Him supplicate for the salvation of our souls.

The Stavro-theotokion : The all-spotless one and God's Bride seeing the One born of her condemned and nailed to the cross, cried out : Glory to Thy long suffering, O my Son, and to Thy great compassion.

The Troparion from the Typicon ; but if there be no Typicon, say this Troparion. Tone 1 :

Through the sufferings of Thy saints which they did endure for Thy sake, be moved, O Lord, and all our infirmities cure, Thou, O Lover of man, we implore Thee.

[*Glory...Both now...the Theotokion or the Stavro-theotokion.*

At the Matins, for God is the Lord, the same Troparion.
After the first Stichologia, the Cathisma, Tone 4. *Similar to:*
Thou hast appeared...

Ye divine martyrs, warriors of Christ, as the greatest stars, ever illumine the venerable firmament of the church and enlighten the faithful. [*Twice.*

Glory...Both now...the Theotokion : Thou, O most pure Virgin, dost receive the imploration from us fleeing under thy shelter ; do not cease to supplicate the Lover of man to save thy servants.

GENERAL SERVICE TO THE MARTYRS. 153

After the second Stichologia, the Cathisma, Tone 4. *Similar to :* He that was lifted up...

With manful thoughts going through your martyrdom, O wondrous martyrs, ye have passed through fire and water and crossed unto the breadth of salvation receiving as inheritance the Kingdom of heaven; do therein make your divine supplications for us, O wise great martyrs. [*Twice.*

Glory...Both now...the Theotokion : In order gratefully and heartily to hymn thee and persistingly to entreat thee, O Theotokos, Sovereign-Lady, for thy mercies, thy servants cry out unto thee saying: O most holy Virgin, do prevent and free us from enemies both visible and invisible and from every threatening, for thou art our protection.

After Praise ye the name of the Lord, the Refrain:

We magnify you, O holy martyrs, and honour your precious sufferings which for Christ ye have endured.

The selected Psalm : God is our refuge and strength...
After the Polyeleon, the Cathisma, Tone 8.

Bound by the enemies were ye led and shut up in dungeons for long periods, yet, preserved by faith, ye did remain unhurt, and having been separated from your bodies by swords, ye, O holy ones, manifestly became bound by the divine desire. Wherefore ye have shone forth in the world as lights, illumining all by the grace of the Spirit, O blessed martyrs; supplicate Christ the God to grant remission of sins unto those that celebrate with love your holy memory. [*Twice.*

Glory...Both now...The Theotokion : As Virgin and one among women we, all the generations of men, bless thee that without seed gavest birth unto God in the flesh, for the divine fire did find abode in thee and thou dost suckle as a babe the Maker and the Lord. Wherefore we, both the angelic and human kind, worthily glorify thy divine child-birth and unanimously cry unto thee: Supplicate Christ the God to grant remission of sins unto those who with faith adore thy most holy child-birth.

The Graduals, the first Antiphon of the 4*th Tone. The Prokeimenon :* The righteous have cried, and the Lord hath heard them. *The Verse:* **Many** are the afflictions of the righteous, and from them all will the Lord deliver them. Let every breath... *The Gospel of the martyrs (Matth. 10, 16-22).*

After the 50th Psalm, the Sticheron, Tone 2.

Come, O ye lovers of festivals, let us rejoice in the Lord, in memory of the martyrs! Come, let us mystically hymn forth, praising the sufferers for Christ, that have broken up the enchantment of idols and before the judgment seat clearly proclaimed Christ; wherefore, O all blessed and great sufferers, cease not supplicating for our souls.

If it be the Forty Martyrs, the following Prokeimenon should be read: We went through fire and through water, but Thou broughtest us out into a place of rest. *The Verse:* Thou hast tried us as silver is tried. [*The Sticheron, Tone 2.*

Whereas David in his Psalms prophetically cried out: We went through fire and through water, but Thou broughtest us out into a place of rest, ye, O martyrs of Christ, carrying out the words in your deeds, actually did go through fire and through water and have entered the Kingdom of heaven. Wherefore supplicate, O ye forty sufferers, that great mercy may be granted unto us.

The Canon, Tone 5, Ode 1. The Heirmos:

To God the Saviour Who hath in the sea made His people go with unmoistened feet and drowned Pharaoh with all his host, unto Him alone let us sing : For He is glorified.

Let us, O ye faithful, God-wisely hymn the warriors of Christ and martyrs, as the destroyers of enchantment and illustrious vanquishers, singing to God the ode of victory: For He is glorified.

Ye have, O sufferers, cheerfully struggled on earth, have endured torments and obtained crowns in heaven, harmoniously singing the ode of victory: For He is glorified.

Linked together by the sure tie of the unity of souls, ye have turned away from the illusion and have appeared crown-bearing vanquishers, harmoniously singing the ode of victory: For He is glorified.

The Theotokion : O most pure Mother of God! Do unceasingly supplicate the God that was incarnate of thee and did not forsake the bosom of the Begetter, to save from every attack those whom He created.

Ode 3. The Heirmos:

By the power of Thy cross, O Christ, strengthen my mind that I may hymn and glorify Thy saving ascension.

Adorned with Christ's understanding, ye warriors have drowned the wicked enemy in the streams of your blood.

Having given your bodies over unto the bitter and cruel tortures, ye, O laudable martyrs, have received through faith divine inheritance.

By command of the tyrant being destroyed with the shower of stones hurled, ye, O great sufferers, have unflinchingly preserved the might of orthodoxy. [*The Theotokion:*

O pure one! Do unceasingly pray, together with the martyrs, unto Him Who hath proceeded from thy loins, to deliver from the enchantment of the devil those hymning thee, O all-spotless one.

The Cathisma, Tone 4. Similar to: Thou that wast lifted up...

The valiant warriors of Christ, having fought well, have utterly drowned in the streams of their blood the cunning enemy; being broken with stones and cut up with swords, burnt in the fire or thrown into the water, they have shewn themselves as crown-bearers; wherefore they are honoured and glorified in faith. [*Glory...Both now...the Theotokion:*

We, thy servants, O Theotokos-Virgin, will never cease gratefully and heartily to hymn thy mercies, O Sovereign-Lady, vociferating and saying: O most holy Virgin, prevent and deliver us from enemies, both visible and invisible, from every need and every threatening, for thou art our protection.

The Stavro-theotokion: The Virgin and ewe seeing on the cross and pierced with a lance the Lamb Whom she without seed hath brought forth, and being hit with the arrows of grief vociferated exclaiming in pain: What is this new mystery? How dost Thou die Who art the Sole Lord of life? Wherefore do rise Thou raising the fallen ancestor.

Ode 4. *The Heirmos*:

I heard the rumour of the power of the cross that the paradise is opened thereby and I cried out: Glory to Thy power, O Lord

Sustained by the God-favoured customs, the choir of sufferers, have vanquished the God-opposing enemy, being strengthened by the grace of the Saviour.

The God-called company of martyrs of Christ have vanquished a whole multitude of the God-opposing, impious enemies, hymning: Glory to Thy power, O Lord.

Seeing the Light unapproachable, whilst in prison, the martyrs have destroyed the polytheistic darkness of the idol-deceit, being strengthened by the power of God.

The Theotokion: The power of the Highest did overshadow thee, O Virgin, and hath made thee paradise, that had in her midst the Tree of life, the Mediator and Lord.

Ode 5. *The Heirmos*:

Watching early we cry out unto Thee, O Lord: Save us, for Thou art our God, beside Thee we know none other.

Educated on the words of the Holy Spirit, the martyrs have abolished the dumbness of idols.

The martyrs were like unto the light-bearing stars and unto the flowers of faith, emitting sweet smells.

Ye, O holy and all-laudable, have appeared as a cornfield, cut down with the sickles of tortures. [*The Theotokion*:

Cease not, O Theotokos, supplicating Him Whom thou didst bear, to save the souls of us that assiduously hymn thee.

Ode 6. *The Heirmos*:

Abyss hath encompassed me, a whale hath become my grave, but I called out unto Thee, O Lover of man, and Thy right hand hath saved me.

Rejoicing the martyrs called out: In Thy hands, O Master, Lover of man, take up our spirits and rest them, for we love Thee, the only One Plenteous in mercy.

The choir of Thy martyrs, O Lover of man, have become co-dwellers with the angels, for having finished their course they pray now that our souls may be saved.

O choir of martyrs, O God-selected, the glory and beauty of martyrs! Do assiduously supplicate that all those may be saved who flee unto you. [*The Theotokion:*

The marvel of thy seedless conception—what word can express, O most spotless one? For thou didst conceive God that hath come unto us for mercy's sake.

The Contakion from the Typicon; but if there be no Typicon, say this Contakion, Tone 8. Similar to: Seeking the highest...

Having appeared as bright lamps, ye, O divine martyrs, enlighten the whole creation with the shine of your miracles, releasing from maladies, ever driving away the profound darkness and supplicating continually Christ the God for us all. [*The Oikos:*

O beautiful choir, shining and divine lamps, ever standing before the Great Light and by the rays of the Never-setting Godhead therefrom proceeding, being ever illumined and deified! Do, O God-blessed martyrs, enlighten us that in faith celebrate your divine memory, and deliver us from darkness and passions, from dangers and malice, praying continually for us all.

Ode 7. The Heirmos:

He Who in the burning furnace hath saved the youthful psalmodists, blessed is the God of our fathers.

In the furnace Thy martyrs, O Christ, called out: Blessed is the God of our fathers.

Enlightened with the Triune Light, the sufferers have with joy given up their souls, singing: Blessed is the God of our fathers.

Standing before God and rejoicing, O ye crown-bearing sufferers, supplicate Him for us. [*The Theotokion:*

As our salvation we implore thee, O Theotokos, to pray for us unto Him Who was incarnate of thee.

Ode 8. The Heirmos:

The Son and God born of the Father before the ages and in these last days incarnate of the Virgin-Mother, hymn, O ye priests, and ye, people, extol Him unto all the ages.

Let our prayer, O ye faithful, be with the martyrs, and we

shall be participators of their heritage, hymning Christ and extolling Him unto the ages.

With heartfelt joy the choir of the patient sufferers God-beseemingly receive from Christ the crowns and cheerfully hymn and extol Him unto the ages.

Dyed red with the streams of your blood, ye-worthy of all laud—will reign with Christ unto the ages in the heavens, piously singing and extolling Him unto the ages.

The Theotokion: Higher than the cherubim hast thou appeared, O pure Theotokos, having carried in thy womb Him that sitteth on them; Him we earth-born together with the bodiless doxologize and extol unto the ages.

Ode 9. *The Heirmos:*

Thee that art above understanding and word, the Mother of God, that hast ineffably brought forth in time the Eternal One, we the faithful with one mind magnify.

Standing before Christ, for Whose sake ye have endured even tortures, do, O most glorious martyrs, pray for the salvation of all.

With your powerful arm, O invincible ones, ye have put down the stronghold of deceit, and now are accounted worthy to live together with angels in the celestial habitations.

With lawful manners of martyrs ye have obtained victory over the proud tyrant and have received the crowns of the righteous, O all-honoured ones.　　　　　[*The Theotokion:*

Hail thou, O Theotokos, Mother of Christ the God, Whom thou broughtest forth. Him supplicate to grant remission of sins unto those that in faith hymn thee.　　　[*The Photagogicon:*

Ye, the passion-bearers, were taken up into the lustrous habitations of paradise, having been vested in bright garments which ye have woven by the multifarious tortures, and ye stand now before the throne of the Maker, assiduously supplicating for all.　　　　　　　　　　　　　　[*The Theotokion:*

With thy sovereign shelter do, O pure one, always preserve us, thy servants, unhurt by the slanders of the enemy; for in thee alone we have acquired a refuge in attacks.

With the Lauds, the Stichera, Tone 8. *Similar to :* O most glorious...

O most laudable martyrs of Christ! Having considered the impetuous rash of the persecutors and violent death as of no account, and having boldly made yourselves ready for the manfully-wise struggle, ye have been invested with the glory of victors and numbered among all the righteous ; with these ever-praising you, we bless you. [*Twice.*

O most blessed martyrs of Christ ! Ye have given up yourselves unto the voluntary slaughter, and sanctified the earth with your blood and clarified the air with your demise ; and now ye tabernacle in the heavens, in the never-setting light, always praying for us, O God-seers.

O invincible martyrs of Christ ! The red heat of tortures ye have passed unhurt by the dew of the divine grace and were accounted worthy to dwell beside the still water, having received the crowns of victory ; wherefore with joy we celebrate to-day your holy memory, glorifying Christ.

Glory...Tone 8 : Carrying on war for Christ, ye have forsaken the delights of earthly life, and having taken up the cross on your shoulders, ye have followed Him for the sake of many and various tortures, never denying Him before any number of kings or tyrants ; the angels have adorned your heads with crowns of victory and ye have boldly and joyfully entered with your souls into the great palace. Wherefore, possessing boldness unto the Saviour of all, supplicate for our souls.

Both now...the Theotokion : Attuning our voices unto that of archangel Gabriel, let us say : Hail thou, O Mother of God, that hast brought forth unto the world the Creator, even Christ.

The Stavro-theotokion : O Lord, when the sun beheld Thee — the Sun of righteousness—hanging on the cross, he hid his rays and the moon hath changed light into darkness, and the all-spotless, Thy Mother, was pierced through in her innermost soul.

CHAPTER XVI.

THE GENERAL SERVICE TO ONE HIEROMARTYR.

At the Vespers, for O Lord, I have cried, the Sticheron, Tone 1.
Similar to: All-laudable martyrs...

O God-wise, blissful (*mentioned by name*), with the purple dye of thy blood, thou hast brightened thy sacred and divine raiment, for thou hast piously gone from strength to strength and from glory to glory; do now supplicate that peace and great mercy may be granted to our souls.

Offering first unto God the bloodless sacrifice, as a priest truly lawful, afterwards, as an entire and acceptable sacrifice, hast thou, O God-spoken and all-honoured one, offered thyself in thy blood, as a most true martyr, unto Christ; Him entreat for those that hymn thee.

A whole troop of martyrs hast thou, O father, brought to Christ by thy precepts and teaching, not only instructing and teaching in words, but offering manifestly thyself as an example, O God-wise one; pray together with them that peace and great mercy may be granted to our souls.

Glory...Both now...the Theotokion: Being the sport of the abyss of transgressions and having run up unto the calm haven of thy supplication, I call out unto thee, O most pure Theotokos: Save me by extending thy sovereign right hand unto thy servant, O most spotless one.   [*The Stavro-theotokion:*

Standing at the cross of thy Son and God and considering His long suffering, thou, O pure Mother, thus spakest in tears: Woe unto me, O my sweetest Child! Why dost Thou unjustly suffer this, O Word of God, that Thou savest mankind?

If Idiomelion be appointed, Glory, Tone 6.

Most lawful priest didst thou, O blissful (*mentioned by name*), remain unto thy very end, for performing the divine and ineffable mysteries, thou hast shed thine own blood for Christ the God and offered thyself as a sacrifice well acceptable to Him; wherefore having boldness before Christ, do assiduously supplicate for those who in faith and with love celebrate thy most honoured memory and who honour it, that they may be saved from attacks, all dangers and calamities.

Both now...the Theotokion: The God incarnate of thee we have come to know, O Theotokos—Virgin, entreat Him for the salvation of our souls.   [*The Stavro-theotokion:*
Beholding Thee, O Christ, crucified, she that bare Thee vociferated: What a strange mystery I see, O my Son! How dost die, being in the flesh hung on the tree, Thou—the Giver of life.

If the Celebration be with the Polyeleon, say the Theotokion of the resurrection: Who would not bless thee...

The Entrance. The Prokeimenon of the day. The three Readings of Hierarchs (see Appendix).

With the Versicles, the Idiomelic Stichera, Tone 6:

Having steeped thy sacred vestment in blood, thou hast, O glorious (*mentioned by name*), entered into the Holy of Holies, being thyself holy, and manifestly art in continuous enjoyment, being adorned with deification, shining in thy martyrdom and taking part in a communion purer than that of angels; wherefore we honour thee and lovingly celebrate thy most sacred festival, O worthy of bliss.

The Versicle: The righteous shall flourish like the palm-tree; he shall grow like a cedar in Lebanon.

Bound with irons, thou hast trodden, without stumbling, thy path, O holy one, which leadeth unto the heavenly city, being trimmed with the precious wounds as with ornaments, O all-wise (*mentioned by name*); therein having entered as the truest vanquisher and invincible martyr and most sacred minister, thou dost clearly sing with the angels the divine hymnology: Holy, Holy, Holy art Thou, O Trinity Consubstantial.

The Versicle: Those that be planted in the house of the Lord, shall flourish in the courts of our God.

Thy sacred deeds as an ascending gradual hath acquired the church which thou, O hieromartyr (*mentioned by name*), dost preserve unshaken and unassailable for the mighty wolves, and which proclaimeth thy virtues and magnifieth thy sufferings, lawfully endured by thee for Christ's sake, O blissful one.

Glory...Tone 4. Into the heavenly church hast thou as a holy one entered, being besprinkled with blood, and dost now, O blissful one, stand before the Trinity, richly besprinkled, shining with the lustres proceeding therefrom, O most opulent one, wherefore celebrating to-day thy, O (*mentioned by name*), light-bearing memory, we enlighten the senses of our souls.

The Theotokion of the resurrection; but if there be no Celebration, say the following Theotokion:

With the clouds of the Most Holy Spirit do thou bedew my thoughts, O most pure one, who hast given birth unto the drop, even Christ, that washed out, through compassions, the countless and immeasurable lawless deeds of men; do thou dry up the source of my passions, and vouchsafe unto me the stream of ever living food by thine intercessions.

The Stavro-theotokion: Beholding Thee, O Lord, nailed to the cross, she-lamb and Thy Mother wondering called out: What is this spectacle, O my desired Son? Is it thus that the treacherous and lawless assembly hath repaid Thee for Thy many miracles in which it had taken delight? Howbeit, glory be unto Thine unspeakable descent, O Master.

The Troparion from the Typicon; if there be no Typicon, say the following Troparion, Tone 4 :

Having been a participant of the character and a successor of the apostles on the throne, thou, O God-inspired one, didst find work in coming into visions; whilst therefore rightly dividing the word of truth, for the sake of the faith didst thou suffer even unto the shedding of thy blood. O hieromartyr (*mentioned by name*), intercede before Christ the God that our souls may be saved.

Glory...Both now...the Theotokion or the Stavro-theotokion.

THE GENERAL SERVICE TO A HIEROMARTYR.

At the Matins, for God is the Lord, the same Troparion.
After the 1st Stichologia, the Cathisma, Tone 3. Similar to:
Of the divine faith...

O sea of confession of the faith! Thou hast put an end to the heterodoxy of the enchantment, having put to shame the godlessness of idol-worship, and having been made a divine burnt offering, thou dost illumine the ends of the world with thy miracles; O holy father, entreat Christ the God to grant us great mercy. *Twice.*

Glory...Both now...the Theotokion:

A divine tabernacle of the Word wast thou, O only most pure Virgin and Mother; thou that hast with thy purity excelled angels, do cleanse me—dust that I am—defiled above all by the sins of the flesh, with the divine waters of thine entreaties, granting, O pure one, great mercy.

After the 2nd Stichologia, the Cathisma, Tone 4. Similar to:
Thou hast appeared...

Having shone forth as a ray of the sun, thou dost sparkle brilliantly unto all the world in thy teaching, O God's voice, light-bearing, holy *(mentioned by name)*, the glory of the martyrs. *Twice. Glory...Both now...the Theotokion:*

Stretching out thy most pure arms, shelter, O Virgin and Mother, those that trust in thee and call out unto thy Son: grant unto all, O Christ, Thy mercies.

After Praise ye the name of the Lord...*the Refrain:*

We magnify thee, O hieromartyr *(mentioned by name)* and honour thy holy memory, for thou dost supplicate for us Christ our God. *The selected Psalm:* Hear this all ye people...

After the Polyeleon the Cathisma, Tone 8. Similar to:
Of the wisdom...

Steered by the all-effecting might and winged by the sail of the cross, thou hast easily swum across the storms of life and hast truly reached the divine haven, having acquired a goodly supply of virtues, which thou didst present unto the Master of all and from Him heard: Well done, thou good and faithful servant and words following these; wherefore, O blissful *(mentioned by name*), supplicate Christ the God to grant remission of sins unto those that with love venerate thy holy memory. *Twice.*

Glory...Both now...the Theotokion: Having fallen a prey unto the greatly complicated assaults from the enemies both visible and invisible, and being held back by the storm of mine innumerable sins, I have recourse unto the refuge of thy loving kindness, O pure one, as to my warm defence and protection; wherefore, O most pure one, do assiduously supplicate Him Who was seedlessly incarnate of thee, for all thy servants that ceaselessly implore thee, O most pure Theotokos, ever entreating Him to grant remission of sins unto those that worthily hymn thy glory.

The Graduals, the 1st Antiphon of the 4th Tone. The Prokeimenon: Precious in the sight of the Lord is the death of His saints. *The Verse:* What shall I render unto the Lord for all His benefits towards me? Let every breath... *The Gospel of a hierarch (St. Luke* 12, 32-40). *After the 50th Psalm, the Sticheron, Tone* 4:

Having cleansed thy soul from passions, thou wast, O holy one, a sacred vessel of the Holy Spirit, and having received from Him the divine holy unction, thou wast a hierarch and preceptor of the God-wise people and an invincible martyr of Him Who for our sake endured passions and made impassiveness to flow, O sufferer (*mentioned by name*).

The Canon, Tone 2, Ode 1. *The Heirmos:*

Come, O ye people, let us sing an ode unto Christ the God Who hath divided the sea and instructed the people whom He brought out of the Egyptian bondage, for He is glorified.

Enlightened with the light emitted by Christ, do thou, O glorious hierarch (*mentioned by name*), with thine intercessions enlighten my darkened soul, that I may hymn thee, O most blissful one.

Having shone forth as an untarnished mirror of thy pure heart in the enlightenment of the salutary preaching, thou, O father, hast emitted rays unto all.

By thy fasting thou hast put down the activity of passions, and by abstemiousness hast thou changed the desire itself and by divers exploits wast thou raised to the height of impassivity. [*The Theotokion:*

We know God that was incarnate of thee without seed or man's desire, that existed before every creature and before all the ages; wherefore we hymn thee as the true Theotokos.

Ode 3. The Heirmos:

Fix us firmly unto Thee, O Lord, that hast slain sin on the tree, and plant Thy fear in the hearts of us that hymn Thee.

As an all-perfect living sacrifice hast thou brought thyself up unto Christ in thy martyrdom, with the conscience of a martyr, having suffered before in the life of abstemiousness.

Thy sacred life, thy divine word and divine deeds taking ascent in thy heart unto the true contemplation of God, thou hast attained it.

Having God-wisely directed thy word in accordance with the injunctions of the Saviour, thou didst appear worthy and wast an invincible defender of the faith. [*The Theotokion:*

Thou hast shaken our minds off deadliness, having given birth unto the Immortality itself, and with thy bringing forth thou hast, O Virgin, woven unto us a vestment of incorruption.

The Cathisma, Tone 3 : Enlightened of the Divine Spirit, thou hast, O hieromartyr, with thy great wisdom and pastoral boldness put to shame the ferocity of tyrants, and having been carried across the abyss of enchantment, hast reached the divine refuge. O holy father! supplicate Christ the God to grant us great mercy. [*Glory...Both now...the Theotokion:*

Everyone hath recourse thither where he can be saved, and what other such recourse is there that can shelter our souls but thou, O Theotokos. [*The Stavro-theotokion:*

Having acquired the staff of might in the cross of thy Son, we put down therewith the surgings of the enemies, unceasingly magnifying thee with love.

Ode 4. The Heirmos:

I have hearkened unto Thy glorious economy and glorified Thine incomprehensible might, O Lover of man.

As a divine burnt-offering and a pure sacrifice wast thou brought up unto the Saviour of all, O most wise hierarch.

Instructing in the light of the knowledge of God the flock of Christ, thou hast driven away the darkness of godlessness.

With the streams of thy sweat hast thou, O father, as hierarch dried up the depths of godlessness. [*The Theotokion*:

With thy light do thou, O most pure one, enlighten my darkened soul, since thou didst give birth unto the Sole Hypostatical Light.

Ode 5. *The Heirmos*:

O Granter of light and Creator of ages! Do Thou, O Lord, lead us in the light of Thine injunctions, for beside Thee we know no other God.

Christ, the true wisdom, hath granted thee, O blissful one, both riches and glory, both longevity and life eternal, for having loved Him exceedingly.

The snares of heresies dost thou drive away with the staff of faith and, having united thy flock with the bonds of love, by love and faith dost thou preserve it unhurt.

Having refused food in thine abstemiousness, thou hast satisfied thy soul, having as food incessant prayers and instruction, and humility that raiseth one up to God. [*The Theotokion*:

We all have acquired in thee, O pure one, protection, sure hope, might and shelter, a wall and a bridge that leadeth into the Kingdom of heaven.

Ode 6. *The Heirmos*:

Wallowing in the abyss of sin, I call unto Thine unfathomable abyss of mercy: Bring me up, O God, from corruption.

Having been both the sacrifice and priest, thou hast sacrificed thyself unto God for the sake of the faith, and dost preserve undefiled the accomplishment of thy ministry to Him.

Having been slain unto the whole world, but remaining alive unto God alone, thou, O God-spoken one, went over to Christ being enriched with incorruptible life.

Having now gone over from earth into the never-ending glory, do thou, O holy one, by assiduous cleansing of thy supplication heal my soul accursed through the passions.

The Theotokion: Having conceived Christ that taketh away the sins of the whole world, cease not, O most pure and all-spotless one, to supplicate for the remission of sins unto thy servants.

The Contakion from the Typicon; but if there be no Typicon, say this Contakion, Tone 4. *Similar to:* Thou that wast of Thine own will lifted...

Having lived piously among hierarchs and having gone through the path of martyrdom, thou, O God-wise one, hast extinguished the sacrifices of idols and wast a protector unto thy flock. Wherefore, in honouring thee, in our hearts we cry out unto thee: Do ever deliver us from dangers through thine intercessions, O *(mentioned by name)*, our father. [*The Oikos:*

Faithfully and with love having come together in memory of the sacred sufferer, let us praise him to-day in odes that we may obtain the enjoyment of his grace, for he doth deliver the souls from passions and dangers, as a martyr and as a faithful hierarch and champion of those that heartily implore him; wherefore let us cry out unto him: Do ever deliver us from dangers through thine intercessions, O *(mentioned by name)*, our father.

Ode 7. *The Heirmos:*

Whilst a golden image in the planes of Dura was being worshipped, Thy three youths have not taken heed of the godless command, and thrown into the midst of the fire, but bedewed, they sung: Blessed art Thou, O God of our fathers.

Thou hast appeared as a cup of wisdom full of virtue, and having by the preaching of thy sublime life gathered thy flock, thou hast, O God-wise one, well tended it and dost now, together with thy sheep, call out: Blessed is the God of our fathers.

Unto the temples there existing, unto the habitation of honour hast thou reached; thou, O father, dost tabernacle with angels and with them rejoicest; wherefore honouring thee, O most blissful one, we with boldness call out: Blessed is the God of our fathers.

Happy art thou and it is now well with thee in thy tabernacle where the troops of the righteous, the numbers of martyrs and the choirs of the most wise apostles vociferate: Blessed is the God of our fathers. [*The Theotokion*:

Thou alone, O most pure Virgin, hast become known as the Mother, innocent of marital life, of God Who created everything in His wisdom; wherefore piously calling unto thee, we say: Blessed art thou that gavest birth in the flesh unto God.

Ode 8. The Heirmos:

The God that hath descended unto the Hebrew youths in the fiery furnace and hath changed the flame into dew—hymn ye the works as the Lord and exalt unto all the ages.

Having piously performed the service of the mysteries of Christ, thou—an intellectual sheep—wast thyself offered up unto Him as an acceptable and well-pleasing sacrifice, perfected with the blood, O most blissful one.

Having adorned thy hierarchical vestments with thy virtues, O most wise one, thou didst appear as keeper of chastity, true food of abstemiousness, teacher of prayer, instructor in repentance and law unto life.

Let us at the time of offering always bring the fruit worthy of repentance, since the barren fig-tree is continually threatened with being cut off; O my soul, fear the curse and receive Christ —the abundant fruit of virtue. [*The Theotokion*:

Do not despise, O dreaded defender, the voice of thy servants and snatch us all away from every danger and from every cruel menace, O holy Virgin, for thy motherly supplication doth move God to mercy.

Ode 9. The Heirmos.

The Word of God, that in unspeakable wisdom came down from God to renew Adam who hath deeply fallen into corruption through eating, and became for our sake ineffably incarnate of the holy Virgin,—Him let us, O faithful, with one mind magnify in odes.

Thou, O father, hast blighted manifold arrows of the enemy with the fire of abstemiousness and having burnt up the fleshly mud with the coals of purity, wast gloriously accounted worthy of the true limpidity existing on high.

Thy light-bearing memory, O father, having shone forth, illumineth the souls of those who reverently celebrate it, and maketh them manifestly the partakers of the divine light, O worthy of admiration; which we do worthily magnify in odes, O God-wise one.

Thee, O father, that dost wear the crown, having received from the right hand of God the reward of thy victory, finished thine exploits and been filled with divine light,—we the faithful offer unto Christ in faith as a fervent intercessor.

The Theotokion: Thee as the Theotokos, Virgin and Mother of the Word, our mediatrix that hast shone forth unto us the Ever-existing Life of God and the Sun of righteousness, we the faithful with one mind magnify in odes.

The Photagogicon. Similar to: The heaven with the stars...

As hieromartyr having the power to bind and to loose, do thou, O blissful one, loose the bonds of mine evil deeds and unto those loved of God number me and partaker of the Kingdom make me through thine intercession. [*The Theotokion:*

Do thou, O pure one, illumine my soul darkened by my sins and through thine intercession deliver me from the eternal flame and darkness, that I may joyfully laud thy majesty.

With the Lauds the Stichera, Tone 4. *Similar to:*
Thou hast given a sign...

The spiritual grace having shone forth unto thee, O father (*mentioned by name*), did greatly illumine thee; thenceforth the night of passion was shortened and the day of impassivity hast thou reached when thou wast united unto the purest Light; abiding therein, forget not, O God-voiced hieromartyr, those who in faith hymn thy memory. [*Twice.*

Possessing the desired grace of heaven, thou, O hieromartyr (*mentioned by name*), hast left unheeded earthly possessions; wherefore as a bodiless one and desirous of enjoying the food of the ever-existing source, thou, O God-pleasing one, hast selected the life of suffering and, having dried up with tears the troubled source of passions, thou hast filled the ears with the food of the soul.

Thy body hast thou given over to affront, since it was covered with wounds from beating and exposed to the fire, for thy mind hast thou fixed with an invincible desire on the divine Bestower for the sake of His beauty, having been transfixed by His sweet desire, O thou ornament of martyrs, adornment of hierarchs, martyr (*mentioned by name*), associate of angels.

Glory...Tone 4. Like a new plant, like unto a green olive-tree wast thou set in the house of God as the son of those that walk in the ways of the Lord; on account of thy martyrdom the Lord hath blessed thee and thou shalt see the good of the heavenly Zion, taking delight in the divine joys together with all the saints, O hieromartyr (*mentioned by name*), worthily hymned ; make us also partakers thereof through thine intercessions. [*Both now...the Theotokion :*

O Theotokos, the Queen of all and the glory of the orthodox ! Do thou put down the rays of the heretically inclined and put to shame their countenances, since they neither bow down before thy precious image, O most pure one, nor venerate it. [*The Stavro-theotokion :*

Seeing Christ—Lover of man crucified and pierced in His side with a lance, the most pure one bewailed crying out : What is this, O my Son ? What have the ungrateful people rendered unto Thee for all the good Thou hast done unto them, and Thou dost most lovingly take care of my childlessness ? I wonder, O Compassionate One, at Thy voluntary crucifixion.

CHAPTER XVII.

THE GENERAL SERVICE TO TWO OR MANY HIEROMARTYRS.

At the Vespers, for O Lord, I have cried, the Stichera, Tone **1**.
Similar to : The all-lauded martyrs...

Having truly and brightly adorned your hierarchical raiment with the blood of martyrdom, and having become lustrously ornate on both sides, ye have presented yourselves together with the angels unto the Creator ; Him supplicate, O ye glorious saints, to grant peace unto our souls and great mercy.

Ye have appeared unto us truly as God-inspired organs ; proclaiming the unspeakable mysteries of God in the divine scriptures and proving the foolishness of idol-worship, you have brought all to Christ; Him supplicate to grant peace unto our souls and great mercy.

With the word of God's understanding, ye, O most wise ones, have delivered the people from their utter ignorance, and having saved them, ye have brought them unto the Word that hath shone forth, born of the Father, even to Christ our God; do supplicate Him to grant peace unto our souls and great mercy.

Glory...Both now...the Theotokion:

O all-hymned Virgin! The mystery that is in thee, Moses with his prophetic eyes saw in the bush burning, yet unconsumed, for the divine fire hath not burnt thy womb, O pure one; wherefore we implore thee as the Mother of our God to obtain peace for the world and great mercy. [*The Stavro-theotokion:*

Standing at Thy cross, O Word of God, she-lamb and Thy Mother bewailing thus vociferated: Woe unto me, O my Son! How dost Thou die on the cross? Woe unto me, O my sweet Light! Where is now gone down the image of Thy beauty, O Thou—the fairest above men?

If Idiomelion be appointed, Glory...Tone 8:

Ye, O God-called ones, have passed out of the temporary cycles, after having endured sevenfold beating, paring and whole crucifying for Christ's sake, but neither fire, nor wounds and instruments of torture, could weaken the strength of your souls, and ye have trodden under your feet the strength of demons, O glorious hieromartyrs; wherefore supplicate Christ the God to save our souls. [*Both now...the Theotokion:*

Unto thy shelter, O holy Virgin—Theotokos, I flee, and know that I shall find salvation through thee, for thou, O pure one, canst help me.

The Stavro-theotokion. Similar to: O most glorious wonder...

Seeing Thee nailed to the cross, O Jesus, and voluntarily accepting Thy passion, the Virgin, Thy Mother, O Master, cried out: Woe unto me, O my sweet Child! How dost Thou endure the unrighteous wounds?—O Physician, that hast healed the infirmity of mankind and hast delivered all from corruption through Thy compassion!

THE GENERAL SERVICE TO HIEROMARTYRS.

If the Celebration be with the Polyeleon say the Theotokion of the resurrection : The King of heavens...

The Entrance. The Prokeimenon of the day. The three Readings of the martyrs (see Appendix.) With the Versicles, the Stichera, Tone 4. Similar to :
As a virtuous...

As the multi-lustrous stars that are spiritually shining forth upon the firmament of the church, you illumine all creation, driving away darkness by the power of light and the brilliancy of miracles, wherefore rejoicing to-day we celebrate your light-bearing and holy memory, O glorious hieromartyrs.

The Versicle : Let Thy priests be clothed with righteousness and let Thy saints shout for joy. Of equal honour with the apostles were ye, O hierarchs, and had withal equally zealous mind, not fearing the godlessness of the inhuman tyrants, but having manfully and earnestly preached the Saviour, ye have endured manifold sufferings; on that account ye are now in the enjoyment of the future rewards, O all-wise ones.

The Versicle : Blessed is the man that feareth the Lord, that greatly delighteth in His commandments.

Accomplishing the honourable services and offering unto the Master, Christ, the blameless sacrifice, ye have, O powerful and blissful hierarchs, offered unto Him yourselves as the perfect burnt-offerings in your martyrdom; Him supplicate to deliver from corruption and dangers those that in faith celebrate your honoured memory. [*Glory...Tone* 4 :

Ye were invincible martyrs, most laudable hierarchs and the lights of the universe, the pillars unassailable of the divine church and standard of learning, instructors of the pious and exterminators of heresies, O God-wise fathers, bright preceptors of our souls, associates of angels and champions of the Trinity. [*Both now...the Theotokion :*

O Theotokos all-hymned! Do thou wash off my passionate heart the filth, and cleanse, O pure one, all the wounds and suppurations of the heart proceeding from sin, and make my mind steadfast, that I, thine accursed and unprofitable servant, may magnify thy might and great intercession.

THE GENERAL SERVICE TO HIEROMARTYRS. 173

The Stavro-theotokion. Similar to: As a virtuous...

Seeing Christ—Lover of man—crucified and pierced in His side with a lance, the most pure one bewailed, crying out: What is this, O my Son? What have the ungrateful people rendered unto Thee for all the good Thou hast done unto them, and Thou dost most lovingly take care of my childlessness? I wonder, O Compassionate One, at Thy voluntary crucifixion.

The Troparion from the Typicon; but, if there be no Typicon, say the following Troparion, Tone 4:

O God of our fathers that ever dealest by us according to Thy kindness, do not withdraw from us Thy mercy, but at their intercessions direct our life in peace.

[*Glory...Both now...the Theotokion or the Stavro-theotokion.*

At the Matins, for God is the Lord, the same Troparion. After the 1st Stichologia, the Cathisma, Tone 8. *Similar to:* Of the wisdom...

Imparting an abyss of wisdom—the spiritual depths, ye, holy ones, have preached the One Godhead in the Trinity and have detailed the orders of angels and the mysteries of their brightness, O God-wise ones; wherefore, setting in order the lower priesthood also, ye were led up into the one communion, O hieromartyrs. Do supplicate Christ the God to grant remission of sins unto those that with love venerate your holy memory.   *Twice. Glory...Both now...the Theotokion:*

O cloud of the Reasonable Sun, the lamp wrought in gold of the Divine Light, unblemished, untainted, all-spotless Theotokos ! Do thou enlighten my soul, darkened with the blindness of passions, with the brightness of impassivity, and wash off my defiled heart with the streams of emotion and the tears of contrition, and cleanse me from the mist of my deeds that I may lovingly call unto thee: O Theotokos—Ever-virgin, supplicate Christ the God to grant me remission of sins, for in thee I thy servant possess the hope.

After the 2nd Stichologia, the Cathisma, Tone 5. *Similar to:* The Co-unoriginate Word...

Having instructed your minds with apostolic discourses and

having well tended the communities of the faithful, ye have, O holy ones, offered a pure sacrifice unto the King and Creator that was incarnate for us of the Virgin-Theotokos and rose again in glory, Whom ye have confessed before the tyrants, O hieromartyrs. *Twice. Glory...Both now...the Theotokion:*

O fervent and invincible intercession, a hope sure and unassailable, a wall and shelter and refuge unto those that flee unto thee, O pure Ever-virgin! Supplicate thy Son and God, together with the angels, to grant unto the world peace and salvation and great mercy.

After Praise ye the name of the Lord, the Refrain: We magnify you, O hieromartyrs of Christ, and honour your holy memory, for ye do supplicate for us Christ our God.

The selected Psalm: Hear this, all ye people...

After the Polyeleon, the Cathisma, Tone 1. Similar to:
Whilst the stone was sealed...

Having cultivated the fruit of God's knowledge by your labours, ye have plucked out of the root of godlessness the stamina of doctrine, and having been anointed with grace as with an oil, have well tended the people in your charge, and having lawfully suffered martyrdom, ye were made worthy by Christ of double honour, O hieromartyrs. Glory unto Him Who hath granted you the strength; glory unto Him Who hath crowned you; glory unto Him Who through you granteth healing unto all.

Twice. Glory...Both now...the Theotokion:

Stretching out thy divine hands on which thou, O most holy Virgin, hast borne the Maker that was incarnate for the sake of mercy, do thou obtain from Him by entreaties that may be delivered from temptations, passions and dangers those who lovingly laud thee and vociferate: Glory unto Him Who hath tabernacled in thee; glory unto Him Who hath come forth from thee; glory unto Him Who hath delivered us through thy delivery.

Thereupon the Graduals, the 1st Antiphon of the 4th Tone. The Prokeimenon: Precious in the sight of the Lord is the death of His saints. *The Verse:* What shall I render unto the Lord for all His benefits towards me? Let every breath...*The Gospel of* the hieromartyrs, St. Luke 12, 32-40. *After the 50th Psalm, the Sticheron, Tone 4, Idiomelion:*

Being as pillars in the church of Christ, ye have destroyed the strong walls of unbelief; wherefore ye, O martyrs of separate orders, have before your death brought to utter failure the heretical storm, praying for our souls.

The Canon, Tone 4. Ode 1. The Heirmos:

The red abyss of the sea with unmoistened steps having crossed on foot, the Israel of old hath through the cruciform arms of Moses obtained victory in the wilderness over the forces of Amalek.

Being resplendent through the shedding of God's light, do, O glorious ones, deliver from the mist of passions those who piously glorify this light-bearing and bright festival of yours.

Put to shame was the wicked one by Thy martyrs and ministers, O Christ the King; although he assiduously attacked them and emptied his seditious quiver, yet was he unable to overcome their strength.

Being filled with the life-effecting and spiritual waters, ye have given drink unto those that were exhausted by the sultriness of the wicked godlessness, and have directed them unto the holy and saving water. [*The Theotokion:*

Pardoned was the crime of the forefathers rather through thy bringing forth, O most pure one, and the first entry into paradise hath been accorded to those who are loudly praising thee.

Ode 3. The Heirmos:

Delighted on Thine account is Thy church, O Christ, calling unto Thee: Thou art my strength, O Lord, both refuge and support.

Kindled mentally with the fire of the Comforter, ye have, O hieromartyrs, extinguished the flames of enchantment of the wicked one, rejoicing thereat.

With the light of the Spirit ye, O glorious ones, have attracted to the light of the holy baptism those that were in darkness profound.

As gold refined through the fire of martyrdom, have ye, O holy ones, appeared, having the seal of your sufferings as martyrs. [*The Theotokion:*

Thou hast given birth, O most pure and all-spotless Virgin, unto the Strong God that delivereth men from the violence of the enemy. *The Cathisma, Tone* 8. *Similar to:* Of the divine faith...

Sanctified by the unction with the holy oil, ye have appeared as pastors unto the God-wise people and, having been sacrificed as pure lambs, ye were presented unto the Word—the Chief Pastor—that was slaughtered as a lamb, O all-praised martyrs and lamps of all the universe; wherefore we all celebrate with love your divine memory. [*Glory. Both now...the Theotokion:*

O Theotokos—our refuge and strength, mighty help of the world! With thine intercessions shelter thy servants from every want, O only blessed one. [*The Stavro-theotokion:*

Having acquired the staff of might in the cross of thy Son, we put down therewith the surgings of the enemies, unceasingly magnifying thee with love.

Ode 4. *The Heirmos:*

Elevated on the cross seeing Thee, the Sun of righteousness, the church stood up in her order worthily calling out: Glory to Thy power, O Lord.

Let the choir of the hieromartyrs be hymned, since they are adorned with the grace of episcopacy and with martyrdom, and joyously sing: Glory to Thy power, O Lord.

Having been taught the divine mysteries, ye have, O God-bearing fathers, well and truly tended the people in righteousness and truth, and have found the divine end in martyrdom.

Having been adorned with the divine gifts of the apostles and prophets, the divine choir of the hieromartyrs calleth out joyfully: Glory to Thy power, O Lord. [*The Theotokion:*

Catechized by God's word and seeing the realization of what was spoken of thee, O Theotokos, we call unto thee: Hail, O most spotless Virgin, having been delivered by thy bringing forth.

Ode 5. *The Heirmos:*

Thou, my God, didst come into the world as light, as a holy light that bringest out of the darkness of ignorance those who in faith hymn Thee.

With the divine brightness of the most wise preaching, ye have shone forth the light of grace unto those sitting in the darkness of enchantment.

Beholding now Christ face to face, ye are in the enjoyment of the ineffable light; do supplicate Him for us.

The divine river of Christ's teaching having been filled in you, ye have stopped the streams of enchantment and have filled the minds of the faithful with good drink. [*The Theotokion*:

Having selected thee alone out of all generations, the Lord was incarnate of thee, O Theotokos, and hath deified mankind.

Ode 6. The Heirmos:

I will sacrifice unto Thee, O Lord, with the voice of praise—crieth out unto Thee the Church, having been cleansed of the demon's blood with the blood that mercifully ran out of Thy side.

In manliness and wisdom having passed the life, the choir of Thy saints, O Lord, doth now rejoice in Thee in truth, in prayer and in chastity.

Sustained by the hope of eternal life, fracturings of your bodies ye have cheerfully endured, O valiant and holy ones, emulators of the divine prophets.

Having been educated on spiritual laws, ye have, O most wise ones, offered unto the lawless salutary laws and have led them unto the light of orthodoxy.   [*The Theotokion*:

From life unto death was Adam dragged in paradise, but with thy life-effecting bringing forth, O Virgin, he was made immortal, O most pure God's Bride.

The Contakion from the Typicon; but if there be no Typicon, say the following Contakion, Tone 3. Similar to: The Virgin to-day...

As the never-setting lights of the reasonable Sun, we that are to-day assembled, will praise you in odes; for ye did shine forth unto those in the darkness of ignorance, and are now calling all to the height of piety, O hieromartyrs. Therefore we cry up to you: Hail, O ye the foundation of all those that keep fasts.   [*The Oikos*:

Shed unto me, O Jesu the Life-giver, the primordeal beauty that I may hymn Thy hierarchs who have striven to emulate Thee even unto death and having severely beaten the forces of the enemy, and exposed the impious wickedness, under the strengthening power of the cross, have worthily obtained glory from Thee, O Christ; wherefore we call unto them : Hail, O ye the foundation of all those that keep fasts.

Ode 7. *The Heirmos*:

In the Persian furnace the youths, descendants of Abraham, burning rather with the love of piety than with the flame of fire, have called out: Blessed art Thou in the temple of Thy glory, O Lord.

Made illustrious through the chrism of episcopacy and through the divine blood of martyrdom, ye are, O God-wise ones, glorified God-beseemingly on account of both, crying out: Blessed art Thou in the temple of Thy glory, O Lord.

As if instantaneously have ye, O most praised ones, set at rest the earthly subtleties, when ye were elevated in a vessel of the most pure glory, calling out: Blessed art Thou in the temple of Thy glory, O Lord.

Being not ignorant of the designs of the adversary, ye have, O glorious hieromartyrs, repelled every seditious insinuation of the tyrants, singing: Blessed art Thou in the temple of Thy glory, O Lord. [*The Theotokion*:

The Lord that doth clothe the earth with mist and the heaven with clouds, hath Himself put on mortal flesh taken from thy blood, O Virgin, clothing men with the raiment of the glory of immortality.

Ode 8. *The Heirmos*:

Having spread his hands Daniel did close the jaws of the lions in their den; and the force of the fire was deadened by the zealously pious youths who girded themselves with virtue and called out: Bless the Lord, all ye works of the Lord.

Scourged with lashes and bodily pains, ye have, O hieromartyrs, obtained by your intercessions incorruptible life for all those who were serving inanimate gods and who, having been saved, are ever calling out with you: Bless the Lord, all ye the works of the Lord.

Being clusters of intellectual grapes, ye do now, O hieromartyrs, shed the wine of healing and gladden the hearts of all those who in faith praise you and vociferate: Bless the Lord, all ye the works of the Lord.

The tombs of hieromartyrs have shed miracles unto the universe, dissipating the enchanting illusions of the all-malicious demon, and they vouchsafe magnificent healings unto those that vociferate: Bless the Lord, all ye the works of the Lord. [*The Theotokion*:

The Ever-existing that was born of thee, O most pure one, was seen as a man, double in nature, deeds and desires, having voluntarily put on the likeness and appeared; unto Him we sing in faith: Bless the Lord, all ye the works of the Lord.

Ode 9. *The Heirmos:*

A stone cut out without hands from an untouched mountain—from thee, O Virgin, was separated—that corner-stone, even Christ, Who hath joined together the distant natures; rejoicing thereat, we magnify Thee, O Theotokos.

Celebrating the sacred memory of the holy hieromartyrs, come O ye all, let us with loud and sacred odes honour them, that supplicate for us our God the All-compassionate.

Having been consoled by the Word, having cleansed your souls of every defilement and having been divested by martyrdom of your fleshly raiment, ye have put on the beautiful garment of salvation.

We are, O people, gathered together in memory of the martyrs to take up the grace of the saints, and to hymn the valiant hieromartyrs who suffered manfully and put down the origin of evil.

Carrying in your hands Christ that beareth everything with His mere nod, do incline Him as thy Son with your entreaties, O most pure one, to deliver me from the assaults of the enemy, to encompass me with an abyss of mercy and to save me.

The Photagogicon. Similar to: Hearken, O ye women...

This day appeareth as a day specially set apart for us, since it is the day of the sacred successors of the holy apostles and at the same time both of the God-bearing teachers of the faith and of the invincible martyrs, whose prayerful memory we all are faithfully celebrating. [*The Theotokion:*

Thou, O most hymned Maiden, hast given birth unto the Angel of the great council of the Father—even Christ, the King of glory, preaching of Whose cross the hieromartyrs have enlightened the nations and have taught them to glorify thee as Theotokos and to adore thy bringing forth.

With the Lauds, the Stichera, Tone 4. *Similar to:*
As a virtuous...

With the sacred unction and the blood of martyrs ye have

drawn near unto God, O all-glorious hieromartyrs, being blossoms of nature, ornament of reason, summits of wisdom, orthodoxy in theology, rule of the faith, discipline unto every community and unto the church magnificence. *Twice.*

Enjoining glorification unto sufferers and magnification unto martyrs, ye have, O God-wise ones, well taught yourselves to venture valiantly upon multifarious tortures, bonds and prisons, upon being stripped unto nakedness, bound in chains, fearfully frozen, and thereafter upon wounds and death, O hieromartyrs.

Through the multiformous tortures having thrown off the garment of death, ye have, O glorious martyrs, put on the raiment of incorruptibility and now are tabernacling in heaven, ever standing before the throne of God; wherefore in faith we celebrate your all-bright memory, embracing the shrine of your relics. [*Glory...Tone* 8 :

You have passed your lives amidst the hierarchs and martyrs, appeared as faithful pastors and drunk of the cup of Christ; wherefore, having in both become acceptable to Christ, together with the highest servants, do supplicate before Him, now that ye are tabernacling in the light. [*Both now...the Theotokion:*

Taking up the voice of the archangel Gabriel, let us say: Hail thou, O Mother of God, who hast given birth to Christ the Life-giver unto the world. [*The Stavro-theotokion:*

The undefiled heifer seeing the Steer voluntarily being nailed upon the tree, compassionately bewailing, vociferated: Woe unto me, O my most beloved child! What hath the ungrateful Hebrew rabble rendered unto Thee, desiring to deprive me of Thee, O my all-beloved one.

CHAPTER XVIII.

THE GENERAL SERVICE TO A MONK-MARTYR.

At the Vespers, for O Lord, I have cried, the Stichera, Tone 6.
Similar to: Of three days...

Let us, O faithful, in dutifully praising the exploits of the wise abstainer and the pains of the soldier of Christ, cry out unto the Lord: Through his intercessions, O Christ the God, deliver us from every calamity.

An abundance of the most noble peace will be given of God unto thee, O holy father (*mentioned by name*), that hast endured the frightful storm of torments, thou invincible warrior and intercessor for those that praise thee.

Thou, O wise one, hast suffered in a righteous cause and wast most wise unto God, and hast appeared, O God-bearing martyr, as another house of the Maker of everything—a light of the church, ornament of the ascetics.

Glory...Both now...the Theotokion: O Theotokos, pure Virgin, supplicate the Lord that through thine intercessions He may grant unto our souls remission of sins, peace and great mercy.

The Stavro-Theotokion: Beholding our Life hung on the tree, thou, O all-spotless Theotokos, motherly bewailing didst cry out: O my Son and my God, save those that lovingly hymn Thee.

If Idiomelon be appointed, Glory...Tone 5:

O holy father, thou didst not give sleep unto thine eyes or slumber to thine eyelids until thou didst free both thy mind and body of passions and hast prepared of thyself a habitation unto the Spirit; for Christ having come unto thee with His Father hath made an abode in thee. Having received the grace of the Consubstantial Trinity, O great preacher and ascetic, supplicate for our souls.   [*Both now...the Theotokion:*

We bless thee, O Theotokos-Virgin, and dutifully glorify thee as an unassailable city, invincible wall, firm intercession and a refuge for our souls.

The Stavro-theotokion. Similar to: We bless thee...

Seeing of old her Lamb elevated upon the cross, the Virgin-Mother, the all-blessed Maiden, with tears vociferated: Woe unto me, O my Son! How dost Thou die, being immortal by nature as God?

If the Celebration be with the Polyeleon, say the Theotokion of the resurrection: In the Red Sea...*The Entrance. The Prokeimenon of the day. The Readings of the Martyrs. (See Appendix).*

With the Versicles, the Stichera, Tone 1. *Similar to:*
The all-praised martyrs...

Thy life, O most famous (*mentioned by name*), hast thou given unto the cultivation of virtues; for the faithful that in psalmody praise Christ in faith, were subdued by thy doctrines. That these may take root in the world, do entreat the Divine Spirit, standing before Him.

The Versicle: Precious in the sight of the Lord is the death of His saints. Thy life, O God-inspired martyr (*mentioned by name*), was manifested unto the earthly as equal to that of angels, and unto the heavenly thy confession was carried up as a fragrant sacrifice and precious incense. Do now supplicate that unto our souls may be granted peace and great mercy.

The Versicle: Blessed is the man that feareth the Lord, that delighteth greatly in His commandments. Having been most successful vanquisher of passions, thou, O (*mentioned by name*), didst obtain victory over the tyrant; exulting together with the crown-bearers, remember, O blissful one, all those that celebrate thy memory, and supplicate Christ to grant unto our souls peace and great mercy. [*Glory...Tone* 4:

Having with the help of the Spirit vanquished the embittered enemy as an invincible warrior, thou hast, O ascetic martyr (*mentioned by name*), with the weapon of the faith cut up the intellectual Ethiopians, and having accomplished the law in thine exploits, thou wast crowned together with all the choirs of martyrs, O ascetic and most wealthy martyr.

Both now...the Theotokion: Deliver us from our wants, O Mother of Christ the God, who hast given birth unto the Creator of all, that we may call unto thee : Hail, thou—the sole intercession for our souls.

The Stavro-theotokion. Similar to : As a virtuous...Seeing Christ—Lover of man—crucified and pierced in His side with a lance, the most pure one bewailed crying out : What is this, O my Son ? What have the ungrateful people rendered unto Thee for all the good Thou hast done unto them, and Thou dost most lovingly take care of my childlessness ? I wonder, O Compassionate One, at Thy voluntary crucifixion.

The Troparion from the Typicon ; but if there be no Typicon, say the following Troparion, Tone 8 :

In thee, O father, was manifestly preserved what is in the image of God, for having taken up the cross, thou didst follow Christ and by thine own example hast taught that the flesh is to be despised as transient, but that particular care should be bestowed on the soul as a thing immortal ; wherefore together with the angels rejoiceth also thine, O ascetic (*mentioned by name*), spirit.

Glory...Both now...the Theotokion or the Stavro-theotokion.

At the Matins, for God is the Lord the same Troparion. After the 1st Stichologia, the Cathisma, Tone 4. Similar to : Thou that wast of Thine own free will lifted up...

The enjoyment of the earthly and corruptible things hast thou despised and loved the life of a hermit, thou hast held in detestation the beauty of the world and the temporal food and hence wast made worthy to be counted in the choir of martyrs and abstemious. Do pray together with them that thy servants may be saved. [*Twice.*

Glory...Both now...the Theotokion : He that sitteth on the cherubic throne and abideth in the bosom of the Father, doth sit in thy womb, O Sovereign-Lady, as upon His holy throne ; for God is become incarnate, He hath truly assumed the rule over all the nations, and with understanding we now sing unto Him ; do entreat Him that thy servants may be saved.

After the 2nd Stichologia, the Cathisma, Tone 8. Similar to:
Of the wisdom...

Imitating in thine abstemiousness the manners of John the Baptist and the virtues of Elijah the Tishbite, thou hast lived the life of a bodiless one, glorifying with the angels the Holy and Divine Trinity and beating off by thy valiance the incursions of the demons; wherefore, in suffering hast thou, O blissful (*mentioned by name*), also manfully carried thy combat, adoring Christ's divine incarnation and Godhead; Him supplicate to grant remission of sins unto those who lovingly celebrate thy holy memory. *Twice.* [*Glory...Both now...the Theotokion:*

As Virgin and one among women we, all the generations of men, bless thee that without seed gavest birth unto God in the flesh; for the divine fire did find abode in thee and thou dost suckle as a babe the Maker and Lord. Wherefore we, both the angelic and human kind, worthily glorify thy divine child-birth and with one voice cry unto thee: Supplicate Christ the God to grant remission of sins unto those who worthily sing thy glory.

After Praise ye the name of the Lord...the Refrain:

We glorify thee, O ascetic martyr (*mentioned by name*), and honour thy holy memory, O preceptor of monks and associate of angels. *The selected Psalm:* I waited patiently for the Lord...

After the Polyeleon, the Cathisma, Tone 4. Similar to: Thou hast appeared...

Having been an expert in fasting, thou didst shine forth in martyrdom and hast enlightened the faithful with thine exploits, O blissful (*mentioned by name*); wherefore we all with one voice magnify thee. *Twice.* [*Glory...Both now...the Theotokion:*

O hope unfrustrable of those trusting in thee, the only one that above nature hast given birth in the flesh unto Christ our God! Supplicate Him with the ascetic martyrs to bestow upon the universe the expiation of sins and unto us all amendment of life before the end.

THE GENERAL SERVICE TO A MONK-MARTYR. 185

The Graduals, the 1st Antiphon of the 4th Tone. The Prokeimenon: Precious in the sight of the Lord is the death of His saints. *The Verse:* What shall I render unto the Lord for all His benefits toward me? Let every breath...*The Gospel (St. Mark* 8, 34-38; 9, 1).

After the 50th Psalm, the Sticheron, Tone 8: Having preserved that which is in the image, unhurt, thou didst, O holy father (*mentioned by name*), with regard to the faith in Christ patiently withstood, without fear, the injunctions of the tyrant, and hast slain him with the spiritual sword; wherefore having attained boldness unto God, do save from all calamities, O ascetic martyr, those who honour thee.

The Canon, Tone 6. *Ode* 1. *The Heirmos:*

Whilst travelling on foot along the depths of the sea as if upon dry land, Israel seeing Pharaoh, their pursuer, drowned, cried out: Unto God let us sing an ode of victory.

From the seductions of life and from passions that torment me, do set my mind at rest, O ascetic sufferer, and make me worthy to keep in peace thy memory unto thy praise.

Having obtained as a martyr the crown of suffering, thou, O ascetic (*mentioned by name*), wast translated from earth into the world free from combat, and unto the true Light and Life, O most blissful one.

With the streams of thy blood having extinguished the flames of the tyrants, thou, O pious martyr, hast watered the souls of the faithful and caused the desire for life eternal to bud in them, O ascetic. [*The Theotokion:*

Thou that hast given birth unto the Unconfinable Word Which did find place in thy womb, O God-harbouring tabernacle, do thou deliver me, O pure one, from the fierce storm of the evil one, that oppresseth me.

Ode 3. *The Heirmos:*

There is none holy as Thou, O Lord my God, that hast, as Good One, exalted the horn of Thy believers, and established us upon the rock of Thy confession.

Thou wast fortified by God's strength, when thou, O most blissful one, hast set out for these exploits and hast endured afflictions and torments from the persecutors, O ascetic sufferer, our father.

The great Agonothete, even Christ, hath endowed thee with strength to destroy the illusion and to put to shame the enemy, impudently boasting and in vain raging everywhere.

Beautiful appear thy feet, O ascetic, going cheerfully along the path of martyrdom and covering with shame the heads of the wicked, O great sufferer (*mentioned by name*).

The Theotokion: Let us hymn pure Mary—the palace of the Master which Jacob of old clearly saw as a divine ladder that was stretched from the earth into the heavenly heights.

The Cathisma, Tone 4. *Similar to:* Wonder struck was Joseph...

Three times wast thou truly baptized and hadst three baptisms—that of water and fire and of the Holy Spirit—the first in tears, the second in the manifold restraints thou didst subject thyself to, having lived on earth the life equal to that of angels, O blissful (*mentioned by name*), the third, when thou, as a selected lamb, wast slain for Christ our God. Him do unceasingly supplicate that our souls may be saved.

Glory...Both now...the Theotokion:

Wonder struck was Joseph contemplating that which is above nature, and with respect to thy seedless confession, O Theotokos, he took into consideration the dew on the fleece, the bush that was not consumed by fire, Aaron's staff that sprouted, and bearing witness, thy betrothed and guardian called out unto the priests: Virgin giveth birth and after the birth remaineth still Virgin.   [*The Stavro-theotokion:*

The thoughts of many a heart are being laid bare and mine own mind is pierced with the lance of Thy passion, in Thy voluntary sufferings: O Child! Who seeing my lamentations and bodily sufferings will recognize in Thee the most truly existing God? I hymn, O Word, Thy compassion for the sake of which dost Thou endure the crucifixion.

Ode 4. *The Heirmos:*

Christ is my power, my God and Lord—the venerable church God-beseemingly singeth, thus calling out, with pure mind feasting in the Lord.

Legitimately hast thou kept fasts, legitimately suffered and legitimately wast thou crowned, being fortified by God's word and preserving thyself unhurt, O most blissful one.

Not enduring to follow the illusion, in thy wisdom hast thou, O ascetic, entered joyfully the path of God's knowledge, and having had bestowed on thee the spiritual light, thou hast appeared as a lamb.

In the sacred act as a voluntary and holy sacrifice wast thou brought up, O (*mentioned by name*), unto Him, Who was slain for thee, and thou didst rejoicingly find rest in the temple of the first fruits. [*The Theotokion*:

Virgin didst thou remain after having given birth, just as thou wast Virgin also before thy bringing forth, for thou hast given birth unto God the Word Who delivered us from corruption through thine intercession, O most spotless one.

Ode 5. *The Heirmos*:

With Thy divine light, O Good One, do illumine, I pray Thee, the souls of those who lovingly watch early unto Thee, that they may know Thee, O Word of God, as the true God recalling them out of the darkness of sin.

The enemy was hit with the weapon of the great endurance of the wise martyr; by the latter having been trodden under foot and put to shame, he hath become the laughing stock.

Having repulsed thy tyrant's malice, thou, O all-honoured martyr, hast appeared meek and benign, and through thy bloody end wast thou decorated with an incorruptible crown.

With the honours of a martyr and with the labours of fasting hath truly crowned thee, O ascetic (*mentioned by name*), the Sole Agonethete, our God Who hath fortified thee against the murderer. [*The Theotokion*:

The God-seeing choir of prophets hath from afar mystically perceived the ineffable depth of thy divine bringing forth, O Virgin—God's Bride, and typified thee in sacred prototypes.

Ode 6. *The Heirmos*:

Beholding the sea of life swelling with the storm of temptations, and taking refuge in Thy calm haven, I cry unto Thee: Lead up my life from corruption, O greatly Merciful One.

Steered by the vivifying arm, thou didst sit upon the waters and wast preserved, O our father, whereas the injunctions of the persecutor were drowned therein through thine assiduous prayer, O sacred one.

With small means effecting great changes, thou, O ascetic, hast given thyself up to martyrdom and thou, O God-manifested one, hast slain by the spirit the serpent—seducer of Eve.

The power of thy speech could not stand even the inventor of the evil; wherefore the flatterer hath savagely given thee over unto the chains, wounds and violent death, O *(mentioned by name)*. [*The Theotokion*:

Behold, the Lord now becometh incarnate of thy pure blood, O Virgin-Mother, and uniteth Himself unto men in an extraordinary manner, effecting our salvation on account of His unspeakable mercy.

The Contakion from the Typicon; but if there be no Typicon, say the following Contakion, Tone 2. Similar to: The trusty...

As a keeper of fasts pious and skilled, as an honoured voluntary martyr and one that in the desert led the life of a hermit,—let us worthily extol in hymns *(mentioned by name)*, the ever to be praised; for he hath trodden the serpent under his feet. [*The Oikos*:

Emulating the Lord's passion, thou, O most blissful one, didst conceive the desire to die for Him and having manfully fought against the enemies, thou hast destroyed the illusion of idol-worship, brought to nought the cunningly contrived allurements and wiles of the enemies and hast obtained the crown of honour, O *(mentioned by name)*, the ascetic sufferer; wherefore we in faith have recourse unto thy shelter and call unto thee: From the enemies both visible and invisible do thou deliver us, for thou hast trodden the serpent under feet.

Ode 7. *The Heirmos*:

Dew-yielding hath an angel made the furnace unto the pious youths, and God's injunction burning the Chaldeans hath inclined the tyrant to cry out: Blessed art Thou, O God of our fathers.

Withdrawing thy mind from compassion towards the flesh, O blissful one, and being burnt and consumed with the fire, thou, O wise one, didst chant the ode of the youths: Blessed art Thou, O God of our fathers.

THE GENERAL SERVICE TO A MONK-MARTYR. 189

By thy mere invocation are driven away the evil spirits that have come to know thee, O ascetic, as fasting man and martyr of Christ, who fervently singest: Blessed art Thou, O God of our fathers.

Thine end was announced to thee, O most blissful (*mentioned by name*), by the all-effecting will; wherefore didst thou give thyself up unto yet greater fasting and ascending from glory to glory wast slain for the sake of Christ, the God of all.

The Theotokion: Raise me up, O most pure one, held down by despondency, unto the accomplishment of God's works, and fortify me against the enemies that ever and fiercely fright me and allure me with contrarious thoughts.

Ode 8. The Heirmos:

Unto the pious hast Thou made dew out of the flame to flow and the sacrifice of a righteous man didst Thou consume with water, for everything makest Thou, O Christ, just as Thou willest; Thee we exalt unto all the ages.

Adorned with the virtues of fasting and tormented with the pains of wounds hast thou, O most glorious one, appeared before the Granter of victories and hast obtained from Him the honours of victory.

Kindled by love unto the Almighty, thou, O most glorious (*mentioned by name*), hast laid low the haughty neck of the enemy, and through thy desire of God hast thou obtained His abiding in thee unto the ages.

Of God's mercy make me worthy, O God-blessed martyr, and from temptations and calamities deliver me, O ascetic (*mentioned by name*), honouring thee and having recourse unto thy shelter. [*The Theotokion:*

Hail thou, O holy mountain, through which God hath passed; hail thou, manifestation of sacred mysteries, awe-inspiring tidings and a vision not easily seen; hail, O Virgin, the recall of the fallen.

Ode 9. The Heirmos:

It is not possible for men to behold God on Whom the angelic orders dare not cast a glance; but through thee, O all-pure one, was seen of man the Incarnate Word; Him magnifying, with heavenly hosts we call thee blessed.

Thou, O God-wise (*mentioned by name*), our father, hast

reached unto the last beauty and sweetness, and standing near God dost sing with the bodiless: Holy, Holy, Holy art Thou, O Trinity all-effecting and all-powerful.

Having escaped from the snares of thy persecutors, thou, O ascetic (*mentioned by name*), hast found rest in the heavenly abodes and hast joined the troops of martyrs; do now with the bodiless ones supplicate for us all that we may glorify thee.

Holding Christ as strength and power, thou hast repelled the ferocious attacks of the demons and hast attained the highest harbours, being thoroughly adorned and richly resplendent with the divine shedding of light. [*The Theotokion:*

Unable to understand the incomprehensible wonder of thy bringing forth, O Mother-Virgin, and rather in silence glorifying it, we doxologize thee, O most-blessed one, the only good one among women and most unblemished.

The Photagogicon. Similar to: Hearken, O ye women...

Having been well proved first by suffering and having secondly accomplished thy divine life of fasting, thou didst ascend into heaven and standest before Christ; do, O ascetic father (*mentioned by name*), fervently supplicate for us, hymning thee. [*The Theotokion:*

Having given birth unto the ineffable Joy, even the Lord, do thou make partakers of the heavenly joy all those that honour thee, O most pure one, as the true grace, and from the depth of the soul call out unto thee: Do not forsake thy servants, O blessed Mary.

With the Lauds, the Stichera, Tone 6:

Having dyed thy sacred vestment in the purple of thy blood of a martyr, thou hast worthily entered into the Holy of Holies, wherein the Light ineffable doth shine, wherein there is the divine glory and wherein is heard the voice of those feasting; wherein thou also hast obtained the reward of thy labours—thy victory as a martyr—the never-fading crown, good fame for ever and the life in paradise. Do thou, O most wise (*mentioned by name*), with boldness supplicate for our souls. [*Twice.*

The storm of torments did not produce any wavering in thy soul, neither the long confinement in a dark dungeon could hide thee, O glorious martyr; but thou hast shone forth as light unto those distressed in the darkness of vanity whom thou hast shewn to be the sons of day through the bath of baptism—the great and saving birth and divine life, as a God-pleasing martyr, O most wise (*mentioned by name*).

Who can worthily testify unto the victories of thy virtues? Whose mouth can describe thy torments and endurance? For in both hast thou been pleasing Christ, O (*mentioned by name*). And now, O ascetic martyr, do not cease to supplicate, since thou hast great boldness, that our souls may be saved.

Glory...Tone 2: O come, let us crown with odes the sufferer of Christ as a field-lily and a God-grown flower of the divine paradise; as a sheep of the orthodox, a beauty of purity, confirmation of the faith, glory of abstemiousness wast thou clearly manifested unto the world; wherefore hast thou obtained also the never-fading crown. [*Both now...the Theotokion*:

All my hope I lay upon thee, O Mother of God, preserve me beneath thy shelter. [*The Stavro-theotokion*:

When thou, O pure one, beheldest hanging on the cross the all-ripest Cluster Whom, without cultivating, hast thou carried in thy maiden womb, thou didst bitterly and loudly bewail Him, calling out: O Child, do Thou, O Benefactor, let fall the sweetness which removeth every drunkenness of passions by divine consolations, for my sake, since I gave Thee birth, O Compassionate One.

CHAPTER XIX.

THE GENERAL SERVICE TO TWO OR MANY MONK-MARTYRS.

At the Vespers, for O Lord, I have cried, the Stichera, Tone 8.
Similar to: What shall we call you...

Having fought valiantly, ye have, O ascetics, manfully endured the assaults of the tyrants; with love ye have laid your souls under the sword and have put on the crowns of martyrs and are worthily exulting together with angels. Your endurance was great and still greater the gifts,—do supplicate for our souls.

Ye have lived well, O holy ones, emulating the exploits of martyrs, O valiant ones; for the torments you have manfully treated with contempt, by fasting you have consecrated your bodies and with love ye have shed your blood, that you might together put on the crowns of your sufferings; do supplicate that our souls may be saved.

O ascetic martyrs of Christ! Ye have fought well, utterly neglecting the temporary life and by will having manfully overcome the wisdom of the flesh, and having thus finished your course in Christ, ye are now worthily tabernacling with angels; wherefore honouring your memory we entreat you: Supplicate the Lord that He may have mercy upon our souls.　　　　　[*Glory...Both now...the Theotokion:*

Unto whom canst thou be likened, my wretched soul, since thou never dost rise to repentance and dost not dread the fire awaiting the wicked? Arise, then, and call upon the only one that is swift for protection, vociferating: O Virgin-Mother! Supplicate thy Son and our God to deliver me from the snares of the evil one.　　　　[*The Stavro-theotokion:*

Beholding the Lamb voluntarily stretched on the tree of the cross, the she-lamb, suffering motherly pangs and bewailing, vociferated: O my Son! What is this strange sight? Giving life unto all as Lord, how dost Thou, O Long-suffering One, undergo death in granting resurrection unto the earthly? I glorify Thy great condescension, O my God.

If Idiomelon be appointed, Glory...Tone 8:
Having lived the lives like unto those of angels in the labours of fasting, and by abstemiousness having brought your bodies into subjection unto the spirit, you were the true workers of the commandments of the Lord; ye have preserved the archetypal beauty of the image and accomplished feats of suffering in the pains of fasting and of martyrdom, wherefore ye were adorned with double crowns. Do assiduously supplicate the Saviour that we may be saved.

Both now...the Theotokion: Thy shelter, O Theotokos-Virgin, is a spiritual medicine; for fleeing unto it we obtain deliverance from the maladies of the soul. [*The Stavro-theotokion:*
Standing before Thy cross, O Lord, she that hath given Thee birth without seed, motherly bewailing, said: Woe unto me, O my Child! How have you gone down from mine eyes, O Reasonable Sun, Light unto the eyes? Rise up, O All-powerful, shine forth with Thy light unto all that confess Thee as true God and man?

If the Celebration be with the Polyeleon, say the Theotokion of the resurrection: The King of the Heavens...*The Entrance...The Prokeimenon of the day and the Readings of the ascetics.* (*See Appendix.*)

With the Versicles the Stichera, Tone 8. Similar to: Thy martyrs, O Lord...
Thy ascetic martyrs, O Lord, emulating the bodiless, by their prayers and abstemiousness have driven away the passions of the flesh, and having shone forth in miraculous deeds, have enlightened the hearts of all; through their intercessions, grant unto Thy people, great mercy.

The Versicle: Precious in the sight of the Lord is the death of His saints. O ascetic martyrs! Animated with virtuous zeal, ye have manifestly destroyed the heresy of Arius and Nestorius, and having been the champions of the orthodox, have become famous unto all; through their supplications, O Christ, grant unto Thy people great mercy.

The Versicle: Blessed is the man that feareth the Lord, that delighteth greatly in His commandments. Being the stars upon the firmament of abstemiousness, ye have enlightened the souls of ascetics and have driven away whole myriads of demons, O ascetic martyrs; wherefore after your demise ye are being blessed, since ye supplicate for the salvation of all those who celebrate your holy memory. [*Glory...Tone* 6:

Blessed are ye, O ascetic-martyrs of Christ our God; as ascetics, since you have loved the truth and received grace, and as martyrs, since the sword did not separate you from the love of Christ, and therefore ye are now rejoicing, for great is your meed in the heavens. [*Both now...the Theotokion:*

No one that hath recourse unto thee, O most pure Theotokos-Virgin, goeth away from thee with shame; but asking for grace he obtaineth the grant of a profitable demand.

The Stavro-theotokion: Beholding Thee crucified, O Christ, she that gave Thee birth, vociferated: What is this strange mystery I see, O my Son? How dost Thou die—hung in the flesh, O Giver of life?

The Troparion from the Typicon; but if there be no Typicon, say the following Troparion, Tone 4:

O God of our fathers, that ever dealest by us according to Thy kindness, do not withdraw from us Thy mercy; but at their intercessions direct our life in peace.

Glory...Both now...the Theotokion or the Stavro-theotokion.

At the Matins, for God is the Lord, the same Troparion.
After the 1st *Stichologia, the Cathisma, Tone* 4. *Similar to:*
Thou that wast of Thine own will lifted...

Neglecting the delight of earthly and corruptible things, ye were animated with loving attachment to the desert-life and detestation of the beauties of the world and of temporal food, and therefore were accounted worthy to be numbered among the choirs of martyrs and ascetics; supplicate together with them that your servants may be saved. *Twice.*

Glory...Both now...the Theotokion: He that sitteth on the cherubic throne and abideth in the bosom of the Father, doth sit in thy womb, O Sovereign-Lady, as upon His holy throne; for God is become incarnate, He hath truly assumed the rule over all the nations, and with understanding we now sing unto Him; do entreat Him that thy servants may be saved.

After the 2nd Stichologia, the Cathisma, Tone 8. Similar to:
Of the wisdom...

Imitating, in your abstemiousness, the manners of John the Baptist and the virtues of Elijah the Tishbite, ye have lived the life of the bodiless, glorifying with the angels the Holy and Divine Trinity, and beating off by your valiance the incursions of the demons; wherefore in suffering ye have manfully carried your combats, adoring Christ's divine incarnation and Godhead, O blissful (*mentioned by name*); Him supplicate to grant remission of sins unto those who lovingly celebrate your holy memory.   *Twice.*   [*Glory...Both now...the Theotokion :*

As Virgin, and one among women, we, all the generations of men, bless thee that without seed gavest birth unto God in the flesh, for the divine fire did find abode in thee, and thou dost suckle as a babe the Maker and Lord. Wherefore we, both the angelic and human kind, worthily glorify thy divine child-birth, and with one voice cry unto thee: Supplicate Christ the God to grant remission of sins unto those who worthily sing thy glory.

After Praise ye the name of the Lord...the Refrain: We glorify you, O ascetic-martyrs, and honour your holy memory, O preceptors of monks and associates of angels. *The selected Psalm:* I waited patiently for the Lord...

After the Polyeleon, the Cathisma, Tone 8. Similar to: Of the wisdom...

Brightly illumined with the light of the Trinity, ye, O light-bearing fathers, have forsaken the deep darkness of sweet things, and as lamps illumining with divine works the hearts of the faithful, ye have appeared blessed for your asceticism and your sufferings; wherefore we venerate to-day your light-bearing and honourable memory, and with one voice call out: O ye, God-voiced and abounding in riches! supplicate Christ the God to grant remission of sins unto those who lovingly honour your holy memory. *Twice.* [*Glory...Both now...the Theotokion:*

As the all-undefiled Bride of the Creator, as the innocent of marital life Mother of the Deliverer, as one that was the receptacle of the Comforter, do hasten, O all-hymned one, unto me, a defiled habitation of wickedness and a sport of demons, although endowed with understanding, and deliver me from the villany of these, making me a bright habitation of virtues; O thou, light-granting and incorruptible, disperse the cloud of passions, and make me worthy both of the communion of the Highest and of the Light never growing dim, through thine intercessions.

The Graduals, the 1st Antiphon of the 4th Tone. The Prokeimenon: Precious in the sight of the Lord is the death of His saints. *The Verse:* What shall I render unto the Lord for all His benefits toward me? Let every breath... *The Gospel* (St. Matth. 10, 16-22).

After the 50th Psalm the Sticheron, Tone 4: Having brightly illumined your souls with the most brilliant rays, ye have, O ascetics, adorned the earth with your virtues; having Christ in your hearts, ye were enlightening, as a never-setting sun, the communities of heathens, and are adorning us with your martyrdom, O ascetic martyrs.

The Canon, Tone 4. *Ode* 1. *The Heirmos:*

The red abyss of the sea with unmoistened steps having crossed on foot, the Israel of old hath, through the cruciform arms of Moses, obtained victory in the wilderness over the forces of Amalek.

Through asceticism having become luminous, ye have, O most blissful ones, appeared as God-shining lights through the shedding of your blood, wherefore you are exulting together with the ascetics of Christ and martyrs.

In the sea of your tears having first drowned the spiritual Pharaoh, ye, O wise ones, have afterwards vanquished him in the streams of your blood, and given him over unto ruin.

Let us praise the ascetic fathers that were slain for Christ, the martyrs that lived as ascetics, singing unto our God—the Deliverer, for He is glorified. [*The Theotokion:*

He that is God by nature, and Whom nothing could comprise, hath confined Himself in thee, O Theotokos-Virgin, having, for the sake of compassion, become earthly that He may save the earthly through His ineffable mercy.

Ode 3. The Heirmos:

Neither in wisdom nor in power and riches we glory, but in Thee, O Christ, the Hypostatical Wisdom of the Father, for there is none more holy than Thou art, O Lover of man.

Having pleased God with the contrition of your hearts, ye have broken down the self-exultation of the enemies, O most blissful ones, whilst ye were being cut up with the sword and slain.

Meditating on the everlastingness of the future, ye, O wise ones, have repulsed the fleeting and corruptible things that drag one down, wherefore ye are being blessed, O ascetic martyrs.

Glorifying in Thy power, the God-bearing ones have mightily vanquished the armies of the ruiner, and having been slain for Thee, O Saviour, and shown doubly great exploits, were crowned for the same.

The Theotokion : O most pure one, that hast given birth unto the Most Holy Word of God! Do sanctify souls and bodies of those that bless thee, O most unblemished one.

The Cathisma, Tone 4. Similar to: Speedily prevent...

As strangers and emigrants ye have appeared on earth, O ascetics; in the wilderness ye have made tents for you and have valiantly fought, adorning your nakedness with the raiments of virtue and emulating the sufferings of Christ; wherefore ye have endured the immolation of martyrdom.

Glory...Both now...The Theotokion: To the Theotokos let us, sinners and humbled, now flee, and in penitence fall down before her, calling out of the depth of our souls : O Sovereign-Lady, help us, taking pity on us, do hasten to our assistance, as we are perishing from the multitude of our transgressions, neither turn thy servants empty away, for thou art the only hope that we have.   [*The Stavro-theotokion :*

The Virgin and the lamb beholding on the cross and pierced with a lance the Lamb that was without seed born of her, and feeling wounded with the arrows of affliction, vociferated painfully exclaiming: What is this new mystery? How dost Thou die—the Sole Lord of life? Wherefore arise, raising up the fallen fore-fathers.

Ode 4. The Heirmos:

Elevated on the cross seeing Thee, the Sun of righteousness, the church stood up in her order worthily calling out: Glory to Thy power, O Lord.

Having refused to obey the passions of the flesh, ye, O most blissful ones, have subjugated the enemy, and having been slain with the sword, ye in exultation were together translated unto the life eternal.

Having of your own free will, before death, slain yourselves with abstemiousness, ye, O ascetics, were involuntarily and cruelly murdered with the sword by the wicked, hoping to live after the death also.

Although ye, fathers, have departed this life through being slain with the sword by the wicked, yet before your end have ye endured cruel attacks, being dead unto the world.

The Theotokion: The Child—God Eternal—doth renew the human race afresh, having appeared from the Virgin and having become man; let us sing unto Him: Glory to Thy power, O Lord.

Ode 5. The Heirmos:

Thou, my God, didst come into the world as light, as a holy light that bringeth out of the darkness of ignorance those who in faith hymn Thee.

Your blood hath appeared as a beautiful paradise, having in your midst the Lord as the tree of life, Who accepted thereof as a pure offering.

Having commingled the drops of blood with the streams of your tears, ye have, O God-bearers, immersed therein the multiformous serpent.

Ye were vouchsafed to behold the divine beauty, and have obtained eternal joy in the place of labours and pains, O blissful ones. [*The Theotokion:*

Thou hast given birth, above word and understanding, unto God, and didst remain Virgin after the birth, just as thou wast before the birth, O pure God's Bride.

Ode 6. *The Heirmos:*

I will sacrifice unto thee, O Lord, with the voice of praise,—crieth out unto Thee the church, having been cleansed of the demons' blood with the blood that did mercifully run out of Thy side.

Having repulsed the bonds of passions with abstemiousness, and by violent death having been freed of the bonds of the body, ye have been called unto the indissoluble goodness of the Master.

Having appeared as mountains through your exalted life, ye have by Christ's might brought down under your feet him who is striving to destroy the mountains and the whole creation.

Through abstemiousness and labours ye have, O holy fathers, attenuated your bodies and have virtuously offered your blood unto Christ and were deservedly crowned.   [*The Theotokion:*

Lull to sleep the unappeasable storm of my passions with thine unceasing supplication, O Virgin,—I implore thee,—and do not permit me to sleep the heavy sleep of sin.

The Contakion from the Typicon; but if there be no Typicon, say the following Contakion, Tone 2. Similar to: Seeking the highest...

Through the multitude of waves dry-shod passing, with the streams of your tears did ye submerge the incorporeal enemies, O Godly-wise ascetic martyrs; having now received the gift of miracles, intercede incessantly for us all.   [*The Oikos:*

O ascetic martyrs! Ye have mortified your flesh on earth with the life-bearing deadliness and typified the passion of Christ the God—firstly in your asceticism and secondly once more in your sufferings; wherefore Christ did send down unto you the double crowns and hath made ready for you an abode in heaven and eternal tabernacle wherein ye joyfully have entered as consanguineous both of martyrs and ascetics. Do incessantly supplicate for us all.

Ode 7. *The Heirmos:*

In the Persian furnace the youths, descendants of Abraham, burning rather with love of piety than with the flame of fire, have called out: Blessed art Thou in the temple of Thy glory, O Lord.

Adorned with the brilliant light of virtues and illumined by the sacred sufferings, ye have passed unto the never-dimning Light and have appeared as the sons of day.

Having voluntarily avoided the sweets of this world, ye have, O holy ones, given yourselves over entirely unto the One Who hath strangely appeared in the flesh among men, and have acquired the future and incorruptible good things.

Blessed art Thou, O God, that hast this day completed the course of the sufferers—the God-bearing fathers, and hast manifested them as participators of Thy heavenly Kingdom.

The Theotokion: Thee carrying in thy womb the Manna of life, the ancient pot of manna hath truly and clearly typified. Blessed art Thou among women, O most spotless Sovereign-Lady.

Ode 8. *The Heirmos:*

Having spread his hands, Daniel did close the jaws of the lions in their den; and the force of the fire was deadened by the zealously pious youths who girded themselves with virtue and called out: Bless the Lord, all ye the works of the Lord.

The great choir of the ascetic martyrs, adorned with the valours of asceticism, sheweth to-day the members of all the divine choirs lauding and together with themselves hymning Christ: Bless the Lord, all ye the works of the Lord.

As lambs have ye stood whilst ye were slaughtered with your tormentors' swords, and were brought up unto the sacrificed Word as a perfect sacrifice; ye have also appeared in the habitations of the firstlings, singing: Bless the Lord, all ye the works of the Lord.

Both the body and soul have ye, O ascetics, dedicated unto the Lord, having been moved thereto by abstemiousness, and with the streams of your blood having dried up the wicked sea of the tyrants, singing: Bless the Lord, all ye the works of the Lord. [*The Theotokion:*

Through thee, O pure God-hailed, doth once more open the first paradise, therein is led again the man that was first condemned and becometh truly deified unto the restoration of men that sing: Bless the Lord, all ye the works of the Lord.

Ode 9. The Heirmos:

A stone cut out without hands from an untouched mountain—from thee, O Virgin, was separated—that corner stone, even Christ, Who hath joined together the distant natures ; rejoicing thereat, we magnify thee, O Theotokos.

O come, let us loudly laud in sacred odes the holy ascetic fathers who have holily lived in deserts and caves and piously suffered martyrdom.

How exceedingly laudable are your labours in asceticism, O martyrs ; how great the exploits with which ye have hurled down the flatterer ; how wonderful are the sufferings which ye have lawfully endured and for which ye have obtained the crowns.

Your God-reflecting memory is illumined by the brilliant light of the labours which ye have endured for Christ's sake, and by the grace of the All-effecting Holy Spirit, doth illumine the consciences of all. [*The Theotokion:*

The cherubim dread beholding the Word that in an unspeakable manner sitteth on them,—the Child that is being carried on thy motherly arms, O most pure Sovereign-Lady, and is the Highest above all creation.

The Photagogicon. Similar to: By the Spirit in the sanctuary...

With the pains of asceticism ye have utterly destroyed the serpent—the origin of evil, and, at your end, obtained the crown of martyrdom,—O ye, ornament of the fathers, glory of the martyrs, multitude of the ascetic martyrs—the wonderful fathers. [*The Theotokion:*

The most glorious wonder of thy giving birth, which is above all understanding, doth astound every mind both of angels and men : being a Virgin thou hast given birth, a Virgin thou didst remain, just as thou wast Virgin before that birth. What a strange mystery ! How wonderful and most glorious is the birth !

With the Lauds, the Stichera, Tone 4. Similar to:
As a virtuous...

Let us joyfully hymn the wise martyrs and ascetic fathers, for in obedience to Christ's injunctions, and having abolished every unclean service, the holy ones have honourably and trustfully served the One God and Lord, Whom they, in the presence of the tyrants, valourously confessed, and therefore were crowned from above. *Twice.*

Ye, O most laudable, have forsaken the life that draggeth down, the delights of food and flourishing glory as transient things, and have attached yourselves unto Christ, kindled by His exceeding beauty, cleaving unto Him as sweet-smelling wild roses, and ye were God-beseemingly crowned with the crowns of the incorruptible Kingdom.

Ye that have detested this world, have appeared above the world, joined unto the church of the first-born, and with the angels you sing now incessant odes, standing all together before God; having also repulsed as martyrs the filthy illusion of idols, ye have put to shame the mad conceit of the tyrants.

Glory...Tone 4: Adorned with the raiment of purity and enlightened by divine prayer, having in you Christ also that was born of the Virgin, you were not taken up with the love unto this world nor would partake of the delights of flesh, but, assiduously working up unto the Fire, with the divine fire ye have consumed the transient fire of passions; wherefore do supplicate, O blissful ascetic martyrs, that we also may be delivered from the all-destructive and eternal fire.

Both now...the Theotokion: We have comprehended the God that is incarnate of thee, O Theotokos-Virgin; do supplicate Him for the salvation of our souls.   [*The Stavro-theotokion:*

Seeing how the most lawless people were unrighteously nailing Thee to the tree, the Virgin and Thy pure Mother, O Saviour, had her heart pierced, as Simeon hath foretold.

CHAPTER XX.

THE SERVICE TO A FEMALE MARTYR.

At the Vespers, for O Lord, I have cried, the Stichera, Tone 4.
Similar to: As a virtuous...

Having adorned thy soul with the beauties of virginity and with the blood of martyrdom, thou hast, O glorious martyr (*mentioned by name*), handed thyself over unto thy Maker Who doth indeed preserve thee in incorruption for ever; wherefore thou dost exult, O all-praised one, together with the hosts of angels and archangels, and with the choirs of apostles, prophets and martyrs.

Tied to the wheels, torn by ferocious beasts, tortured both by fire and water, having sharpened thy mind with the Divine Spirit, thou hast manfully smothered the prince of darkness with the rush of thy blood and hast passed over unto the intellectual palaces, bringing unto thy Bridegroom, O Virgin, martyrdom as thy marriage portion.

Having been sanctified with the blood of the Bridegroom, even Christ, thou hast, O most laudable one, adorned with thine own blood the garment of flesh; being therefore refined both inwardly and outwardly thou wast, O most laudable (*mentioned by name*), made worthy of His bright palace; Him supplicate that may be delivered from corruption and dangers those who in faith celebrate thine all-honoured memory.

Glory...Both now...The Theotokion: Since thy supplication unto the Lord is indefatigable and thine intercession incessant, do thou, O most pure one, lull to sleep the attacks and lay down the waves of my wretched soul; vouchsafe, O Maiden—I implore thee—consolation unto my heart that is now in affliction and grant grace unto my mind that I may worthily glorify thee.   [*The Stavro-theotokion:*

Beholding thee, the Lamb and the Shepherd, on the tree, the ewe that gave Thee birth wept and motherly spake unto Thee:

O Son most desired! How is it that Thou art hung on the tree, O Long-suffering? How is it that Thy hands and feet, O Word, were nailed by the lawless and that Thou, O Master, hast shed Thy blood?

If there be Idiomelon, Glory, Tone 6: Upon the right hand of the Saviour there stood virgin, great sufferer and martyr (*mentioned by name*), arrayed in unassailable virtues and adorned with the oil of purity and with the blood of martyrdom, holding joyfully the lamp and vociferating unto Him: Unto the sweet smell of Thy myrrh have I directed my steps, O Christ the God, since I was struck with the love for Thee; do not drive me away, O Heavenly Bridegroom! Through her intercessions send down unto us, O All-powerful Saviour, Thy mercies.

Both now...the Theotokion: No one that hath recourse unto thee, O most pure Theotokos-Virgin, goeth away from thee with shame, but asking for grace, he obtaineth the grant of a profitable demand. [*The Stavro-theotokion:*

Beholding Thee hanging on the cross, the most pure one with lamentations vociferated motherly: O my Son and my God, my sweet Child, how dost Thou endure the infamous passion?

If the Celebration be with the Polyeleon, say the Theotokion of the resurrection: Who will not bless thee?...*The Entrance. The Prokeimenon of the day. The Readings of the martyrs* (*see Appendix*).

<blockquote>With the Versicles the Stichera, Tone 4. Similar to:
As a virtuous...</blockquote>

Having manfully and wisely stood in thy mind against the rage of the tormentor and his insolent harshness, thou, O God-wise one, foresawest the ever and immovably abiding unto the ages delights of the future; which thou, O glorious one, hast also obtained, having passed over from earth unto the heavenly palaces and unto the choir indestructible.

The Versicle: Wonderful in His holy ones is God, the God of Israel.

The magnificence of the Kingdom and the handsome fairness of thy Bridegroom, even Christ, wast thou made worthy to behold, having been adorned with the wounds of thine unyielding martyrdom, and unto the source of all good didst thou worthily approach; wherefrom hast thou, O blissful one, richly obtained the fruit of divine joy and the immortal glory.

The Versicle: In the congregations bless ye God, even the Lord, from the fountains of Israel:

Neither the laborious yoke, nor womanly weakness, neither famine nor sores could prevent thee, O all-praised one, from shewing firmness in thy martyrdom, and thou hast suffered the torments with all the fervour of thy soul; whence hast thou obtained the heavenly habitation and art adorned with the crown of grace, standing before thy Maker?

Glory...Tone 5: The beauty of thy virginity hath desired the King of glory, even Christ, since He hath betrothed thee unblemished as a bride unto Himself in uncorrupted union; for, having granted of His own will unto thy virtue strength against the enemies and passions, He hath shewn thee invincible in thine enduring the most painful sores and atrocious torments, adorned thee with double crown and placed thee on His right hand as a resplendent queen. Him supplicate, O martyr honourable and long-suffering (*mentioned by name*), that unto thy psalmodists may be granted salvation and life and great mercy.

Both now...the Theotokion: We the faithful bless thee, O Theotokos-Virgin, and glorify, as in duty bound, thee—the immoveable city, the wall unassailable, firm intercession and refuge of our souls. [*The Stavro-theotokion:*

Beholding of old her Lamb lifted up on the cross, the Virgin and Maiden blessed of all, vociferated tearfully: Woe unto me, O my Son! How dost Thou die, being God, immortal by nature?

The Troparion from the Typicon; but if there be no Typicon, say this Troparion, Tone 4:

Thy Lamb, O Jesus, (*mentioned by name*), is calling with a loud voice: Thee, O my Bridegroom, I love and, whilst Thee seeking, for Thee I endure martyrdom, I become crucified together with Thee and buried with Thee unto Thy baptism, and I suffer for Thy sake, so that I may reign in Thee, and I die for Thee that I may live with Thee; but as unblemished sacrifice do

Thou receive me that in love sacrificed myself to Thee. At her intercessions, as the Merciful One, save our souls.

Glory...Both now...The Theotokion or the Stavro-theotokion.

At the Matins, for God is the Lord, the same Troparion. After the 1st Stichologia, the Cathisma, Tone 5. Similar to: The Co-unoriginate...

Having piously enslaved thyself unto the Almighty, thou, O honoured one, wouldest not become a slave of the impious tyrant, but hast firmly endured the dark confinement and the sores from fire, and art gone over unto God, O Godly-wise martyr (*mentioned by name*). Supplicate for us that celebrate thy memory. *Twice.*

Glory...Both now...the Theotokion: O pure Ever-Virgin, intercession both fervent and invincible, hope both certain and unassailable, wall, shelter and refuge of those that flee unto thee! With the angels do supplicate thy Son and God to grant unto the world pacification and salvation and great mercy.

After the second Stichologia, the Cathisma, Tone 1. Similar to: Thy sepulchre...

The fire of torments hast thou, O honoured one, extinguished with the dew of thy spirit, and art gone unto the light both divine and immaterial; and after thy blessed demise dost thou, O (*mentioned by name*), cause the drops of healing to flow, removing the flame of passions by the power of the spirit. *Twice.*

Glory...Both now...the Theotokion: Do accept, O Theotokos, the entreaties of thy servants, and deliver us from every calamity, since thou gavest birth unto the Saviour-Christ, the Deliverer of our souls.

After Praise ye the name of the Lord, the Refrain:

We magnify thee, O Christ's martyr (*mentioned by name*), and honour thy honourable passion which thou hast endured for Christ's sake.

After the Polyeleon the Cathisma, Tone 4. Similar to: Thou that wast lifted up on the cross...

Let us—the multitude of the faithful—gracefully hymn (*mentioned by name*), that came unto Christ of her own will and adorned her heart with virtues, for she hath put to shame the insolence of her tormentors, and having shone forth as the sun in the midst of the lawless, after her demise she did appear unto the earthly, both as a divine confirmation and power also. *Twice.* [*Glory...Both now...The Theotokion:*

Having from the angel received in thy womb the Word and having given birth unto Emmanuel—the God Incarnate, do thou, O Theotokos, supplicate for our souls.

The Graduals, the 1st Antiphon of the 4th Tone. The Prokeimenon: Wonderful in His holy ones is God, the God of Israel. *The Verse:* In the congregations bless ye God, even the Lord, from the fountains of Israel. Let every breath. *The Gospel, (St. Mark, 5, 24-34). After the 50th Psalm the Sticheron, Tone 6:* (*Glory...for O Lord, I have cried*).

The Canon, Tone 8. Ode 1. The Heirmos:

Let us sing unto the Lord Who hath led His people over across the Red Sea, for He alone hath gloriously triumphed.

The all-praised maiden by her wonders doth incite unto the singing of hymns both the hosts above and the choirs of the earthly.

Having desired the beauty of thy most fair heart, O all-praised one, the Master of all hath made thee worthy of the heavenly palaces.

For execution, pains and multiform sores didst thou, O martyr, go in without fear; for thou hadst the grace of the Saviour assisting thee and helping thine endurance.

The Theotokion: We hymn thee, O most pure Theotokos, that hast above nature given birth unto the Incarnate Word Ever-existing and Most Divine.

Ode 3. The Heirmos:

Thou art the stablishing of those having recourse unto Thee, O Lord; Thou art the light of those in darkness, and my spirit doth hymn Thee.

Thou didst appear before thy judges with courageous soul, O all-praised one, and hast vanquished the enemy as one destitute of courage.

Thou hadst neither blemish in thy beauty, nor failing in thy soul, and Christ hath received thee as a bride in the incorruptible palaces.

Do thou, O all-praised martyr of Christ (*mentioned by name*), heal the eschars of my soul and pacify with thine intercessions the storms of my life. [*The Theotokion:*

We all the Christians have acquired in thee a refuge and wall, and we unceasingly doxologize thee, O innocent of marital life.

The Cathisma, Tone 8. *Similar to:* Of the wisdom...

With the streams of thy blood thou dost, O all-praised martyr of Christ, ever form a deluge unto the wicked, and with the heavy clouds of grace ever watering the intellectual fields, thou dost rear up thereon the ears of faith; wherefore after thy demise also hast thou gloriously appeared as a cloud, shedding the testimony of thy life. O all-praised great sufferer (*mentioned by name*), supplicate Christ the God to grant the remission of sins unto those that lovingly honour thy holy memory. [*Glory...Both now...the Theotokion:*

As Virgin, and one among women, we, all the generations of men, bless thee that without seed gavest birth unto God in the flesh, for the divine fire did find abode in thee, and thou dost suckle as a babe the Maker and Lord. Wherefore we, both the angelic and human kind, worthily glorify thy divine child-birth, and with one voice cry unto thee: Supplicate Christ the God to grant the remission of sins unto those who worthily sing thy glory. [*The Stavro-theotokion:*

Seeing the Lamb, the Shepherd and the Redeemer upon the cross, the lamb exclaimed in tears, and loudly lamenting, thus vociferated: The world indeed rejoiceth receiving through Thee the deliverance, but my innermost is consumed at the sight of Thy crucifixion which Thou dost endure on account of the mercifulness of Thy compassion. O Longsuffering Lord, abyss of mercy and a source inexhaustible, take compassion and grant the remission of transgressions unto those who in faith hymn Thy divine passion.

Ode 4. *The Heirmos:*

I have hearkened, O Lord, unto the mystery of Thine economy, comprehended Thy works and glorified Thy Godhead.

Having made thyself an unstained mirror of divine understanding, thou, O martyr, hast shone forth in the midst of the female sufferers as a golden lamp of exquisite workmanship.

Unto the dark demon thou didst not bring sacrifice, O invincible martyr (*mentioned by name*), for thou hast lovingly desired to receive the life-bearing death for thy piety.

Bearing thy body, O unblemished one, painlessly with the passion-bearers, thou didst remain insensible to the sores through the working of the divine love. [*The Theotokion:*

Grant unto us the purification of ignorance, as Sinless One, and pacify Thy world, O God, through the intercession of her who gave Thee birth.

Ode 5. *The Heirmos:*

Watching early we call unto Thee, O Lord: Save us, for Thou art our God, beside Thee we know no other.

Having learned the opposites of the day and the world, thou didst not desire to love the contentious demon.

Having imagined he would be able to weaken thy divine strength, O martyr (*mentioned by name*), the most cunning in snares hath made of himself a laughing stock.

Grant unto me, O all-praised one, enlightenment and peace, dispersing with thine intercessions my great agitation and confusion. [*The Theotokion:*

We hymn thee, O Theotokos, as Virgin after the birth, for thou hast brought forth unto the world in the flesh God the Word.

Ode 6. *The Heirmos:*

A bright garment do grant me Thou that puttest on light as a garment, O Multi-merciful Christ, our God.

Bearing in thy feminine body manly wisdom of the mind, thou, O glorious one, hast disdained the beasts that are in waters.

Thou hast vanquished the pride of thy tormentors, hast remained unhurt, O invincible martyr, and obtained the crown of victory.

As good and beautiful, as honourable and shining with the lustre of virginity, doth the Bridegroom, even the Lord, bring thee unto Himself, O all-praised one. [*The Theotokion:*

The only one that by the word hath given birth in the flesh

unto the Word, do thou deliver our souls from the snares of the enemy,—we implore thee.

The Contakion from the Typicon ; but if there be no Typicon, say this Contakion, Tone 2. Similar to : Seeking the highest...

Having found thine all-revered temple to be the healer of souls, we all the faithful with a loud voice cry unto thee, O virgin-martyr (*mentioned by name*), the greatly renowned : Christ the God entreat incessantly for us all. [*The Oikos :*

Coming together let us worthily honour (*mentioned by name*), that became affianced unto Christ through martyrdom, so that having been, through her intercessions, delivered from soul destructive ruin, from destruction, earthquake and plague, we may pass our lives in humility, and be vouchsafed, together with all the saints that pleased God in past ages, to walk in the light and to sing with them : Thou, O Saviour, hast astonished with Thy mercies all men that in faith praise her. Wherefore we call unto her : Supplicate unceasingly for us all.

Ode 7. *The Heirmos :*

The youths that came from Judea have once in Babylon, by the faith in the Trinity, trodden under their feet the flame of the furnace, singing : O God of the fathers, blessed art Thou.

Above understanding hath appeared the valour of the divine martyrs, for the Maker of all subdueth the creation unto those who in their suffering call out : O God of our fathers, blessed art Thou.

The illustrious maiden hath shut up the dissolute mouths of the tormentors and laid low the pride of the lawless, whilst by the Holy Spirit she divinely sang : O God of our fathers, blessed art Thou.

The trio of the pious youths hath of old burned those that made the furnace extremely hot ; and now the God-wise maiden, hymning the Trinity, hath inclined the servants to sing unto the God of the fathers : O God, blessed art Thou.

The Theotokion : When Thou, O Saviour, didst desire to accomplish our salvation, Thou hast entered the womb of the Virgin and hast shewn her as intercession unto the world : O God of our fathers, blessed art Thou.

Ode 8. The Heirmos.

The King of the heavens, Whom the hosts of angels sing, praise ye and extol Him unto all the ages.

The most blissful among women, having the rewarding grace of the Most High, sang praising Christ unto all the ages.

Strengthened by the thought of the Bridegroom and caring for things immaterial, thou didst give up thy body unto death and liveth unto all the ages.

The Bridegroom, having secretly descended into the furnace unto the most pure bride, hath, by the dew of the Spirit and through the good pleasure of the Father, saved her that was hymning Christ unto all the ages.

The Theotokion: Do not despise, O Virgin, those that seek thine aid, and sing and extol thee unto the ages.

Ode 9. The Heirmos.

Thee, innocent of marital life—the Mother of the Most High God, thee that above understanding hast by the word given birth unto the True God, and that is higher than the most pure powers, in unceasing doxologies we magnify.

The flow of live blood is a sign of incorruptible life from above granted unto thee, O all-praised martyr, for thou hast appeared as an inexhaustible treasury of healings unto those that draw thereof.

The death hath touched thee in accordance with the law of nature, O God-wise one, and the life-bearing deadlyhood hast thou put on impassively;—therein, as thine inspirited, all-precious body was laid, thou livest incorruptibly and the flow of thy blood is the witness thereof.

As a ray of the sun illumining all and as the fairest bride of Christ, as a turtle-dove fond of cleanliness and as an olive tree, as a cedar and as a truly chosen dove—we all praise thee, O *(mentioned by name),* divinely eminent.   [*The Theotokion:*

As a bride innocent of marital life, as a receptacle of sweet smell, as the true and spotless Virgin and Mother, that hast received in thy womb a cloud of the divine light, heavenly rain, —we magnify thee.   [*The Photagogicon:*

As a bride wast thou adorned, betrothed unto the Bridegroom by the good-effecting passions, and as a chosen one hast thou entered into the resplendent palace, carrying the lamp of a maiden, and now dost thou (*mentioned by name*) reign exultingly with the One Existing unto the ages. [*The Theotokion*:

We all sinners possess in thee, O most pure Virgin, an intercession; do make by thy supplication thy Son easily reconciled unto us.

With the Lauds, the Idiomelic Stichera, Tone 3:

Seeing the celebration of the female martyr God-wisely performed, let us, O ye faithful, sing thanksgiving psalmody unto our God, wonderful in His counsels, for He hath vanquished the invisible might of the enemy in the nature of a female, and hath put forth His divine power in the weakness of the good martyr, since He through her intercessions doth save our souls. *Twice*.

The all-praised martyr of Christ (*mentioned by name*), having mingled the cup of truth with her blood of a martyr, ever doth offer it in the church unto which, with the voice of wisdom, she gathereth the church's nurslings, saying: Draw the beer—a pledge of the resurrection, that driveth away the infidels and purifieth the passions, but is preservative unto the souls of the pious, that call unto the Saviour: Thou that hast filled us from the stream of the sweetness of the Spirit,—save our souls.

Let us whose souls were sealed with the blood of Christ in the day of redemption, with spiritual exultation, prophetically, draw the holy blood that is flowing unto us from the source of martyrdom, and is prefigurative both of the life-bringing passion of the Saviour and of the eternal glory; let us therefore cry unto Him: Thou that art glorified in thy saints, O Lord, save our souls through the intercessions of Thy most glorious female martyr. [*Glory...Tone* 6:

Proceeding along the path of martyrdom, thou, O all-honoured (*mentioned by name*), hast escaped the counsel of thy tyrant; since as a wise maiden, carrying the lamp, thou hast entered into the courts of thy Lord, and as a valiant martyr thou hast obtained the grace to cure the passions of the flesh. Do thou, with thine intercessions before God, cure from spiritual maladies also us that are hymning thee. [*Both now...the Theotokion*:

We have learned the God that was incarnate of thee, O

Theotokos-Virgin; Him supplicate for the salvation of our souls. [*The Stavro-theotokion*:

When the all-pure one saw Thee hanging on the cross, with lamentations she thus vociferated motherly: O my Son and my God, my sweetest Child, how dost Thou endure the ignominious passion?

CHAPTER XXI.

THE SERVICE COMMON TO TWO AND MANY FEMALE MARTYRS.

At the Vespers, for O Lord, I have cried, the Stichera, Tone 4. *Similar to:* Thou hast given a sign...

The virgin-maidens, united by the law of nature and manifestly sustained by the love unto their Maker, were by faith freed from the ties of the body; the impotent enemy they have valiantly destroyed under their feet, became resplendently adorned with the honours of victors and are rejoicing having found their abode in the intellectual bridal chambers.

The all-honoured have endured fire and multiformous tortures and deaths, possessing in faith the fairest beauty of the Bridegroom, and, having been adorned with various wounds, were numbered unto Him; wherefore Jesus—the Lover of man and Saviour of our souls—hath crowned them with divers gifts.

Incorrupt virginity, most admirable virginity have ye, O good maidens, brought unto Christ, having with manly minds by the power of the cross put down the rage of the enchantment of godlessness; wherefore all the churches of Christ celebrate your holy memory, O most bright and all-glorious.

Glory...Both now...the Theotokion: Since thy supplication unto the Lord is indefatigable and thine intercession incessant, do thou, O most pure one, lull to sleep the attacks and lay down the waves of my wretched soul; vouchsafe, O Maiden,—I implore thee,—consolation unto my heart that is now in affliction, and grant grace unto my mind that I may worthily glorify thee. [*The Stavro-theotokion*:

Beholding thee, the Lamb and the Shepherd, on the tree, the ewe that gave Thee birth wept and motherly spake unto Thee: O Son most desired ! How is it that Thou art hung on the tree, O Long-suffering ? How is it that Thy hands and feet, O Word, were nailed by the lawless, and that Thou, O Master, hast shed Thy blood ?

If there be Idiomelon, Glory...Tone 8: Let every tongue be moved unto the laudation of the most praised female martyrs; let every generation and age, all the youths and maidens, crown with praises the great martyrs of Christ; for, having put forth lawful boldness and discarded female weakness, they have put down the tormenting enemy, and having been adorned for their labours of martyrs with the heavenly and divine crowns, they supplicate their Bridegroom and God to grant us great mercy. [*Both now...the Theotokion*:

O Sovereign-Lady accept the supplication of thy servants and deliver us from every need and woe. [*The Stavro-theotokion*:

The most pure one, when she beheld Thee hanging on the tree in the flesh, was pierced in her heart, and with lamentations vociferated : O Word, whither art Thou gone down, most beloved Jesu, my Son and Lord ? Do not, O Christ, leave me alone who bare Thee.

If the Celebration be with the Polyeleon, say the Theotokion of the resurrection : The King of the heavens...*The Entrance. The Prokeimenon of the day. The three Readings of the martyrs (see Appendix).*

With the Versicles the Stichera, Tone 4. *Similar to:* As a virtuous...

The choirs of angels have been certainly amazed at your hearty-zeal, divine love and the unity of your sufferings, O blissful ones, since, having by manful united efforts put down the invisible enemy, ye have worthily and openly received from the life-bearing Hand the crowns of victory. *The Versicle : Wonderful in His holy ones is God, the God of Israel.* Being put to death for Christ's sake by the enraged sophistry, ye have extinguished the vain flame, and, having the lamps of your souls preserved unextinguished, ye have entered together into the heavenly palace of Christ; wherefore, we all, enlightened by your grace, piously hymn your holy memory, O great female sufferers.

The Versicle: In the congregations bless ye God, even the Lord, from the fountains of Israel. Ye have endured sufferings of many tortures, O all-praised ones, and have stood them firmly; thereupon were ye translated unto the reception of the never-setting brightness, serene joy and eternal divine light; wherefore we bless you and perform to-day your holy commemoration, O female martyrs God-comprehending. [*Glory...Tone* 4.

The life dragging down, the food-delights and the glory of prosperity ye have set aside, O most laudable ones, as transient, but attached yourselves unto Christ in martyrdom, being moved thereto by His fair beauty, ye have approached as the sweet-smelling roses and were adorned with the crowns of the incorruptible Kingdom, O God-renowned.

Both now...the Theotokion: O most pure Sovereign-Lady, lamp inextinguishable, throne most admirable, do supplicate that our souls may be saved. [*The Stavro-theotokion:*

Seeing Christ—the Lover of man—hung and being pierced through His side with a spear, the most pure one did bewail, crying out: What is this, O my Son? What have the ungrateful people rewarded Thee with for all the good Thou hast done unto them? and Thou most lovingly takest care of my childlessness. I wonder at Thy voluntary crucifixion, O Compassionate One.

The Troparion from the Typicon; if there be no Typicon, say this Troparion, Tone 1: Ye reasonable lambs unto Christ, the Lamb and Shepherd, were conducted through martyrdom, having finished your course and preserved the faith; wherefore with gladsome hearts do we recall to-day your, O wonder-worthy, holy memory, magnifying Christ. *Glory...Both now... the Theotokion or the Stavro-theotokion.*

At the Matins, for God is the Lord, the same Troparion. After the 1st Stichologia, the Oathisma, Tone 1. *Similar to:* Thy sepulchre...

Burning with the fire of the divine desire, ye were not at all burned by the contact with the material fire, O blissful ones, but with that fire you have destroyed the allurement, and being mercilessly dragged about, ye have, O ever-memorable female martyrs, found your end and obtained glory. *Twice.*

Glory...Both now...the Theotokion: O blessed Mary, innocent of marital life—refuge of the despairing, God's abode! Do set in the path of repentance us who constantly stray into the roadless paths of evil and anger the Good Lord.

After the 2nd Stichologia, the Cathisma, Tone 4. Similar to:
Wonder-struck was Joseph...

The heavenly choirs of the bodiless powers have been wonder-struck by your great endurance; it was as if ye were witnessing somebody else's sufferings, whereas your own legs and joints were broken and ye suffered the bitter death, destroying with your female bodies the apostate serpent, O ye virgins, brides of the Giver of Life, champions of the faith. *Twice.*

Glory...Both now...the Theotokion: Wonder-struck was Joseph contemplating that which is above nature, and with respect to thy seedless conception, O Theotokos, he took into consideration the dew on the fleece, the bush that was consumed by fire, Aaron's staff that sprouted, and bearing witness thy betrothed and guardian called out unto the priests: Virgin giveth birth and after the birth remaineth still Virgin.

After Praise ye the name of the Lord, the Refrain: We magnify you, O holy female martyrs, and honour your honourable sufferings which for Christ ye have endured. *The selected Psalm:* God is our refuge and strength...

After the Polyeleon, the Cathisma, Tone 8. Similar to:
Of the wisdom...

Having been God-beseemingly affianced unto the Lord, ye—passion-enduring maidens—have brought Him as dowry your blood and immolation, and have worthily obtained the divine palace wherein ye are unceasingly filled with ineffable enlightenment; wherefore, in spiritually celebrating your holy and honourable memory, we glorify the Saviour and in faith call out: Supplicate Christ the God to grant remission of sins unto those who lovingly honour your holy memory. *Twice.*

Glory...Both now...the Theotokion: Being moved by the entreaties of Thy bodiless, Thy precursor, of apostles and prophets, of martyrs and all saints and of the Theotokos—Thine innocent of marital life and kind Mother, do grant, O Christ, that we may walk in thy light and vouchsafe unto us that we may obtain Thy Kingdom, for the sake of Thy compassionate mercy.

The Graduals, the first Antiphon of the 4th Tone. The Prokeimenon. Wonderful in His holy ones is God, the God of Israel. *The Verse:* In the congregations bless ye God, even the Lord, from the fountains of Israel. Let every breath. *The Gospel, St. Mark 5, 24-34. After the 50th Psalm, the Sticheron, Tone 4:* The life dragging down...(*See Stichera with the Versicles*).

The Canon, Tone 4. Ode 1. The Heirmos:

I will open my mouth, and it shall be filled with breath, and I will break forth in speech to the Queen Mother; yea I will appear as one keeping bright festival and will joyfully hymn her wonders.

Valiantly have ye, female martyrs, combated the enemy—first by fasting and thereupon—secondly—by the cruel shedding of your blood; wherefore we honour in faith your memory.

Moved by the desire of Him Who for our sake hath suffered both the cross and the death, ye holy female martyrs—followed in His footsteps, forgetting your bodily weakness.

Sacrificial temples of Hellens and armies of demons have ye, O most honourable female martyrs, overthrown with the weapon of your martyrdom, and have been brought into the heavenly church as burnt-offerings.   [*The Theotokion:*

Strengthened with the grace of Him Who hath shone forth from thy loins, O most spotless one, the virgin-maidens have undergone the pains of martyrdom and were led in after thee rejoicing.

Ode 3. The Heirmos:

The bow of the mighty hath become impotent and the infirm have girded themselves with strength; wherefore my heart hath become strengthened in the Lord.

Strengthened of God with mighty power, ye have overthrown the might of the opposing wrestler, and therefore have become famous as invincible victoresses.

Vain appeared the gapings of the beast through Christ's

divine power, and ye, O God-wise ones, were delivered unhurt, glorifying God.

Your minds were enlightened with wisdom and grace, and ye—female martyrs of the Saviour—were not frightened by the threats of your tormentors, being sustained by God's strength.

The Theotokion : Orthodoxly conceiving, we proclaim thee to be the true Mother of God and all-spotless, for through thee the Maker was pleased to come into union with us.

The Cathisma, Tone 1 :

Having acquired in you the sources of miracles, we, O most-laudable female martyrs, abundantly draw health, singing your pains and divine zeal, the valiant sores and feats; yea it is unto the glory of our God that we celebrate your wonder-worthy memory. [*Glory…Both now…the Theotokion :*

The entreaties of thy servants do receive, O Theotokos, and deliver us from every misfortune, for thou hast given birth unto Christ the Saviour and Deliverer of our souls.

The Stavro-theotokion : Possessing intercession in thee, O most pure one, and being delivered from afflictions through thy supplications and everywhere preserved by the cross of thy Son, we all dutifully and piously magnify thee.

Ode 4. *The Heirmos :*

He that sitteth in glory upon the throne of the Godhead, even Christ the most divine, hath come in a light cloud and with incorruptible hand saved those that call: Glory unto Thy power, O Christ.

Having suffered tortures and bodily sores in various forms, such as breaking of limbs and burning, ye have inherited the heavenly abodes, taking delight in the Tree of life, O wonder-worthy.

The heavenly powers were astonished at the feat of the blissful female martyrs, whilst they in their female nature vanquished the enemy, being strengthened by the power of Him Who hath shone forth from the Virgin.

Having rejected all the vanity of the world, ye have with the whole of your souls attached yourselves unto God alone; wherefore ye have endured the pains of fasting and of tortures, O ye, Christ's brides, long-suffering.

The Theotokion : Into thy womb, O most unblemished one,

the Lord hath descended like the dew upon the wool, as the prophet hath said of old; Him hast thou brought forth in two natures and unto Him we call: Glory to Thy might, O Christ!

Ode 5. The Heirmos:

The wicked will not see Thy glory, O Christ, but we, rising early in the night, hymn Thee, the Only-Begotten, the Brightness of Thy Father's divine glory, the Lover of man.

As unblemished lambs and acceptable sacrifices ye were brought unto the True Shepherd, even Christ, perfect offerings and pleasing holocausts.

Having died bodily, ye have revived in your souls, O female martyrs, being like unto Him Who hath slain the might of death and endured the cross and death and the voluntary passion.

The God-wise ones having one mind in many bodies were pared in different ways and burned with the fire, whilst they confessed One Jesus, the Lord of all. [*The Theotokion:*

Raise me up fallen into the pit of passions and set me straight, O thou the only all-unblemished, who hast brought forth God and Governor that hath by the grace joined together those separated at first.

Ode 6. The Heirmos:

I will sacrifice unto Thee, O Lord, with the voice of praise,—crieth out unto Thee the church, having been cleansed of the demons' blood with the blood that mercifully ran out of Thy side.

The first mother doth divinely rejoice, seeing overthrown and trodden under the female feet the serpent that hath first driven her from Eden through flattery.

Having joined fasting unto the lawful suffering, ye are now incorruptibly conjointed unto the spiritual Bridegroom and with gladsome souls settled in the heavenly palace.

The waves raised by tormentors were unable to immerse the martyr-ships, for they have reached the divine haven by a strong arm. [*The Theotokion:*

Of thy speech now seeing the fulfilment, we yet more magnify thee, O God's Mother, and Him Who hath exalted thee; for truly all generations now bless thee.

The Contakion from the Typicon; but if there be no Typicon, say this Contakion, Tone 4. Similar to: Thou hast appeared...

Of Christ's female martyrs the memory we are now celebrating and in faith praying for help, that from every affliction may be delivered we all that call out: With us is our God that hath glorified these as He willed. [*The Oikos*:

Having acquired in you, O female martyrs of Christ, the sources of miracles, we abundantly draw health, honouring your pains and divine zeal, the valiant sores and feats, and celebrate your wonder-worthy memory, calling out: With us is our God that hath glorified these as He willed.

Ode 7. The Heirmos:

Thou that hast saved in the fire Thine Abrahamic youths and hast slain the Chaldeans whom the truth hath rightfully affected, O Most-hymned Lord, God of our fathers, blessed art Thou.

Having the eyes of their hearts turned unto God—the Saviour and King, the lambs of Christ went boldly before every variety of evil snares and vanquished manfully, vociferating: Blessed art Thou, O God of our fathers.

Having all your desires concentrated solely on the Master, ye have, O female martyrs, accounted as a dream all the attractions of life, vociferating: Blessed art Thou, O God of our fathers.

Behold, the palace is open—let us not be dejected, but rather stand up manfully without sparing our bodies, vociferated the valiant female martyrs, whilst standing before the judgment seat, for Christ is holding out the crowns. [*The Theotokion*:

Blessed is the Fruit of thy blessed womb, O pure one; Him bless, O blessed one, the heavenly powers and assemblies of men as One Who hath delivered us from the first curse.

Ode 8. The Heirmos:

The bringing forth of the Theotokos hath saved the pious youths in the furnace; then it was only typified, but now, being enacted, it moveth the whole universe to sing unto Thee: Hymn the Lord, O ye works, and highly exalt Him unto all the ages.

Through the blood of martyrdom ye have vested yourselves in bright garments, having truly put off man corrupted by sins, and are singing: Hymn the Lord, O ye works, and highly exalt Him unto the ages.

Through the shine of the abundant light, through the divine brightness of the intellectual Sun, ye have, O all-praised female martyrs, passed the night of godlessness, singing in the unity of your souls: Hymn the Lord, O ye works, and highly exalt Him unto the ages.

Like lambs and undefiled heifers, like God's doves and voluntary sacrifices were ye, O female martyrs, brought unto the Maker as undefiled sacrifice, unanimously singing: Hymn the Lord, O ye works, and highly exalt Him unto the ages.

The Theotokion: There followed in thy train, O most pure God's Bride, the only one innocent of marital life, the women-martyrs, desirous of the sweet-smelling Myrrh that hath shone forth from thy womb, even thy Son, the only Child, and they truly reign with thee, hymning Christ unto the ages.

Ode 9. The Heirmos:

Whereas Eve through the fit of disobedience hath brought in the curse, thou, O Virgin-Theotokos, hast flowered unto the world the blessing through the sprouting in thy womb.

The most famous female martyrs distribute as if from a spring the drops of healing among those that seek for them allay sufferings of the diseased and drive away the troops of demons; they also water the hearts of the God-loving ones for the fructification of Godly works.

Having obtained power over the enemies, ye have, O God's brides, become exalted and art like unto the angels; freely ye enjoy in the paradise the delights of the tree of life and of the source of all goodness, supplicating for the world.

Your memory, O female martyrs, shining with the divine lustrous graces, doth illumine the thoughts of those that praise you. [*The Theotokion*:

As abode of the Wisdom, far above understanding, as spiritual throne and door, thou hast appeared, O undefiled Virgin, wherefore women loved thee as their Queen and virgins were led in thy train. [*The Photagogicon*:

Desirous to see by all means the fairness of the Bridegroom, by the call unto Him ye have been taught immortality in your mortal bodies, O God-bearing ones; wherefore you are worthily blessed. [*The Theotokion*:

Spare me, O Christ, when Thou comest in glory to judge the

world, dispel the mist of my passions, through the intercessions of her that bare Thee, and of Thy honourable female martyrs, as Good One and Greatly Merciful.

With the Lauds the Stichera, Tone 4. Similar to: As a virtuous...

Having adorned yourselves with the shedding of your blood, ye, O virgin-maidens, have been incorruptibly united unto the Fair One in quality, even Christ our God, Who doth preserve undefiled your virginity in the immortal bridal-chamber of incorruption, in the heavenly tabernacles, in the palace not made by hand, O most laudable female martyrs. *Twice.*

In imperfect bodies, but with perfect minds, ye, O glorious ones, have, by the power of your spirit, vanquished the ancient serpent—the origin of evil—and have shewn the weakness of his strength; wherefore, O most laudable female martyrs, champions of the Trinity, ye have received the crowns of victory.

Neither breaking of your limbs, nor burning of your bodies, neither tearing with iron teeth, suspending on the trees, nor cutting up with swords could make you, O most laudable female martyrs, reject Christ; wherefore ye have received the crowns of victory, O great female martyrs, most opulent, champions of the Trinity. [*Glory...Tone* 2:

Having lived undefiled life and overthrown the godless judges, ye have stood your ground as victoresses, O honourable ones; wearing as a flower God's lustre, and invested with God's strength, ye have spurned the injunctions of the tyrants and laughed to scorn the vain speeches of the orators, O God-wise female martyrs. [*Both now...the Theotokion:*

All my hope do I lay upon thee, O Mother of God; preserve me beneath thy cover. [*The Stavro-theotokion:*

When the undefiled lamb saw her Offspring being dragged as a man to the willing slaughter, she thus spake with sobs: Dost Thou strive now, O Christ, to make me childless who gave Thee birth? Wherefore hast Thou done this, O Deliverer of all? Howbeit, I hymn and glorify Thine extreme goodness, O Lover of man, which is above the mind and speech.

CHAPTER XXII.

THE GENERAL SERVICE TO A NUN.

*At the Vespers, for O Lord, I have cried, the Stichera, Tone 8.
Similar to :* Thy martyrs, O Lord...

Having endured the pains of asceticism, thou, O honoured mother (*mentioned by name*), hast obtained the grace to cleanse the diseases both of the soul and of the body, to drive away unclean spirits by your spirit, and to be a patron unto all afflicted; wherefore with thy supplications entreat healings for all and great mercies.

The shrine of thy relics doth pour unto the blind the recovery of their sight, and the cure for all the sick that come up in faith and implore for thy visitation, O holy and wonder-worthy mother (*mentioned by name*); wherefore with thy supplications obtain for us great mercy.

Thou hast acquired mercy towards thy neighbour, orthodox faith and love unto God, O God-blissful, honoured (*mentioned by name*); therefore the spiritual grace of God hath particularly rested with thee, O holy mother; wherefore with thy supplications do preserve in the faith those that bless thee.

Glory...Both now...the Theotokion : Held down by afflictions we entreat thee, O most pure one and our intercession, do not forsake thy servants to our utter ruin; but hasten to deliver us from the present anger and misery, O most holy and pure receptacle of God, for thou art unto us an unassailable wall and help.   [*The Stavro-theotokion :*

Seeing Thee, O Jesu, nailed to the cross and willingly enduring the passion, the Virgin and Thy Mother, O Master, thus vociferated: Woe unto me, O my sweet Child! How dost Thou unrighteously suffer the sores—Thou, the Physician that hast cured human infirmity and delivered all from corruption through Thy compassion?

If there be Idiomelon, Glory...Tone 2: The spiritual snares and bodily passions hast thou cut down with the sword of abstemiousness, and the transgressions in thoughts hast thou strangled with the silence of fasting; with the streams of thy tears thou hast watered all the desert, and hast germinated unto us the fruits of repentance; wherefore we celebrate, O holy one, thy memory. [*Both now...the Theotokion:*

Save from dangers thy servants, O Theotokos, for, after God, we all resort unto thee, as an indestructible wall and protection.

The Stavro-theotokion. Similar to: When from the tree...

When the undefiled lamb saw her offspring being dragged as a man to the willing slaughter, she thus spake with sobs: Dost Thou strive now, O Christ, to make me childless who gave Thee birth? Wherefore hast Thou done this, O Deliverer of all? Howbeit, I hymn and glorify Thine extreme goodness, O Lover of man, which is above the mind and speech.

If the Celebration be with the Polyeleon, say the Theotokion of the resurrection: Disappeared the shadow... *The Entrance. The Prokeimenon of the day. The three Readings of the ascetics* (*see Appendix.*)

With the Versicles the Stichera. Tone 1. *Similar to:*
Of the heavenly orders...

Having truly desired the glory of the fathers, thou hast loved the incorruptible glory; having therefore rejected the sweet things, thou hast given thy body over to all kinds of pains, O (*mentioned by name*), and having now obtained the reward of thy labours, thou dost reign with Christ.

The Versicle: Wonderful in His holy ones is God, the God of Israel. Having desired the fair beauty of the Bridegroom, even Christ, and having striven with all kinds of good deeds to affiance thyself unto Him, thou, O (*mentioned by name*), hast adorned thyself with the labours of asceticism; wherefore dost thou now reign with Him in His palace.

The Versicle: Precious in the sight of the Lord is the death of His saints. Having fixed thy course unto the divine haven, thou hast calmly passed over the waves of the worldly agitations, and hast piloted the ship of thy soul, safe from foundering, through the bitterness of sweet things, and filled with secret treasures.

Glory. Tone 6: Thy sacred celebration hath shone forth to-day more brightly than the sun, and doth illumine those that are in the darkness, ever driving away the demoniacal mist, O wonder-worthy one. [*Both now...the Theotokion:*
O Theotokos, thou art the true vine...

The Stavro-theotokion: Beholding Thee crucified, O Christ, she that gave Thee birth, vociferated: What is this strange mystery I see, O my Son? How dost Thou die—hung in the flesh, O Giver of life?

The Troparion from the Typicon; but, if there be no Typicon, say this Troparion, Tone 8: In thee, O mother, was manifestly preserved what is in the image of God; for, having taken up the cross, thou didst follow Christ, and by thine own example hast taught that the flesh is to be despised as transient, but that particular care should be bestowed on the soul, as a thing immortal; wherefore together with the angels rejoiceth also thine, O religious (*mentioned by name*), spirit. *Glory...Both now...the Theotokion or the Stavro-theotokion.*

At the Matins, for God is the Lord the same Troparion. After the 1*st Stichologia, the Cathisma, Tone* 5. *Similar to:* The Co-unoriginate.

Having valiantly endured the feats of asceticism, thou hast overthrown the multi-snaring one, and having lived piously the life of hardship, thou hast now, O holy (*mentioned by name*), passed unto God, supplicating for all who sacredly keep thy holy celebration. *Twice.* [*Glory...Both now...the Theotokion:*
O all-undefiled Mother! Shine forth unto me the ray of repentance, disperse the mist of mine enormous evil-doings and drive away from my heart the evil thoughts, O Virgin.

After the 2*nd Stichologia, the Cathisma, Tone* 4. *Similar to:*
Speedily prevent...

Thy body hast thou crucified with passions, and all thy love hast thou concentrated on Christ, thine eternal Bridegroom, O (*mentioned by name*); wherefore hast thou obtained the crown and wast numbered unto the choirs of angels, assiduously supplicating Him for those who honour Thee, O, holy one. *Twice.* [*Glory...Both now...the Theotokion:*

The storm of sins doth trouble me, and also the agitation of mine unsuitable thoughts; take compassion on me, O all-undefiled one, and stretch out unto me thy helpful arm as gracious one, that having been saved I may magnify thee.

After Praise ye the name of the Lord...this Refrain: We glorify thee, O holy mother (*mentioned by name*), and honour thy holy memory, for thou dost supplicate for us Christ our God. *The selected Psalm:* I have patiently waited for the Lord...

After the Polyeleon, the Cathisma, Tone 8. Similar to: The secretly ordained...

O mother fore-ordained of God! Piloted unto the haven of life, thou hast passed the storm of life without agitation; hymning now, together with angels, the Redeemer, thou ever dost supplicate for us Christ that He may grant us grace and mercy, and preserve the flock which thou hast formed by thy labours. *Twice.* [*Glory...Both now...the Theotokion:*

Hail thou that hast from angel received the Joy of the world. Hail thou that hast given birth unto thy Creator and Lord. Hail thou that wast made worthy to become the Mother of God.

The Graduals, the 1st Antiphon of the 4th Tone. The Prokeimenon: Wonderful in His holy ones is God, the God of Israel. *The Verse:* In the congregations bless ye God, even the Lord, from the fountains of Israel. Let every breath. *The Gospel (St. Matth. 25, 1-13). After the 50th Psalm the Sticheron, Tone 2:* The spiritual snares. (*Glory...O Lord, I have cried*).

The Canon, Tone 8. Ode 1. The Heirmos:

The pursuing Pharaoh with the chariots did once submerge the cruciformly stretched and dividing the sea miraculous rod of Moses, but it hath saved the fugitive Israel who proceeded on foot singing a chant unto God.

Since I am continually submerged by the storms of passions and my soul is agitated by utterances of thoughts, do thou, O holy (*mentioned by name*), set me straight unto the serene haven of Christ's will, that I may worthily hymn thee.

Illumined with virginal virtues, O God-glorified (*mentioned by name*), and having divinely lived the life of abstemiousness, thou hast affianced thyself unto the pure Word and followed in His life-bringing footsteps, having suffered the mortification of passions.

Thou, O glorious (*mentioned by name*), hast followed the instructions of the divine fathers and hast strictly emulated their lives, having lived in abstemiousness as a bodiless one, in purity and virginity and in true humility, O holy one. [*The Theotokion*:

As the divine pot and table that hath borne the Bread of life, as the unploughed land and holy mount we glorify the Theotokos-Virgin in hymns.

Ode 3. The Heirmos:

O Lord, the Roofer of the heavenly firmament and the Founder of the church, do Thou stablish me in Thy love, Thou—the end of desires, the stablishing of the faithful, the only Lover of man.

Having been selected as a bride unto the Almighty, thou hast found thine abode in the heavenly resplendent palaces, and dost cause rivers of healings to flow and to dry up in us the flow of passions, O (*mentioned by name*).

Thou wast adorned with thine extreme desire for Christ Who, through the superabundance of compassion, didst undergo bodily impoverishment, and thou hast followed His words of life, rejecting with contempt all the sweets of this life.

Having acquired the golden wings of virtue, thou hast flown up the heavenly heights as an immortal dove, O blissful (*mentioned by name*). [*The Theotokion*:

The race of man was saved, O Virgin, through the grace of Him Who hath undergone impoverishment in the body which was ineffably taken in thy womb; wherefore we honour and piously bless thee, O most pure Virgin, God-greeted.

The Cathisma, Tone 4. *Similar to*: Thou that was lifted on the cross...

With the beauties of the ascetic, sacred feats hast thou appeared adorned as a virgin and undefiled bride of Christ, and having entered with Him into the incorruptible chamber, dost thou delight in the contemplation of the beauties thereof; but supplicate that we may be saved from every misfortune, lovingly hymning thee. [*Glory...Both now...the Theotokion:*

O pure, all-undefiled and innocent of marital life, the only one that hast in time given birth unto the Ever-living Son and Word of God! Him supplicate, together with the holy and honourable apostles and martyrs, prophets and religious, to grant unto us cleansing and great mercy.

The Stavro-theotokion: O Virgin most undefiled, Mother of Christ the God! A sword pierced thy most holy soul when thou beheldst thy Son and God being voluntarily crucified. Do not cease supplicating Him, O most blessed one, to grant unto us the remission of sins.

Ode 4. *The Heirmos:*

I have hearkened, O Lord, unto the mystery of Thine Economy, comprehended Thy works and glorified Thy Godhead.

Thy bright festival which shineth with the light of God's Spirit, doth illumine our souls who in faith hymn thee, O holy (*mentioned by name*).

With divine miracles hast thou brought unto the faith those who were ignorant of the Master, and unto the knowledge of Him didst turn those who left the darkness of enchantment.

As gifts hast thou brought unto Christ—complete mortification of limbs and labours of abstemiousness, and in return thou hast obtained the Kingdom of heaven and the never-ending delight. [*The Theotokion:*

By humbling do save me, living in arrogance, O most pure one, who hast given birth unto Him that hath exalted our humbled nature.

Ode 5. *The Heirmos:*

Watching early we call unto Thee, O Lord: Save us, for Thou art our God, beside Thee we know no other.

Thine arms, O mother (*mentioned by name*), raised up unto the Creator, have put down the rage of the enemies.

The Highest holding thee by thy right hand, hath conducted thee, O mother, unto His heavenly delight.

Having passed the narrow path of asceticism, thou, O all-honoured (*mentioned by name*), hast succeeded unto the breadth of paradise.

THE SERVICE TO A NUN.

The Theotokion: Those that do not know thee, O God's Mother, as the Theotokos, shall not see the Light that was born of thee, O most pure one.

Ode 6. The Heirmos:

A bright garment do grant me Thou that puttest on light as a garment, O Multi-merciful Christ, our God.

Having mortified the bodily agitations, thou becamest a thorough mistress of thy passions; and now, O all-honoured (*mentioned by name*), hast thine abode in passionless serenities.

Thou, O glorious one, wast accustomed to adore the image of the Saviour, in thy deeds and words observing His saving teaching.

Christ hath shewn thee, O mother (*mentioned by name*), as a cloud that sheddeth the rain of life unto those who in faith ask thee for it, O glorious one. [*The Theotokion:*

Thy Son, O most pure one, is the fairest above all men in the beauty of Divinity, although He was flesh for our sake.

The Contakion from the Typicon; but if there be no Typicon, say this Contakion, Tone 2. Similar to: Having received the grace...

For the love of God thou didst, O religious one, detest the device for rest, having by fasting made thy spirit luminous, for thou didst inflict a severe defeat on the beasts; but through thine intercessions destroy the plots of the enemies. [*The Oikos:*

Streams of speech grant me, O my God, make my mind a fountain of piety and bless my tongue that I may hymn thy lamb whom Thou hast crowned with Thy graciousness. For if Thou Thyself do not impart unto me a worthy word, how can I, a beggar, bring a gift unto her who is so rich both in words and deeds? Wherefore do grant me strength to declare her combats, for she hath capitally vanquished the beasts; but through her intercessions destroy the plots of the enemies.

Ode 7. The Heirmos:

The Hebrew youths have boldly trodden the flame in the furnace and have changed the fire into dew, vociferating: Blessed art Thou, O Lord God, unto the ages.

On corrupt qualities hast thou, O holy (*mentioned by name*), bestowed no care, fixing thy mind on the above existing rewards and light, God's glory and beauty never-growing old, and the divine abode.

This corrupt world hast thou exchanged for life above the world and never-growing old, the temporal food for permanent substance and the carnally betrothed for the heavenly Bridegroom.

God-loving understanding hast thou, O (*mentioned by name*), acquired, in thy body thou didst become like unto the angels, with love fervently watching and singing: Blessed art Thou, O Lord God, unto the ages. [*The Theotokion:*

Behold, O Virgin, mine affliction which the multitude of my evil deeds hath brought over me, and snatch me out of the fire-like flame, vociferating: Blessed art Thou, O Lord God, unto the ages.

Ode 8. *The Heirmos:*

The God-spoken youths, whilst treading down in the furnace the flame with the fire, sung: Bless the Lord, ye the works of the Lord.

The God-spoken youths treading down the flame in the fiery furnace, sung: Bless the Lord, O ye the works of the Lord.

Adorned with the radiance of purity and illumined by the purity of thy life, thou, O mother, dost stand before thy Bridegroom, even Christ, our God.

Thy holy body, most gloriously preserved in the shrine, doth cure various diseases of men and driveth away demons with their villanies.

As a sacred sacrifice and a bright offering, wast thou, O holy mother (*mentioned by name*), brought unto the Master of all, even Christ our God, for a sweet-smelling incense.

The Theotokion: Without corruption and above word hast thou given birth unto the Word that delivereth us all from corruption; wherefore we do in faith magnify thee, O Virgin.

Ode 9. *The Heirmos:*

Everyone became terrified at hearing of the ineffable God's condescension, that the Most High did voluntarily come down even unto the flesh itself, having become man in the Virgin's womb; wherefore we the faithful magnify the most pure Theotokos.

Thou hast desired the intellectual beauty of the Bridegroom and hast purely loved Him. "Where dost Thou take Thy rest?"

or " where dost Thou tend ? "—hast thou ardently called out. Let me rest with Thee and take delight in Thy serenities, magnifying Thy graciousness.

In thy soul thou didst have both understanding and humility, divine benignness, undoubting faith, hope and love that is unto God, approaching Him in thine all-night prayers and being both illumined and enlightened by the above existing serenities, O blessed (*mentioned by name*).

People are gathered to-day with lauds to magnify the Lord that hath glorified this thy holy festival; whereon standing before Christ, thy Bridegroom, O holy and all-honoured (*mentioned by name*), do remember us who are remembering thee. [*The Theotokion*:

Spare me, O God, that wast born of the Virgin and hast preserved her that bare Thee incorrupt after the birth, when Thou wiltst sit to judge my deeds; do overlook my wickednesses and sins, as sinless and gracious God and Lover of man.

The Photagogicon: Having suppressed thy shame before the prince, thou hast shown him foolish in the most inglorious manner, being a virgin in thy soul and body thou wast a man in thine understanding and faith, O holy (*mentioned by name*), beauty of chaste men, adornment of black garmented ones. [*The Theotokion*:

Do shine unto me a day of intellectual joy, for thou, O pure one, art the light and the life of those sitting in darkness. Unto thy desire and what thou hast to do, art thou mistress, since thou art the Sovereign-Lady of all; do deliver all from misfortunes and all the afflicted from temptations of the evil one.

With the Lauds, the Stichera, Tone 4. Similar to:
As a virtuous...

The impulses of the body hast thou duly subjugated unto the soul and hast followed Christ; thou hast taken thine abode among ascetic women, with all kinds of fasting, extinguishing the flames of sweet things with the divine clouds of tears and heating up to yet greater degree thy desire for the Creator. *Twice.*

A sacred abode for the benefit of many hast thou erected unto God, having seen in the purity of thy soul, O all-wise one, the temple of the Holy Spirit; thou hast also guided the souls unto the beneficial exertions in abstemiousness and hast as dowry brought them saved unto the Master; with these we in faith honour thee, O (*mentioned by name*).

Following thy teaching, maidens loved their Bridegroom and Lord, and having in spirit contemned the bodily weakness, with assiduity have piously kept down their passions; together with thee, O (*mentioned by name*), they were also brought into the heavenly and divine palace, ever rejoicing. [*Glory...Tone* 8.

O most glorious wonder! With what fervour hast thou given thyself up unto God in ascetic labours and ascetic tears? Thou hast fulfilled the divine love, vanquished the bodily passions, trodden under thy feet the demons through abstemiousness and wast a Bride unto the Almighty. [*Both now...the Theotokion*:

Taking up the voice of archangel Gabriel, let us say: Hail, O Mother of God, since thou hast brought forth unto the world the Life-giver, even Christ. [*The Stavro-theotokion*:

When the most pure one beheld Thee hanging in flesh on the cross, her heart was breaking, and she vociferated tearfully: O Word, how art Thou gone down, O most beloved Jesu, my Son and Lord? Do not leave me alone that gave Thee birth.

CHAPTER XXIII.

THE SERVICE COMMON TO TWO AND MANY NUNS.

At the Vespers, for O Lord, I have cried, the Stichera, Tone 1.
Similar to: Of the Heavenly orders.

Shining above as God-like rays, with intellectual rays ye enlighten the world, disperse the darkness and drive away the troops of the evil demons; wherefore we celebrate your light-bearing and divine festival.

THE SERVICE TO NUNS. 233

Having beheld the beauties of paradise and been abundantly filled therewith, ye, O all-honoured ones, have sprouted unto the world as the never-fading flowers of the divine intellect; partaking thereof to-day in spiritual love, we effectuate every good fruit for our souls.

With your ascetic life ye have adorned a great multitude of ascetics, shining forth unto all as the sun; wherefore with them are ye being glorified, O most honoured ones, taking delight in the divine glory and supplicating that we may be saved.

Glory...Both now...the Theotokion: Tossed about in the abyss of transgressions, I flee unto the calm haven of thy most pure prayer and call out unto thee, O God's Parent: Save me by stretching out unto thy servant thy mighty right hand, O all-unblemished one. [*The Stavro-theotokion:*

Behold, I have already seen, as it was foretold to me of old, the] sword piercing my heart, O my Child, when I saw Thee the Fairest of all the sons of the earth; for voluntarily wast Thou, O Christ, with robbers, as a malefactor, hung up on the cross.

If there be Idiomelon, Glory...Tone 8:

With the outpouring of tears ye have extinguished the fire of the bodily passions, and having kindled the desire for the care of things divine and the love unto the King, even Christ, ye were impassively united unto Him; wherefore, now that ye have entered into the intellectual palace, supplicate for those that honour you, the Provider thereof.

Both now...the Theotokion: O Sovereign-Lady, accept the prayers of thy servants and deliver us from every want and woe.

If the Celebration be with the Polyeleon, say the Theotokion of the resurrection: The King of the heavens...*The Entrance. The Prokeimenon of the day. The three Readings of the martyrs* (*see Appendix*).

With the Versicles, the Stichera, Tone 8. *Similar to:* As a virtuous...

Ye have proceeded along the narrow path that leadeth unto the life, without your spirit being agitated in your progress, for being of the female ascetics the glory, ye have successfully destroyed the snares of demons; wherefore ye have obtained the title of inheritrices of the heavenly Kingdom and are now enjoying the delights of the never-fading beauty thereof.

The Versicle: Wonderful in His holy ones is God, the God of Israel. Your most illustrious life hath astonished angels and manifestly frightened the rage of demons; it hath also brightly adorned the companies of the faithful, enjoining them always to continue in the way unto the heavenly habitation of Christ; Him supplicate that may be delivered from corruption and misfortunes those who in faith celebrate your all-honoured memory.

The Versicle: Precious in the sight of the Lord is the death of His saints: Song and praise bringing daily unto Christ whilst ye lived in the desert, ye have given up your souls and thoughts entirely unto God alone, and have, as the great Moses, entered unattainable regions; wherefore ye have obtained victory over the invisible enemy and become a pure receptacle of the divine Spirit. [*Glory...Tone* 4:

Maidens have loved the Bridegroom, even the Lord, and in obedience to His teaching, and disdainful of bodily weakness, in their spirit, with pious fervour, they held down the passion and were led in, together with you, O holy ones, into the heavenly palace, ever rejoicing. [*Both now...the Theotokion:*

O most pure Sovereign-Lady, lamp inextinguishable, throne of righteousness, supplicate that our souls may be saved.

The Stavro-theotokion: Bewail me not, O Mother, beholding hung on the tree thy Son and God, Who suspended the earth over the waters unrestrained and fashioned all the creation; for I shall rise again and be glorified, with My power I shall destroy the strongholds of the hades, shall exterminate the might thereof, deliver the captives from his villanies, as Compassionate, and bring them unto My Father, as Lover of man.

The Troparion unto the holy nuns. Tone 2:

Having affianced yourselves unto the true desire, O ye glorious in Christ, refusing union with the temporal bridegrooms, and having matured in virtuous deeds, you did rise to the height of incorruption, O ye beautiful in your souls and abounding in riches, the pillars and the rule for the women living in convents. Therefore plead incessantly for us that lovingly celebrate your memory.

Glory...Both now...the Theotokion or the Stavro-theotokion.

At the Matins, for God is the Lord, the same Troparion. After the 1st Stichologia, the Cathisma, Tone 3. Similar to : Unto the beauty of virginity...

The beauty of this world ye have forsaken, O holy ones, having exchanged the perishable riches for those that never pass away and are clearly ever present; wherefore we glorify you, together with all the saints, and celebrate your sacred memory, entreating that through your intercessions, O blissful ones, we may obtain great mercy. *Twice.*

Glory...Both now...the Theotokion:

Unthinkable and incomprehensible is the awful divine mystery, that was accomplished in thee, O Sovereign-Lady God-greeted; for having conceived the Immense One, thou hast brought Him forth clothed with the flesh from thy most pure blood; Him, O pure one, do always supplicate as thy Son, that our souls may be saved.

After the 2nd Stichologia, the Cathisma, Tone 5. Similar to: The Co-unoriginate...

Having adorned your life with abstemiousness, and having mortified the fleshly desires, you have, O holy ones, obtained victory over the attacks of the enemy; ye have appeared also both as dwellers of the wilderness and reasonable lamps of the world; wherefore, O blissful ones, entreat the Lord to have mercy on our souls. *Twice.*

Glory...Both now...the Theotokion: Having acquired in thee both haven and wall, refuge and lofty shelter and warm intercession, we the faithful flee unto thee, assiduously vociferate and cry out unto thee in faith: Have mercy, O Theotokos, upon those that trust in thee, and deliver from transgressions.

After Praise ye the name of the Lord, the Refrain: We glorify you, O holy mothers, and honour your holy memory, for ye supplicate for us Christ, our God.

The selected Psalm: I have patiently waited for the Lord...

After the Polyeleon, the Cathisma, Tone 8. Similar to: The ordained...

Watching in secret prayers and finding delight in the God-inspired writings, ye, O blissful ones, have taken upon your shoulders the cross of the Lord and, following it in abstemiousness, ye have put down all the fawning of the serpent, crying out unto Christ: O heavenly Bridegroom, be Thou unto us the mainstay. *Twice.*

Glory...Both now...the Theotokion: Thou that for our sake wast born of the Virgin and didst endure crucifixion, O Good One, Who, as God, by death hast overthrown death and made resurrection manifest, despise not those whom Thou hast fashioned with Thy hand; shew forth Thy love to man, O Merciful One; receive the Theotokos that bare Thee, who intercedeth for us, and save, O Saviour, Thy despairing people.

The Graduals, the 1st Antiphon of the 4th Tone. The Prokeimenon: Wonderful in His holy ones, is God, the God of Israel. *The Verse:* In the congregations bless ye God, even the Lord, from the fountains of Israel. Let every breath. *The Gospel (St. Matt. 25, 1-13). After the 50th Psalm, the Sticheron, Tone 8:* With the outpouring of tears...(*see Glory, for O Lord, I have cried*).

The Canon, Tone 8. Ode 1. The Heirmos:

The pursuing Pharaoh with the chariots did once submerge the cruciformly stretched and dividing the sea miraculous rod of Moses, but it hath saved the fugitive Israel who proceeded on foot, singing a chant unto God.

In bodily weakness have ye, O holy women, put down the powerful enemy and assigned yourselves unto God, supplicating Him to grant the saving strength unto us all.

Struck by the beauty of the Bridegroom and attaching yourselves unto His train, according to the psalmist, ye have followed in His life-bringing footsteps; therefore ye have also put down the inimicable serpent.

Having withered the fair bodily qualities with your labours of abstemiousness, ye have adorned your souls, and together with Christ—the Bridegroom—ye have entered the resplendent chambers, O holy ones. [*The Theotokion:*

Thy womb, O Virgin, was shown to be a resplendent receptacle, for the sake of the mercy of the Lord, Who was incarnate of thee in the flesh and hath illumined everything with the rays of the knowledge of God.

Ode 3. The Heirmos :
O Lord, the Roofer of the heavenly firmament and the Founder of the church, do Thou stablish me in Thy love, Thou—the end of the desires, the stablishing of the faithful, the only Lover of man.

Ye, O most honoured ones, despised the fair traits of the body, and as a dream accounted the transient glory, but with humility and watchfulness have sought and found God, O blessed of God.

The sacred relics do send forth beams in vouchsafing cures unto those who in faith have recourse thereunto, the holy women having drawn the grace from the Saviour's source Whose voluntary passion they have emulated.

Ye have rejected the world and the subtleties of the flesh, but by abstemiousness and labours have acquired the most pure Bridegroom, even Christ, Who granteth you the heavenly palace for the divine enjoyment. [*The Theotokion :*

The sacred trumpets of the sacred prophets have of old foreannounced thee, O most pure Virgin, as a door that gavest birth unto the Light, and as a live book in which, above words and without hands, was written the Word.

The Cathisma, Tone 4. Having taken upon your shoulders the cross of Christ, ye have, O all-bright and holy ones, faithfully followed Him in your ascetic works and have appeared as a rule unto all religious women; but having through your divine labours inherited the Kingdom on high, do unceasingly pray that our souls may be saved.

Glory...Both now...the Theotokion: We have learned to know the Word of the Father, even Christ, our God, that was incarnate of thee, O Theotokos-Virgin, the only pure, the only blessed one; wherefore unceasingly hymning we magnify thee. [*The Stavro-theotokion :*

Beholding hung on the cross Thee, O Christ, that wast born of the Unoriginate Father, she, who in these last days gave Thee birth in the flesh, vociferated: Woe unto me, O my most beloved Jesu! How is it that Thou Who art glorified of the angels as God, now of lawless men art Thou, O my Son, voluntarily crucified? I hymn thee, O Long-suffering One.

Ode 4. The Heirmos:

I have hearkened, O Lord, unto the mystery of Thine economy, comprehended Thy works and glorified Thy Godhead.

Having withered the beauty of the body by asceticism, the holy women behold now the most pure beauty of their beloved Bridegroom.

Having thrown the sleep off your mental eye-lids, ye have, O sacred women, lulled to sleep the agitation of your bodies with abstemiousness.

Your bright festival, beaming with the light of the Divine Spirit, doth illumine the souls of us who in faith honour you, O holy ones. [*The Theotokion*:

Having conceived love unto Thee, O Lord, Who wast incarnate of the most pure Virgin, the holy women followed in the wake of the smell of Thy myrrh, being moved thereto by the divine love.

Ode 5. The Heirmos:

Why hast Thou driven me away from Thy presence, O Light never-setting, and why hath covered me, the miserable one, the enemy's darkness? Do howbeit turn me and set my paths unto the light of Thy commandments, I pray Thee.

Doing away with all sicknesses by the power of the Holy Spirit, ye, O all-honoured ones, disperse the mist of maladies by the most glorious lustre of your miracles, and turn the faithful unto the light of the heavenly Kingdom.

Having died unto the world, ye, O God-blissful ones, have inherited the life immortal and were accounted worthy of the divine bridal chamber, since ye, O all-honoured ones, have with the oil of asceticism preserved your lamps unextinguished.

Neglecting the life of short duration and corruptible, ye have, O God-blissful ones, left it unto those remaining on earth having bound yourselves with love spiritual; therefore now ye settle wherein there are habitations of the righteous.

The Theotokion: The Divine Word, even God, hath voluntarily found His abode in the womb innocent of marital life, and was seen as man He Who hath preserved as Virgin thee, O most pure one; Him desiring, the maidens have followed Him in the asceticism of their bright life.

Ode 6. *The Heirmos:*

I will pour out my prayer before the Lord, and unto Him will I make known my sorrows, for my soul is filled with evil and my life is come nigh unto the hades; I will pray with Jonah: Out of corruption lead me up, O God.

Abstemiousness and humble heart, watchfulness and mercy, understanding and faith and perfect love having acquired, ye were, O sacred women, the temple of God and the source of healings inexhaustible.

Ye, O honoured ones, have turned yourselves away from the sweets of life and endured the pains of asceticism for the sake of Him Who hath come down unto the earth and voluntarily peregrinated thereon for our sake; therefore ye have, O wonder-worthy ones, acquired in heaven the Hospitable One.

Ye, O all-honoured ones, have lulled to sleep with many vigils the soul-corrupting passions, and have worthily fallen into the sleep of the righteous, supplicating for the world.

The Theotokion: I know thee, O Virgin, to be the live intercession and powerful preserver, the extinguishing of the noise of attacks and the driving away of the temptations of demons; wherefore I always entreat thee from the corruption of my passions to deliver me.

The Contakion from the Typicon; but if there be no Typicon say this Contakion, Tone 2: Having by fasting attenuated your bodies and in ceaseless prayers implored the Creator for your sins, that ye might obtain their entire forgiveness, you did win of God their remission and the Kingdom of heaven; intercede before Christ the God for us all. [*The Oikos:*

Thou that shuttest up and openest the abyss, that carriest up water into the clouds and grantest rain unto the face of the earth, do grant, O God, unto my barren soul also, for the opening of my mouth, well composed speech and unto my stuttering tongue clear utterance that I may be able worthily to hymn Thy holy ones whom Thou Thyself hast glorified, for for

Thy sake they despised the good things of [this world and attenuated their bodies; by Thy might they vanquished the devil and from Thee received the crowns of endurance; and now, standing in the heaven with all the saints, before Thee they unceasingly intercede for us all.

Ode 7. *The Heirmos:*

From Judea coming the youths did once in Babylon tread down the flame of the furnace by their faith in the Trinity, singing : O God of the fathers, blessed art Thou.

The holy ones by love have changed perishable glory into the incorruptible and, delighting therein, joyful and exulting they sing : Blessed art Thou, O God of our fathers.

Ye have appeared as multi-lustrous stars and, illumining the souls of the faithful with the light of your labours, ye teach them to sing : Blessed art Thou, O God of our fathers.

Ye have appeared as the river of healings, drowning the sea of sufferings and saving those that sing : Blessed art Thou, O God of our fathers.   [*The Theotokion:*

Release my wretched soul from the bonds of sin and attach unto the perfect love of God, O God's Parent, that I may glorify thee in faith and hymn unto the ages.

Ode 8. *The Heirmos:*

Having been, through Thy grace, the vanquishers of both the tyrant and of the flame, and strictly carrying out Thy commandments, the youths vociferated : Bless the Lord, all ye the works of the Lord.

The virgins have subdued the irrational passions unto the mind and being mentally united unto the Bridegroom—the Word, sang: Bless the Lord, all ye the works, and extol Him unto the ages.

Having been crucified unto the world and pierced by the divine love, the sacred virgins have wounded with the arrows of abstemiousness him that wounded Eve through the taste of sweets, and are hymning Christ unto the ages.

Ye have, O holy ones, subdued the irrational lusts unto reason, and affianced yourselves, O honoured ones, blamelessly unto the Bridegroom—the Word, singing: Bless the Lord, all ye the works and extol Him unto all the ages.

The Theotokion: Thou that of thy pure blood hast given birth unto the Incarnate Jesus, O most pure Virgin-Mother, gatheredst all the virgins and dost vociferate together with them: Bless the Lord all ye the works and extol Him unto the ages.

Ode 9. The Heirmos:

As truly the Theotokos we declare thee, being saved by thee, O pure Virgin, and together with the bodiless choirs magnify thee.

Ye, O beautiful and God-spoken turtle-doves and bright and cleanly swallows, were brought into the heavenly beautiful palaces unto the Master.

Ye are numbered with the highest choirs and have found your abode among the assemblies of the elect, supplicating for us God abounding in love.

The memory of the holy women hath shone forth unto the world, enlightening the thoughts of the faithful that ever magnify Christ. [*The Theotokion:*

Being the receptacle of the Light, do enlighten, O Virgin, my soul darkened by passions, and deliver me with thine intercessions from the outer darkness. [*The Photagogicon:*

O holy and all-honoured ones, do, with your supplications unto God, deliver from every kind of calamity those who lovingly and gratefully celebrate your memory, and wash off the defilement of my soul, however little I may have sung you.

The Theotokion: Do not cease, O Virgin, to supplicate for us thy Son, even God, the Lover of man; for in thee we have acquired our hope and through thine intercession we who glorify thee in faith, obtain deliverance from calamities and sufferings, from sins and maladies.

With the Lauds the Stichera, Tone 4. *Similar to:* Thou hast given a sign...

Having preserved your virginity incorruptible, having led unpolluted and pure life and attained opulence, ye, O holy ones, have fulfilled the law of Christ, after Whom you followed, leaving the earth and everything that is thereon; wherefore

Jesus, the Lover of man and Saviour of our souls, hath granted you the heavenly riches and the heaven itself. *Twice.*

Philosophically ye have shewn the self-directing and immortal side of the soul; wherefore ye have striven also to give up the bonds of the flesh free from every pollution of sin and from every impurity, that ye may have neither spot nor wrinkle, O God-acceptable women; ye have stood up before your Bridegroom pure and undefiled.

Your light-like countenances were illumined with lustre at your demise, O most laudable ones, Christ having glorified you as His holy ones—God-like and compassionate, God-loving and God-spoken; for ye have lived on earth the life of angels, and pleased God with the brightness of your life. [*Glory...Tone* 1:

Through abstemiousness and labours having laid aside all the bodily burthen, ye have, O holy women, proceeded up into the heavenly habitations, wherein ye enjoy the ineffable goodness beloved of you. [*Both now...the Theotokion:*

Be hailed from us, O holy Theotokos Virgin, the purest vessel of all the universe, lamp inextinguishable, the receptacle of the Illimitable, the temple unassailable. Hail thou! of whom was born the Lamb of God that taketh away the sins of the whole world. [*The Stavro-theotokion:*

Beholding Thee lifted up on the cross, the Virgin—unblemished lamb—vociferated in tears: O my sweet Child! What is this new and most glorious sight? How is it that Thou Who holdest everything in the palm of Thy hand, art nailed down to the tree in the flesh?

CHAPTER XXIV.

GENERAL SERVICE TO A NUN-MARTYR.

At the Vespers, for O Lord, I have cried, the Stichera, Tone 8.
Similar to: What shall we call you, O holy ones...

Having through abstemiousness subjugated the bodily passions, with thy passion, O all-praised sufferer, female-martyr (*mentioned by name*), hast thou slain the serpent—the enemy, astonishing with thy pains the angels and making men joyful with thy sufferings, O ornament of ascetics, vessel of virginity! Supplicate that our souls may be saved and enlightened.

What shall we call thee, O glorious one? A bride of Christ made illustrious through the beauty of virginity, an elect daughter of Jerusalem on high, cohabitant and associate of angels. Thou art in the enjoyment of the intellectual palace, O great sufferer, ornament of ascetics (*mentioned by name*), do supplicate that our souls may be saved and enlightened.

Thou hast endured the breaking of teeth, cutting off of hands, feet and nipples, and being cut up by the lawless tormentors and suffering pains beyond endurance, thou hast looked up to the beauty of the Bridegroom, O (*mentioned by name*) great sufferer, incorrupt bride of Christ, do supplicate that our souls may be saved and enlightened.

Glory...Both now...the Theotokion: Which of thy deeds of kindness is more to be wondered at, O most pure one? Thou healest the sick, deliverest from passions and drivest away the godless assaults of the enemies; thou deliverest from calamities those who hymn thee and assuagest the afflictions through thy supplications. Be, O Virgin, mediatrix of a greater joy unto thy servants, praying that our souls may be saved. [*The Stavro-theotokion:*

Beholding the Lamb voluntarily stretched on the tree of the cross, the she-lamb, suffering motherly pangs and bewailing, vociferated: O my Son! What is this strange sight? Giving life unto all as Lord, how dost Thou, O Long-suffering One, undergo death in granting resurrection unto the earthly? I glorify Thy great condescension, O my God.

If there be Idiomelon. Glory...Tone 2:

With the voice of gladness and in loud psalmodies let us hymn the holy martyr (*mentioned by name*), since she hath put down the enchantment of idols and manfully brought under her feet the opposing enemy; wherefore, after her demise she hath flown unto heavens, carrying on her head a crown, and calling out: Unto Thee, O my Bridegroom, I desire, and coupling love with the desire, I have given up my body unto torments for

Thee, that I might find abode in the honourable habitations, wherein all the exulting abide. [*Both now...the Theotokion*:

We have laid our trust in thee, O Theotokos, let us not be disappointed; save us from dangers, O thou, the help of those in perplexity, and destroy the counsels of the enemies, for thou art our salvation, O God-blessed one. [*The Stavro-theotokion*:

When the undefiled lamb saw her offspring being dragged as a man to the willing slaughter, she thus spake with sobs: Dost Thou strive now, O Christ, to make me childless who gave Thee birth? Wherefore hast Thou done this, O Deliverer of all? Howbeit, I hymn and glorify Thine extreme goodness, O Lover of man, which is above mind and speech.

If the Celebration be with the Polyeleon, say the Theotokion of the resurrection: Disappeared the shadow...*The Entrance. The Prokeimenon of the day. The three Readings of the Martyrs. (See Appendix).*

For the Versicles the Stichera, Tone 4. Similar to: Thou hast given a sign...

In thy wrestling, O all-praised (*mentioned by name*), thou hast endured double suffering, having mixed with the sweat of abstemiousness the blood of martyrdom; wherefore, O holy one, the Benefactor hath also granted thee a double-crown, unto Whom thou art gone up brightly adorned as a virgin all-unblemished and as a martyr invincible.

The Versicle: Wonderful in His holy ones is God, the God of Israel. The fair qualities of the body and the beauty of thy divine soul have met together in thee, thou hast shone forth as a lily made white in the habitations of the ascetics and imbrued in the streams of blood, O all-undefiled bride (*mentioned by name*); wherefore the heavenly fair Bridegroom hath also received thee in the imperishable palace as virgin and martyr.

The Versicle: In the congregations bless ye God, even the Lord, from the fountains of Israel. The angel hath come round unto thy deliverance, O all-praised (*mentioned by name*), for from childhood hast thou appeared God-fearing and wast presented as an honourable offering set aside unto the Almighty; wherefore thou hast heavily trodden under thy feet the madness of the tyrant and proceedest up unto thy Bridegroom, even Christ.

Glory...Tone 6: Upon the right hand of the Saviour thou hast stood up, O great sufferer and martyr (*mentioned by name*), adorned with the raiment of virtues, unsubdued and embellished with the oil of purity and the blood of martyrdom; thou hast cried out unto Him, joyfully holding up the lamp: Unto the sweet smell of Thy myrrh I was making my way, O Christ the God, since I was struck with love unto Thee, do not send me away, O my heavenly Bridegroom. Through her intercessions do send down unto us, O All-powerful Saviour, Thy mercies. [*Both now...the Theotokion*:

The eye of my heart I raise up unto thee, O Sovereign-Lady, do not despise my weak sigh in the hour when thy Son will judge the world : be unto me the shelter and help.

The Stavro-theotokion: Seeing Thee crucified, O Christ, she who hath given Thee birth, vociferated: What a strange mystery do I see now, my Son? How being hung in the flesh dost Thou die on the tree, O Giver of life?

The Troparion, Tone 4:

Thy lamb, O Jesus (*mentioned by name*), is calling with a loud voice: Thee, O my Bridegroom, I love and, whilst Thee seeking, for Thee I endure martyrdom, I become crucified together with Thee and buried with Thee unto Thy baptism, and I suffer for Thy sake so that I may reign in Thee, and I die for Thee that I may live with Thee; but as unblemished sacrifice do Thou receive me that in love sacrificed myself to Thee. At her intercessions, as Merciful One, save our souls.

Glory...Both now...the Theotokion or the Stavro-theotokion.

At the Matins, for God is the Lord, the same Troparion. After the 1st *Stichologia, the Cathisma, Tone* 8. *Similar to:* Of the wisdom...

With the dew of abstemiousness thou hast vigorously extinguished the flame of passions and with the fire of thy blood hast burned all the enchantment, and unto the Bridegroom—Christ—as dowry hast thou brought honourable virginity and valiant suffering; wherefore He hath led into the palace of glory thee that hast fought illustriously and vanquished the serpent. O greatly-suffering (*mentioned by name*), supplicate Christ the God to grant the remission of sins unto those who lovingly honour thy holy memory. *Twice.*

Glory...Both now...the Theotokion: He that sitteth on the cherubic throne and abideth in the bosom of the Father, doth sit in thy womb, O Sovereign-Lady, as upon His holy throne; for God is become incarnate, He hath truly assumed the rule over all the nations, and with understanding we now sing unto Him; do entreat Him that thy servants may be saved.

After the 2nd Stichologia, the Cathisma, Tone 8. Similar to:
Thy sepulchre...

First asceticism, secondly the blood of martyrdom, as an alabaster of myrrh, hast thou brought unto the Bridegroom, even Christ, for the sake of love, and as the reward hast thou received from Him, O wonder-worthy martyr (*mentioned by name*), divine and incorruptible crown and the grace of healing through the power of the Spirit. *Twice.*

Glory...Both now...the Theotokion: O pure unmarried Virgin-Theotokos—the only intercession and shelter of the faithful! Do thou deliver from dangers, afflictions and ferocious attacks all those that trust in thee, O Maiden, and save our souls with thy divine supplications.

After Praise ye the name of the Lord, the Refrain: We magnify thee, O holy martyr (*mentioned by name*), and honour thy holy memory, for thou dost supplicate for us Christ our God.
The selected Psalm: God is our refuge and strength...

After the Polyeleon the Cathisma, Tone 8. Similar to: Of the wisdom...

Having bound thy soul with love unto Christ, thou, as glorious disciple of the Word, hast passed by the corruptible and transient things in oblivion; thou, O wise martyr, hast first slain the passions with asceticism and secondly hast put to shame the deceiver with thy martyrdom; wherefore thou hast also become worthy of double boldness before thy Maker, since thou hast obeyed Him, O holy, most opulent (*mentioned by name*). Do supplicate Christ the God to grant the remission of sins unto those who lovingly honour thy holy memory. *Twice. Glory...*

THE SERVICE TO A NUN-MARTYR. 247

Both now...the Theotokion: As the all-spotless Bride of the Creator, as the innocent of marital life Mother of the Redeemer, and as the receptacle of the Comforter, make haste, O all-hymned one, to deliver me—filthy habitation of wickedness and conscious play-thing of demons that I am—from the villanies of these latter, by making me into a habitation resplendent with virtues. Thou, O light-giving and incorruptible, disperse the cloud of passions and make me with thine intercessions worthy of communion with the highest and of the Light never setting.

The Graduals. The 1st Antiphon of the 4th Tone. The Prokeimenon: Wonderful in His holy ones is God, the God of Israel. *The Verse:* In the congregations bless ye God, even the Lord, from the fountains of Israel. Let every breath. *The Gospel* (St. Matth. 25, 1-13). *After the 50th Psalm, the Sticheron:* Upon the right hand of the Saviour. (*See Glory...for the Versicles.*)

The Canon, Tone 8. Ode 1. The Heirmos:

Let us sing unto the Lord Who hath led His people over across the Red Sea, for He alone hath gloriously triumphed.

Grant unto me, O God-wise one, honouring this light-bearing thy commemoration, illumination driving away the darkness of my soul.

From swaddling cloths hast thou given thyself entirely unto thy Maker, O (*mentioned by name*), and with the fire of abstemiousness hast burned up thy bodily passions.

Unto the height of martyrdom hast thou ascended, O martyr, not sparing thy body, and as virgin wast thou made worthy of the reasonable palaces. [*The Theotokion:*

We honour thee, O Maiden, as the ladder reaching unto heaven, upon which stood God Who made men heavenly.

Ode 3. The Heirmos:

Thou art the stablishing of those having recourse unto Thee, O Lord; Thou art the light of those in darkness and my spirit doth hymn Thee.

Whilst thou stoodest before the judgment seat of thy tormentor, thou hast, O glorious (*mentioned by name*), preached Christ as the Creator of all and Master, as God the Word.

The kindness of thy heart coming to the outward appearance in thine eyes, hath made thy sight, O glorious (*mentioned by name*), the fairest one.

An inexhaustible treasury of healings was granted thee, O maiden, by Christ, Whose poverty hast thou voluntarily loved. [*The Theotokion*:

The substance of my sins do thou, O Mother of the Light, burn up with the fire of thy supplications, bringing unto me the divine dew of pardon. [*The Cathisma, Tone* 1:

Thou, O reasonable maiden-lamb, unto the Lamb and Shepherd wast brought by asceticism, having finished thy course in martyrdom and having preserved the faith; wherefore we joyfully celebrate to-day, O wonder-worthy (*mentioned by name*), thy sacred memory, glorifying Christ.

Glory...Both now...the Theotokion: The entreaties of thy servants do accept, O Theotokos, and deliver us from every danger, as one that hast given birth unto Christ—the Saviour, Redeemer of our souls. [*The Stavro-theotokion*:

Possessing thine intercession, O most pure one, and through thy supplications being delivered from evils and preserved everywhere by the cross of thy Son, we all, as in duty bound, piously magnify thee.

Ode 4. *The Heirmos:*

I have hearkened, O Lord, unto the mystery of Thine economy, comprehended Thy works and glorified Thy Godhead.

Thee, O female martyr, who from thine youth was bearing the lightest yoke of Christ, the most lawless have condemned to endure a heavy burden.

The drops of thy blood have extinguished the burning coals of polytheism, and the rays of thy miracles, O (*mentioned by name*), have burned up the nature of the passions.

Above the earth hath risen thy fire, having been lighted at thy bosom, O martyr, and impelling thine anxiety, O virgin, about the Master. [*The Theotokion:*

After the birth thou didst remain incorruptible, O Virgin, as thou wast before the birth, for thou gavest birth unto the young Infant that was known before the ages.

Ode 5. *The Heirmos:*

Watching early we call unto Thee, O Lord : Save us, for Thou art our God, beside Thee we know no other.

Thou didst appear unexhausted through the material fire, O *(mentioned by name)*, for the divine fire of thy cordial love unto the Bridegroom was bedewing thee.

Adorned with the slappings on thy face, O *(mentioned by name)*, thou hast repulsed the abominable foolishness.

Stretched upon the tree, thou hast, O God-wise *(mentioned by name)*, typified the divine passion of thy beloved Bridegroom.

The Theotokion : We hymn thee, O all-hymned Sovereign-Lady Theotokos, for thou hast given birth in the flesh unto the most hymned God, O most pure one.

Ode 6. *The Heirmos:*

A bright garment do grant me Thou that puttest on light as a garment, O Multi-merciful Christ, our God.

The ruining of thy body with wounds was shewing the uprightness of thy conscience, O martyr *(mentioned by name)*, before Christ our God.

Whilst suspended and enduring wounds, thou, O praise-worthy martyr *(mentioned by name)*, hath preserved unhurt the nobleness of thy soul.

Whilst thou, O holy and glorious one, didst endure the cutting off of thy breast, thou hast fed the faithful with the milk of the divine care. [*The Theotokion :*

Having given birth unto God the Lover of man, do, O God-loving Sovereign-Lady, supplicate Him that we may be delivered from the fire of Gehenna.

The Contakion, Tone 4. *Similar to :* Speedily prevent...

Thy divine memory, O *(mentioned by name)*, having now arisen, appears to the world as a sun proclaiming thy life : for having by abstinence destroyed the agitations of the flesh, through the blood of thy martyrdom hast thou affianced thyself to Christ; wherefore deliver from all evils those who praise thee, that we may call unto thee : Hail, thou, O holy mother. [*The Oikos :*

Standing before God, O all-glorious holy martyr, do thou open my lips with thy God-acceptable supplications that I may sing thy divine life, O most blissful one, and worthily describe thy sufferings which thou hast, through thy fervent love, endured on earth, and appearedst an invincible female martyr; through thy faith thou hast improved the vigilance of abstemiousness and hast loved purity; wherefore deliver from all evils those who praise thee, that we may call unto thee: Hail thou, O holy mother.

Ode 7. The Heirmos:

The youths that came from Judea, have once in Babylon by the faith in the Trinity trodden under their feet the flame of the furnace, singing: O God of the fathers, blessed art Thou.

Wherein the sound of the voice of those feasting is heard, dost thou, O martyr (*mentioned by name*), exult with other virgins psalmodizing unto God the Maker: Blessed art Thou, O Lord the God, unto the ages.

Seeing thy limbs broken and enduring the tearing of the nails, thou, O (*mentioned by name*), wast brought as a sacrifice unto God psalmodizing: Blessed art Thou, O Lord the God, unto the ages.

Thou hast appeared, O God-wise (*mentioned by name*), as a vine, thy hands and feet being cut off as branches, and thou dost shed unto us the reasonable wine, consoling the hearts and repelling the drunkenness of passions. [*The Theotokion*:

Having put on the whole of man, except sin, the undefiled Flesh-bearer hath come out of thy womb, O pure one; do move Him to save those that honour thee in faith.

Ode 8. The Heirmos:

Sevenfold hath the enraged Chaldean tyrant caused the furnace to be heated for the God-fearing, but seeing these saved by a greater power, unto the Creator and Redeemer he cried out: Bless, O ye youths, hymn, O ye priests, ye people, exalt Him unto all the ages.

Vigorously shewing thy valour, thou, O all-praised martyr, hast raised thy victorious arm against the enchantment: for thou didst endure the deprivation both of the hands and of the feet, and the uprooting of thy breasts and of thy teeth, joyfully psalmodizing: O people, exalt Christ unto the ages.

Thou wast as the sun all-lustrous with the limpidity of virginity, thou hast shone forth with thy qualities of a martyr and thou hast illumined the world with the resplendent brightness of thine endurance, O great sufferer, calling out : Bless, O ye youths, hymn, O ye priests, ye people, exalt Christ unto the ages.

Do thou, O God's Bride, with thy supplications cleanse from evils my soul defiled by passions and blackened with assaults of the serpent, and with thy bright overshadowing, O martyr (*mentioned by name*), enlighten me to call out: Hymn, O ye priests, ye people, exalt Christ unto the ages. [*The Theotokion :*

Desiring thee—the pure and unblemished one, the virgin hath preserved without blemish both her body and soul; the burning passions she hath reduced to ashes by endurance and hath suffered the pains of many temptations, and now, together with thee, she doth exult in the heavenly palaces, rejoicing unto all the ages.

Ode 9. The Heirmos:

Terrified was heaven and the ends of the earth were amazed that God hath bodily appeared unto men and that thy womb hath become more spacious than the heavens; wherefore thee, O Theotokos, the highest among angels and men magnify.

Thou wast hung on the tree, typifying the blessed passion of the Word of God, and hast endured the cutting off of thy hands and feet, the extirpating of thy teeth, the cutting off of the tongue and nipples, O pure (*mentioned by name*), the glory of the ascetics and ornament of the martyrs.

As a bride wast thou arrayed, having affianced thyself in thy good-effecting sufferings, and as a selected one thou hast found thine abode within the inner resplendent chambers, carrying thy virginal lamp; now dost thou radiantly reign, O (*mentioned by name*), with those living for ever.

Thy pains are shedding sweetness that doth away with the bitterness of sin; and thy shrine doth unto the glory of the Saviour, pour out rivers of healings and submergeth all the passions and cruel maladies of those who worthily glorify thee, O honoured (*mentioned by name*). [*The Theotokion :*

Since Thy female martyr, O Lord, knew Thee as having taken flesh from a woman, and was adorned with the rays of virginity and embellished with the blood of martyrdom unto Thee, O God, she was gloriously led in the train of Thy Mother unto Thee that reignest over the creation. [*The Photagogicon :*

As a river dost thou shed healings unto those who in faith have recourse unto thy honoured shrine, O God-seeing (*mentioned by name*),—the vessel of virginity, beautiful flower of nature, king's daughter, enjoying face to face the bliss of the divine glory. *[The Theotokion:*

Do thou, O Virgin, that hast given birth unto the Hypostatic Wisdom, the Word Ever-existing, the Physician of souls and bodies, heal the painful, but temporal sores and wounds of my soul and set a limit unto the malady of my heart.

With the Lauds, the Stichera, Tone 8. Similar to:
O most glorious wonder...

Having forsaken the beauty of the world, the nobleness of thy soul, O all-praised (*mentioned by name*), hast thou made resplendent with the noble qualities from above, having preserved unsullied the grace of the image in thy life, O female martyr invincible, the God-like forefront of virginity and most noble flower of nature. *Twice.*

Having adorned thyself with the word and deed, with the grace and endurance of thy soul, thou hast brought hosts of female martyrs and an assembly of virgins unto Him Who hath shone forth from the Virgin and Who hath manifestly opened unto all the way of martyrdom. O all-wise (*mentioned by name*), together with those, move Him also now to save thy flock.

He that ordereth righteousness, thee as pure virgin and glorious martyr hath God-beseemingly adorned with double-crowns, having granted unto thee a beautiful palace illumined with lustrous rays; having found thine abode therein, thou, O bride of Christ, art now enriched with eternal blissfulness.

Glory...Tone 4, Idiomelon: Whilst thy body was being pared, the illustrious beauty of thy soul hast appeared as the fairest, O holy, wise and most opulent one,—ornament of female ascetics, adornment of female martyrs, ever-flowing source of miracles, disperser of the unclean spirits and supplicant for those who honour thy memory. *[Both now...the Theotokion:*

We have acquired in thee, O most pure Theotokos, a wall, undisturbed haven and establishment; wherefore do entreat for me, that am so afflicted in my life, pilot me and save me.

The Stavro-theotokion: Bewail me not, O Mother, beholding hung on the tree thy Son and God, Who suspended the earth over the waters unrestrained and fashioned all the creation; for I shall rise again and be glorified, with My power I shall destroy the strongholds of the hades, shall exterminate the might thereof, deliver the captives from his villanies, as Compassionate, and bring them unto My Father, as Lover of man.

CHAPTER XXV.

THE GENERAL SERVICE TO A HIERO-CONFESSOR OR MONK-CONFESSOR.

At the Vespers, for O Lord, I have cried, the Stichera, Tone 4.
Similar to: As a virtuous...

As erecter of truth and confirmer of the faith, as propounder of dogmas, harmonist of piety, abode of purity, select receptacle, the sweet smell of the Spirit, the great treasury of doctrines and the foundation of the church of Christ—we know thee, O God-inspired (*mentioned by name*), sacred father.

We praise thee as successor of apostles, of one temperament with martyrs, zealous emulator of ascetics, the seal of teachers, divine representative of Christ's adepts, God-flowing river of understanding that drowneth the notions of the lawless and blasphemers, O God-bearing, all-laudable, wise (*mentioned by name*).

Having increased thy talent of wisdom, thou O opulent one, wast made worthy of the joy of thy Lord; embellished with the grace of the divine beaming and shining with the spiritual lustre, thou dost now stand before the life-bringing right hand, being ever resplendent with the rays thereof, O glorious (*mentioned by name*).

Glory...Both now...the Theotokion: O all-hymned Theotokos! wash off the filth of my passionate heart, and all the sores and wounds thereof caused by sin, cleanse and make steady my wavering mind, that I, thy wretched and unprofitable servant, may magnify thine, O pure one, might and great protection.

[*The Stavro-theotokion*:

Seeing Christ the lover of man, hung and being pierced through His side with a spear, the most pure one did bewail crying out: What is this, O my Son ? What have the ungrateful people rewarded Thee with for all the good Thou hast done unto them ? and Thou most lovingly takest care of my childlessness. I wonder at Thy voluntary crucifixion, O Compassionate One.

If Idiomelon be appointed, Glory...Tone 6.

The grace was poured out through thy lips, O glorious apostle (*mentioned by name*), and thou wast the lamp of the church of Christ, teaching the intellectual sheep to believe in the Trinity Consubstantial, in the One Godhead.

Both now...The Theotokion: No one who fleeth for refuge unto thee, ever leaveth Thee ashamed, O most pure Theotokos-Virgin, but asking for grace, he receiveth the grant of his profitable petition. [*The Stavro-theotokion* :

The all-pure one seeing Thee hung on the cross with motherly tears cried out unto thee: O my Son and my God, my sweetest Child, how is it that Thou sufferest the ignominious death ?

If the Celebration be with the Polyeleon say the Theotokion of the resurrection: Who would not bless thee...*The Entrance...The Prokeimenon of the day...The readings of the monks* (*see Appendix*).

For the Versicles the Stichera, *Tone* 8. *Similar to*: O most glorious wonder...O all-wise father (*mentioned by name*), Thou hast brightened the church of Christ with songs, singing of things divine, striking thy harp, O most glorious father, by the energy of the Spirit and making it like unto that of David's; sounding thereon that hast attracted all with the divine songs. *The Versicle*: *Precious in the sight of the Lord is the death of His saints.* O most glorious father (*mentioned by name*), abandoning the seditious noise of the world, thou, O holy one, didst reach the Christ's calm and wast truly and clearly enriched with most various brightnesses through the contemplation of the divine actions, reflecting the same to the faithful, before whom thou dost shine with the God-beseeming life. *The Versicle: Blessed is the man that feareth the Lord, that greatly delighteth in His commandments.* Come, O ye earth-born, let us to-day piously honour with hymns the sacred and honourable commemoration of the holy (*mentioned by name*); for, behold, he hath truly been deigned to obtain the reflexion of the divine light. O how ineffable is Thy kindness, O Lord and Master, through which we learned to glorify Thee—the most kind One! *Glory...Tone 8.* We, the multitude of monks, honour thee as our preceptor, O (*mentioned by name*), our father; for we have truly learned from thy path rightfully to walk. Blessed art thou for having laboured for Christ and convicted the enemy, O associate of angels, companion of the holy and the righteous ones. Do with these supplicate the Lord that our souls may be saved. *Both now...the Theotokion of the resurrection:* O Virgin unmarried...

But if there be no Celebration, say the following Theotokion:
O holy Virgin-Theotokos! I flee up unto thy shelter and know that through thee I shall find the salvation, for thou, O pure one, art able to help me. [*The Stavro-theotokion:*
The unblemished heifer, beholding the Steer voluntarily nailed to the cross, thus vociferated with sobs and tears: Woe unto me, my most beloved Child! What have the graceless Hebrew rabble rendered unto Thee, desiring to make me childless and to separate me from Thee, O All-beloved?

The Troparion from the Typicon; but if there be no Typicon, say the following Troparion, Tone 8: The teacher of orthodoxy, preceptor of piety and chastity, luminary of the universe, God-inspired instruction of the hierarchs, O (*mentioned by name*), greatly wise, thou hast illumined all by thy teaching, O spiritual flute; entreat Christ the God that our souls may be saved. *Glory...both now...the Theotokion or the Stavro-Theotokion.*

At the Matins, for God is the Lord, the same Troparion. After the 1st Stichologia the Cathisma, Tone 4. Similar to: Thou that wast of Thy free-will lifted up...

Forsaking the enjoyment of the earthly and corruptible things, the fairness of the world and the temporal food, thou didst live the life of a hermit, and wast made worthy to be numbered unto the choir of martyrs and ascetics; do supplicate with these that thy servants may be saved. *Twice.*

Glory...Both now...the Theotokion : O pure, all-spotless and innocent of marital life, the only one that hast in time given birth unto the Ever-existing Son and Word of God ! Together with the holy and venerable apostles, martyrs, prophets and religious, supplicate Him to grant us purification and great mercy.

After the 2nd Stichologia the Cathisma, Tone 4. Similar to : Speedily prevent... Following Christ, thou hast forsaken the world and, having manifestly subdued thy flesh by abstemiousness, thou hast, O most blissful (*mentioned by name*), obtained the unction of consecration and now art thou gone over unto the immaterial choirs, supplicating for us all that praise thee. *Twice. Glory...Both now...the Theotokion :* Do thou, the only one that hast given birth unto the Creator of all, the only one that hast adorned humanity with thy bringing forth, O most pure one, deliver me from the meshes of the flattering Belial, set me upon the rock of Christ's desires, assiduously supplicating Him unto Whom thou gavest flesh.

After Praise ye the name of the Lord, the Refrain for a hiero-confessor : We magnify thee, O hierarch, father (*mentioned by name*)...*The Psalm :* Hearken unto this all ye nations...*And unto a monk-confessor :* We bless thee, O holy father (*mentioned by name*). *The Psalm :* I waited patiently for the Lord...

After the Polyeleon the Cathisma, Tone 3. Similar to : Of the divine faith...

Enlightened by the Divine Spirit, thou didst with boldness proclaim the orthodox tradition, O all-blissful (*mentioned by name*), and hast put to shame the lawless tyrant, although thou hadst to suffer banishments. O holy father ! Supplicate Christ the God to grant the remission of sins unto those who lovingly venerate thy holy memory. *Twice.*

Glory...Both now...the Theotokion : Everyone hath recourse thither where he can be saved, and what other such recourse is there that can shelter our souls but thou, O Theotokos.

SERVICE TO A HIERO-CONFESSOR OR MONK-CONFESSOR. 257

The Graduals, the 1st Antiphon of the 4th Tone. The Prokeimenon: Precious in the sight of the Lord is the death of His saints. *The Verse:* What shall I render unto the Lord for all His benefits toward me? Let every breath... *The Gospel of* (*St. Luke* 12, 8-12). *After the* 50*th Psalm, the Sticheron, Tone* 6: O holy father! Into all the earth is gone forth the echo of thine instructions; wherefore, in heaven hast thou obtained the meed of thy labours, thou hast destroyed troops of demons, comprehended the orders of angels whose life thou didst irreproachably emulate. Having boldness before Christ the God, do obtain by entreaties peace unto our souls.

The Canon, Tone 6, *Ode* 1. *The Heirmos:*

Whilst travelling on foot along the depths of the sea as if upon dry land, Israel seeing Pharaoh, their pursuer, drowned, cried out: Unto God let us sing an ode of victory.

With all his thoughts hath the sacred (*mentioned by name*) loved Thee, O Jesus, and with all his heart he was ready to suffer, enduring sorrows, maladies and suffering, until he attained the everlasting food.

With drops of blood hast thou appeased the bitter sea of unbelief; thou wast Christ's river which ever giveth rightful drink unto the church.

The feats accomplished by thee on earth hast thou brought unto God, O glorious (*mentioned by name*), and wast made worthy to receive the crowns of the heavenly Kingdom and the undisturbed life everlasting. [*The Theotokion:*

Adorned with the beauty of virtues, thou hast, O pure mother of God, conceived the Virtue, even the True God, Who hath illumined us with divine virtues.

Ode 3. *The Heirmos:*

There is none holy as Thou, O Lord my God, that hast, as Good One, exalted the horn of Thy believers, and established us upon the rock of Thy confession.

Thou hast given neither repose unto thine eyelids, nor sleep unto thine eyes, O holy Father (*mentioned by name*), until thou didst appear as a house of the Holy Trinity and a treasury of wisdom, enriching the world with the brilliant as gold teachings of thine, O blissful one.

8

Having been the keeper of the divine injunctions, O God-wise (*mentioned by name*), thou wast locked up in prisons, opening unto the faithful the bars of the instructive path that leadeth unto the breadth of understanding.

Strengthened by the divine might, thou hast put down the arrogant insolence of the lawless with thy firm confession, O all-sacred sufferer (*mentioned by name*), as an armiger of the divine army. [*The Theotokion:*

The Wisdom and the Word of the Father that existed before all ages, and that in these latter days was ineffably incarnate of thee, O Mother, innocent of marital life, hath made thee the Theotokos.

The Cathisma, Tone 4. *Similar to:* Thou hast appeared to-day...

The glorious Sun placed thee on the summit of His church as the morning star, enlightening the faithful with thy teachings, O heavenly adept (*mentioned by name*), our God-wise father.

Glory...Both now...the Theotokion: Do thou, the only one that hast given birth unto the Creator of all, the only one that hast adorned humanity with thy bringing forth, O most pure one, deliver me from the meshes of the flatterer Belial, set me upon the rock of Christ's desires, assiduously supplicating Him unto Whom thou gavest flesh.

When Thy most pure Mother beheld Thee, O Word of God, lifted up on the cross, she called out, motherly bewailing: What is this new and strange wonder, O my Son? How dost Thou—the Life of all—approach the death desiring to revive the dead, as Compassionate One?

Ode 4. *The Heirmos:*

Christ is my power, my God and Lord—the venerable church God-beseemingly singeth, thus calling out, with pure mind feasting in the Lord.

With thy words as with a lance hast thou pierced the godlessness, and with thy sufferings, as with a sword, hast thou obtained victory over the troops of demons, from whose malice do deliver those that venerate thee, O all-laudable (*mentioned by name*).

The sacred martyr (*mentioned by name*) hath called out: I will not sacrifice to idols, neither do I fear death or material tortures, but I confess One God known in the Trinity.

Seeing the most glorious height of thy humility, the Lord hath granted unto thee the word above nature, wherewith thou hast humbled, O father, the devilish-haughtiness of heretics.

The Theotokion: We bless thee, O Virgin, as the door leading unto the divine entrance, as the divine paradise, as the intellectual place of sanctification, and as the beauty of Jacob.

Ode 5. *The Heirmos:*

With Thy divine light, O Good One, do illumine, I pray Thee, the souls of those who lovingly watch early unto Thee, that they may know Thee, O Word of God, as the true God recalling them out of the darkness of sin.

With the flow of thy tears thou hast, O all-wise father (*mentioned by name*), dried up the abyss of sweet things, and with the outpouring of thy teaching thou hast barred up the torrents of heresies.

Thou wast, O father (*mentioned by name*), a truly spacious temple unto the Trinity, being adorned by the grace, by the shine of the honourable virtues, and by thine instructive humility.

Having by thine endurance put down all the risings of the evil one, do thou deliver me from his harm, O glorious (*mentioned by name*), making me by all means bold, and setting me in the paths that lead unto God. [*The Theotokion:*

We hymn, O all pure one, Him Who from thee hath taken the passionate and mortal flesh, and the manifest birth in the commingled, but unmixed Hypostasis.

Ode 6. *The Heirmos:*

Beholding the sea of life swelling with the storm of temptation, and taking refuge in Thy calm haven, I cry unto Thee: Lead up my life from corruption, O Greatly Merciful One.

Having been a luminary and having enlightened the ends of the world with the light of thy sufferings, thou hast confessed the name of Christ before thy tyrants, O all-laudable sufferer of the Lord (*mentioned by name*).

Thy tongue was truly as the calamus of a swift scribe, propounding the all-honourable sense of the spiritual law and writing it on the tablets of hearts, O father (*mentioned by name*).

Those that swim in the calm of thine instruction, O God-spoken father, avoid the abyss of the perfidious tempest, and those coming from heresies are saved by faith. [*The Theotokion:*

The Holy Spirit having come over Thee, O pure one, as the preserver of virginity, hath made thee, O all-blessed one, into an all-undefiled and honourable abode of the Son of the Most High.

The Contakion from the Typicon; but if there be no Typicon, say the following Contakion, Tone 2:

Having found delight in abstinence, thou hast stilled the very desires of thy body, appearing to be reared on the faith, and as the paradisical tree of life hast thou blossomed, O (*mentioned by name*), sacred father.

The Oikos: Do thou open my lips with thy God-acceptable supplications, O all-glorious, most sacred and holy martyr standing before God, that I may hymn thy blessed life and worthily describe thy virtues which thou hast with fervent love practised on earth; for thou wast a fearless confessor, thine abstinence hast thou set aright by the faith and loved vigilance and purity, O sacred father (*mentioned by name*).

Ode 7. *The Heirmos:*

Dew-yielding hath an angel made the furnace unto the pious youths, and God's injunction burning the Chaldeans hath inclined the tyrant to cry out: Blessed art Thou, O God of our fathers.

As thy life was most illustrious on account of abstinence, so firm appeared also thy suffering, O God-wise one, for thou hast openly glorified Christ, vociferating: Blessed art Thou, O God of our fathers.

Having girded thyself with the manliness of the purity of chastity, and by grace obtained the lustrous crown of martyrdom, thou, O God-pleasing father (*mentioned by name*), hast vociferated: Blessed art Thou, God of our fathers.

Those that do not adore Thy most pure icon, O Saviour, these wicked ones have deeply and manifoldly offended Thy servant that is ever saying and vociferating unto Thee: Blessed art Thou, O God of our fathers. [*The Theotokion:*

He that uncircumscribed sitteth in the bosom of the Begetter, having now passed out of thy loins, O most pure one, doth sit circumscribed, being like unto thine image and having become Adam in order to save Adam.

Ode 8. *The Heirmos:*

Unto the pious hast Thou made dew out of the flame to flow and the sacrifice of a righteous man didst Thou consume with water, for everything makest Thou, O Christ, just as Thou willest; Thee we exalt unto all the ages.

Thou didst appear light-bearing, O blissful (*mentioned by name*), as another sun, sending forth instruction unto the ends of the world, and with the light of repentance driving away the darkness of every perplexing sin.

Protected by the streams of divine teaching, thou didst come out as a river from another paradise, O God-pleasing (*mentioned by name*), giving drink unto the face of the earth and drowning the tares of wickedness.

Thou wast adorned with the beauty of thy speech, O all-blissful one, for thou didst appear as a calamus, piously writing down for the faithful the divine understanding and extolling Christ unto the ages. [*The Theotokion:*

Unto thy shelter, O all-spotless one, I flee, and as a protection of my life I now offer thee that above understanding barest God the Word, Whom we extol unto the ages.

Ode 9. *The Heirmos.*

It is not possible for man to behold God on Whom the angelic orders dare not cast a glance; but through thee, O all-pure one, was seen of man the Incarnate Word; Him magnifying, with heavenly hosts we call thee blessed.

As light, as the moon and the great sun, as lightning hast thou shone forth unto the church of Christ, and hast illumined the thoughts of the faithful; having found thine abode in the never-fading light, thou dost sing the trisagion hymn unto the Uncreated Trinity.

The earth hath been enriched with thy holy tomb and with thy sacred body, O all-praised (*mentioned by name*), and the spirits of the righteous began to exult when the angels have taken up thy spirit, O blissful one; together with them do remember us that hymn thee.

Thou wast, O (*mentioned by name*), temple of the Holy Spirit and a river full of living water, an immoveable foundation of the church, standard of orthodoxy, stream ever-flowing, wonder-worthy source of the divine repentance.

The Theotokion: As heavenly drop hath the rain descended into thy womb, O Virgin, and having dried up the streams of flattery, made incorruption and deliverance to flow unto all men, through thee, O full of God's grace. [*The Photagogicon:*

First well tried in suffering, having secondly accomplished thy divine course in asceticism, thou hast ascended into heaven and dost stand before Christ, O holy father (*mentioned by name*). Do fervently supplicate for us hymning thee. [*The Theotokion:*

Having given birth unto the ineffable Joy, even Christ, do thou, O most pure one, make partakers of the heavenly joy all those that honour thee and bring unto thee their heartfelt thanks. Forget not thy servants, O God-blessed Mary.

With the Lauds the Stichera, Tone 4. Similar to: Thou hast given a sign...

The grace of the Spirit, shining forth unto thee, O father (*mentioned by name*), hath brightly illumined thee; therefore hast thou shortened the night of passions and attained the day of impassiveness, purely commingling thyself with the purest Light; abiding therein, forget not, O God's voice, those who in faith hymn thy sacred memory. *Twice.*

Possessing the heavenly grace desired of thee, thou hast, O (*mentioned by name*), forsaken the earthly things; wherefore, as a bodiless one, hast thou selected the life of suffering, since thou, O God-pleasing one, hast desired piously to enjoy of the stream of the ever-existing sweetness, and with thy tears, O holy one, thou hast dried up the turbid spring of passions and given to drink unto the ears of the soul's food.

The grace of healings hast thou, O (*mentioned by name*), worthily obtained from the grace of God; therefore is put down the enchantment of the spirits that were trying to ensnare thee, O holy one, and having avoided the corruption of severe maladies, thou passedst over, for thou dost shed thy streams of the waters of grace, watered with which we hymn thy memory.

Glory...Tone 5: O holy father! Thou didst not give sleep unto thine eyes, nor slumber unto thine eyelids until thou hadst freed both thy soul and body from passions and until thou hast prepared thyself into an abode of the Spirit, for Christ, having come with the Father, hath made an habitation in thee. Having been the favourite of the Consubstantial Trinity, do thou, O great preacher, father (*mentioned by name*), supplicate for our souls.

The Theotokion: We the faithful bless thee, O Theotokos-Virgin, and glorify, as in duty bound, thee—the immoveable city, the wall unassailable, firm intercession and refuge of our souls. [*The Stavro-Theotokion:*

Beholding of old her Lamb lifted up on the cross, the Virgin-Mother and Maiden blessed of all, vociferated tearfully: Woe unto me, O my Son! How dost Thou die being God, immortal by nature?

CHAPTER XXVI.

GENERAL SERVICE TO THE UNMERCENARIES AND WONDER-WORKERS.

At the Vespers, for O Lord, I have cried, the Stichera, Tone 4. *Similar to:* Thou hast given a sign...With spiritual waters being filled and rivers, and manifestly filled to overflowing, ye do water the creation with the knowledge of God and with the most famous gifts of healing, dry up the soul-destroying passions, heal the maladies and drive away the evil spirits, O God-bearing unmercenaries (*mentioned by name*), supplicants for our souls.

Having subdued the irrational passions by the strength of your souls, ye do, O holy ones, vouchsafe benefits both unto men and beasts, having been enriched of Christ with the granting of healings, wherefore celebrating your sacred and light-bearing commemoration, we entreat of you the cleansing of our souls.

Your holy temple hath appeared as a resplendent and saving heaven, and is now as the sun shining with the working of the divine healings, the saving miracles acquired therein being like unto the stars, most blissful (*mentioned by name*), most glorious (*mentioned by name*),—the ministers of the Lord and supplicants for our souls.

264 SERVICE TO UNMERCENARIES AND WONDER-WORKERS.

If Idiomelon be appointed, Glory...Tone 8 : Who would not wonder at, who would not glorify, who would not faithfully hymn the miracles of the wise and most glorious unmercenaries ? For after their holy demise also they vouchsafe abundant healing for all that in faith have recourse unto them, and their honoured and holy relics shed the grace of cures. O holy twins! O honoured heads ! O wisdom and glory of the grace given unto you by God ! Wherefore in odes we call unto the Benefactor— God Who hath shewn us these for the cure of our souls and bodies. [*Both now...the Theotokion :*
Hail thou—the praise of the universe ; hail—the temple of the Lord; hail—the overshadowed mount ; hail—the refuge of all ; hail—the golden lamp ; hail—the honoured glory of the orthodox ; hail—Mary Mother of Christ the God ; hail—the paradise ; hail—the divine table ; hail—the tabernacle ; hail— the golden pot ; hail—the hope of all.

The Stavro-theotokion. Similar to : O Lord, although before the judgment seat...

Seeing Thee, O Lord, hung on the Cross, and standing close by, she that gave Thee birth, with lamentations said unto Thee : O Child! why dost Thou suffer this in the flesh, and strivest to make me childless ? Endeavour to glorify Thyself that I may be magnified through Thy passion !

If the Celebration be with the Polyeleon, say the Theotokion of the resurrection: The King of the Heavens...*The Entrance*...*The Prokeimenon of the day. The Readings of the martyrs.* (*See Appendix.*)

For the Versicles the Stichera, Tone 1. *Similar to :* Of the heavenly orders...

Having with the rays of your miracles made the whole universe resplendent, ye were, O holy unmercenaries, as most brilliant lamps made worthy of the heaven through the grace, being set as stars on account of the virtues of your holy lives. *The Versicle: In the saints that are in His earth, the Lord hath made wonderful all His desires in them.* Ye, O martyrs of the Lord, are the rain-producing clouds abounding in richly-flowing miracles of graces, with which ye spiritually water all the earth and impel the bringing unto God of orthodox psalmodies.

The Versicle: Behold, how good and how pleasant it is for brethren to dwell together in unity. Having truly received from God the art of healing the pains of both the soul and the body, ye do, O martyrs of the Lord, most naturally heal all not by human medical treatment, but by divine inspirations. [*Glory...Tone 4*:

Possessing the source of healings, ye do, O holy unmercenaries (*mentioned by name*), grant cures unto all seeking for them, since ye were made worthy of the greatest gifts from the ever-flowing source, even the Saviour Christ, for the Lord hath said unto you, as emulators of the apostles: Behold, I gave you the power against the unclean spirits, to cast them out, and to heal all manner of sickness and all manner of disease. Wherefore having well lived according to His injunctions, freely ye have received, freely ye give in curing the maladies of our souls and bodies.

Both now...the Theotokion of the resurrection : Look down upon the entreaties...

But if there be no Celebration, say the following Theotokion :

O Theotokos, the Queen of all and the glory of the orthodox! Do thou put down the rays of the heretically inclined and put to shame their countenances, since they neither bow down before thy precious image, O most pure one, nor venerate it. [*The Stavro-theotokion :*

Seeing Christ—Lover of man crucified and pierced in His side with a lance, the most pure one bewailed crying out: What is this, O my Son? What have the ungrateful people rendered unto Thee for all the good Thou hast done unto them, and Thou dost most lovingly take care of my childlessness? I wonder, O compassionate One, at Thy voluntary crucifixion.

The Troparion from the Typicon; but if there be no Typicon, say the following Troparion, Tone 8 : O holy unmercenaries and wonder-workers, visit our infirmities: gratuitously have ye received, disinterestedly bestow it upon us.

At the Matins, for God is the Lord, the same Troparion. After the 1st Stichologia, the Cathisma, Tone 2:

Made worthy of great gifts, ye have, O glorious ones, lived a humble life on earth, going about everywhere and disinterestedly curing the sick of their illnesses and pains. Now that ye have appeared associates of angels, do, O faithful, best brothers (*mentioned by name*), heal through your supplications our pains also. *Twice. Glory...Both now...the Theotokion:* Being a fountain of tenderness of heart, vouchsafe us thy sympathy, O Theotokos: look upon the people that have sinned; shew, as ever, thy power; for hoping in thee, we cry out to thee: Hail, as once did Gabriel, the chief captain of the bodiless ones.

After the 2nd Stichologia, the Cathisma, Tone 1: O martyrs of Christ (*mentioned by name*), supplicate for us that come to you in faith, for through your intercessions, ye grant the grace of healing and drive away many an infirmity, as preservers of our lives. *Twice. Glory...Both now...the Theotokion:* O most pure Theotokos! Thou art blessed in heaven and doxologized on earth; Hail thou, O Bride unmarried.

After Praise ye the name of the Lord, the Refrain: We magnify you, O glorious wonder-workers (*mentioned by name*), and venerate your honourable suffering which ye have endured for Christ. *The selected Psalm:* God is our refuge and strength... *After the Polyeleon, the Cathisma, Tone 5. Similar to:* The Co-unoriginate Word... The feast of the martyrs (*mentioned by name*), doth to-day shine forth, for they are in possession of the heavenly light; the choir of angels triumpheth and the race of men maketh also a festival; wherefore the holy ones do supplicate for our souls. *Twice. Glory...Both now...the Theotokion:* The mystery of the wonderful Virgin hath appeared unto the world as the salvation, for out of her was born the Joy; O Lord, glory to Thee.

The Graduals, the 1st Antiphon of the 4th Tone. The Prokeimenon: In the saints that are in His earth, the Lord hath made wonderful all His desires in them. *The Verse:* I have set the Lord always before me. Let every breath. *The Gospel (St. Matth.* 9, 36-38; 10, 1. 5-8). *After the 50th Psalm, the Sticheron, Tone* 1: The resplendent and holy, beautiful and all-festive memory of the martyrs (*mentioned by name*), illumining all the earth and driving away the darkness of sin, doth shed the grace unto remedies.

The Canon, Tone 8, Ode 1. The Heirmos.

Unto Him Who hath overthrown in the sea the tyranny of Pharaoh and led Israel over the dried land, let us sing unto Christ, for He is glorified unto the ages.

Him that hath manifested throughout the world the unmercenaries and physicians (*mentioned by name*), who through the grace heal the maladies of all, let us hymn Christ the Saviour, for He is glorified unto the ages.

The holy ones make flow the rivers of miracles from the spiritual graces and heal maladies; let us, O faithful, laud Him Who hath granted them this power, for He is glorified unto the ages.

Do bring, O unmercenary physicians, unto God your prayers that He may deliver us from temptations and many afflictions and from the terrible and awful eventual torture.

The Theotokion: Do thou, O incessant protection of the afflicted, salvation and hope of the despairing, Theotokos all-praised, always supplicate Christ that we may be delivered from dangers.

Ode 3. The Heirmos:

My heart is fixed in the Lord, exalted is my horn in my God, my mouth is wide open against mine enemies and I rejoice in Thy salvation.

Unto the earthly hast Thou, O Lord, manifested Thy holy (*mentioned by name*), as secret rays enlightening the whole world; do manifest Thy mercies upon us also.

Since ye have freely received the gift from God, ye do also disinterestedly grant healings, driving away demons, in accordance with the words of the Lord our God.

The world hymneth your benefactions ever great and the multitude of miracles, O holy physicians and wonder-workers, the companions of all angels. [*The Theotokion:*

Thee that hast sprouted forth on earth from David, and hast given birth unto God that was incarnate of thee, we praise thee, O most pure one, as the divine tabernacle, the throne and the door.

The Cathisma, Tone 4. *Similar to:* Thou that wast of Thy free will lifted on the cross...

Having trodden under feet the sweet things that drag down, by the grace ye have cheerfully betaken yourselves up into the divine light of martyrdom, O sufferers and lamps of the universe (*mentioned by name*); wherefore we entreat you to deliver us from the darkness of sin and maladies through your intercessions before God, Who is above all.

Glory...Both now...the Theotokion: Thou, O Theotokos-Virgin, art an unassailable wall unto Christians, for when we flee unto thee, we remain unhurt, and when we sin again, we have in thee our intercession; wherefore in giving thanks we vociferate unto thee: Hail thou, full of grace, the Lord is with thee.

The Stavro-theotokion: O most spotless Virgin, Mother of Christ the God! A sword hath pierced through thy most holy soul, when thou beheldest voluntarily crucified thy Son and God; cease not thy supplications unto Him to grant us the remission of sins.

Ode 4. *The Heirmos:*

Mysteriously foreseeing Thee, O Word, incarnate of the Virgin, the prophet in melody vociferated: Glory to Thy might, O Lord.

Wonderful is the Saviour, our God, for the naked bones of His holy ones lie in their tombs, but they work in the world wonderful and awful miracles; glory to Thy might, O Lord.

Having forsaken the earthly things as corruptible, ye, O holy ones, have become inheritors of Zion and worthy citizens of Christ's Kingdom.

Ye are worthily praised on earth, O healers of the sick and unmercenaries (*mentioned by name*), since after your demise also ye do deliver all from maladies. [*The Theotokion*:

Hail thou—the tabernacle of God's glory; hail—the weapon and the fiery throne; hail—the overshadowed mount, from which was cut the stone, even Christ.

Ode 5. *The Heirmos:*

Watching early we cry out unto Thee, O Lord: Save us, for Thou art our God, beside Thee we know no other.

Having received from God the power, ye heal, O unmercenaries (*mentioned by name*), the diseases of all the infirm.

Having been made worthy of the great gifts of the Lord, ye, O holy ministers, disinterestedly cure all.

For the sake of intercessions of thy holy ministers (*mentioned by name*), do Thou, O our Saviour, grant unto the whole world Thy mercies, as Compassionate. [*The Theotokion:*

As Virgin after the birth we praise thee, O Theotokos, for thou barest unto the world the Word of God in the flesh.

Ode 6. *The Heirmos:*

As Thou didst deliver the prophet out of the abyss-like depth, do Thou, O Christ the God, deliver me also from my sins, as Lover of man, and direct my life,—I implore Thee.

Since upon the sea of life ye have passed the abyss without storm, ye have piously attained unto the salutary haven, the highest kingdom, O unmercenaries.

Ye, holy unmercenaries, shed the wonderful grace as everflowing springs, driving away maladies; do supplicate for our souls.

Joyfully inhabiting the heavens, do, O martyrs, hasten to visit your venerable temple and cure our bodily infirmities and the passions of our hearts. [*The Theotokion:*

As the highest above the cherubim and all creation, let us praise her who alone hath given birth unto the Maker and Lord and opened unto us the gate of paradise.

The Contakion from the Typicon; but if there be no Typicon say this Contakion, Tone 2:

Having obtained the grace of healing, ye do distribute health among those in want thereof, O physicians, most glorious wonder-workers; but through your visitation put down the insolence of the enemies, making whole the universe with your miracles. [*The Oikos:*

The speech of the wise physicians passeth all understanding and wisdom, and yet giveth understanding unto all, for having received the grace from the Most High, they invisibly vouchsafe health; therefrom it is that unto my narration also is granted the grace to hymn them as God-bearing favourites of Christ and ministers granting a multitude of healings, for they deliver the world from all maladies, healing miraculously.

Ode 7. *The Heirmos:*

Thou that hast in the beginning founded the earth and made firm the heavens with Thy word, blessed art Thou unto the ages, O Lord, God of our fathers.

Thou that hast gloriously magnified the memory of the most wise unmercenaries on the earth,—blessed art Thou, O Lord, God of our fathers.

Thou that hast shewn unto all the holy wonder-workers as honourable mile-stones,—blessed art Thou, O Lord, God of our fathers.

Celebrating the venerable memory of the unmercenaries, we joyfully vociferate unto Thee, O compassionate One: Blessed art Thou, O Lord, God of our fathers.   [*The Theotokion:*

Thou that hast tabernacled in the womb of the Virgin and therein renewed Adam, blessed art Thou, O Lord, God of our fathers.

Ode 8. *The Heirmos:*

Him that was glorified on the holy mountain, and in the bush through the fire unto Moses hath shewn the mystery of the Ever-virgin, hymn the Lord and exalt unto all the ages.

Him that hath granted from above unto His unmercenaries the gifts of healing—gratuitously to cure diseases,—hymn the Lord and extol Him unto the ages.

Him that hath given unto the saints the grace to cure the infirmities of those diseased and to deliver the souls from passion,—hymn the Lord and extol Him unto the ages.

What man would not praise the unmercenaries for their virtuous life above that of all men? For they have continually wrought great wonders while on earth. Hymn the Lord and extol Him unto the ages.   [*The Theotokion:*

Him that hath found His abode in the womb of the Virgin and therein renewed, above word and awe, the ancient Adam,—hymn the Lord and extol Him unto the ages.

Ode 9. *The Heirmos:*

In unceasing hymns we magnify the bringing forth of the Ever-virgin unto the salvation of us faithful, which was manifested unto the lawgiver in the fire and the bush on the mountain.

As an universal cure hath appeared your shrine, O holy unmercenaries (*mentioned by name*), running unto which as it behoveth, all the faithful obtain cures.

O ye sickly men, come and be cured of your various diseases; come also ye beasts, for from the shrine of the holy ones floweth the stream of miracles.

Having found your abode in the highest habitations, ye, O holy ones, that were in our midst, invisibly take compassion on us, who in the midst of your temple send up odes unto the Almighty, and assiduously bless you, O all-praised ones.

The Theotokion: Thou, O Theotokos, art our wall and weapon, thou art the protectress of those that flee unto thee; thee we all entreat now that we may be delivered from our enemies.

The Photagogicon. Similar to: The heaven with stars...

O ye wonder-working lamps (*mentioned by name*)! Do cure our diseases both of the souls and bodies, having received from God the grace of healing. [*The Theotokion:*

Of the good things granted by God unto the world, thou, O Theotokos, wast the cause; do also now entreat for universal salvation the God that changeth wrath for mercy.

With the Lauds the Stichera, Tone 2.

O ye, physicians of the feeble, treasuries of cures, saviours of the faithful, all-glorious unmercenaries! Help those that call upon you in their needs and heal the sick, supplicating the good God that we may be delivered from the meshes of our enemies. *Twice.*

The fountain of healing did heal but one sick person in a year, but the temple of the unmercenaries doth heal all the multitude of sufferers; for the opulence of the holy ones is inexhaustible and cannot be spent; through their intercessions have mercy upon us, O Christ.

The choir of the holy ones doth for ever rejoice, for they have inherited the Kingdom of heaven, and the earth, having received their relics, doth emit sweet smells; they were servants of Christ and have entered into the life eternal. [*Glory...Tone* 6:

Endless is the grace which the holy ones have received from Christ; wherefore their relics also uninterruptedly by the divine power work miracles, and, when their names are with faith invoked, they heal incurable diseases; through them, O Lord deliver us also, as Lover of man, from bodily and spiritual sufferings. [*Both now...The Theotokion*:

Do thou, O all-hymned Theotokos—the joy of the sorrowing, the health of the diseased, the peace of the persecuted, the calm of the agitated, the only intercession of the faithful,—save the city and people. [*The Stavro-theotokion*:

The most pure one seeing Thee hung on the cross, with motherly tears cried unto Thee: O my God, my sweetest Child! How is it that Thou sufferest the ignominious death?

CHAPTER XXVII.

THE GENERAL SERVICE TO SAINTS ANDREW OF CONSTANTINOPLE, ISIDORE OF ROSTOW, MAXIM AND BASIL OF MOSCOW, AND OTHER FOOLISH FOR CHRIST'S SAKE.

At the Vespers, for O Lord, I have cried, the Stichera,
Tone 8. Similar to: O most glorious wonder...

O blissful, God-wise (*mentioned by name*), Thy pure soul shining with the orthodox sense, resplendent with the radiance of virtues, doth illumine the fulness of the faithful, driving away the demon's darkness; wherefore as participant of the never-fading grace we all piously praise thee, O wonder-worthy one.

With compassionate soul, pure thoughts, valiant heart, undoubting faith and love truly impartial art thou gone from the earth into heaven and dost find thy habitation with the choirs of the righteous; wherefore we all honour thee with sacred hymns and piously glorify thee, O wonder-worthy (*mentioned by name*).

Strengthened by divine teaching, thou hast driven away the passions of the body and wast unto the Holy Trinity a well-cleansed habitation; wherefore art thou gone over unto the divine life, whereas thy beatified body even now is being preserved in uncorrupted state by God, Who in His divine judgment, as He Himself knoweth, doth manifestly glorify thee, O (*mentioned by name*). [*Glory...Tone* 4.

How can we help wondering at thy life? or how can we abstain from praising, O holy (*mentioned by name*), thine angel-like life, the chastity of thy thoughts, thy humble and silent meekness, thine inexhaustible charity? thou wast adorned with all virtues, O blissful one; wherefore ineffable joy and heavenly Kingdom are waiting for thee.

Both now...the Theotokion: Accepting the supplications of sinners and not despising the sighs of the afflicted, do thou, O most holy Theotokos, entreat the Son of thy most pure womb that we may be saved.

The Stavro-theotokion: Seeing of old how thy Son and Master hath stretched out His hands on the cross, and His side was pierced with a lance, thou, O pure Mother, didst with lamentations vociferate: Woe unto me! How dost thou suffer Who deliverest men from pains, as Lover of men?

If the Celebration be with the Polyeleon, say the Theotokion of the resurrection: Let us hymn Mary the Virgin... *The Entrance. The Prokeimenon of the day. The Readings of the monks (see Appendix.)*

For the Versicles the Stichera. Tone 2. Similar to:
O House of Ephrah....

House and abode of the Most Holy Spirit wast thou, O most wise (*mentioned by name*); wherefore make us also houses of the same who honour thy holy memory.

The Versicle: The righteous shall be glad in the Lord, and shall trust in Him. Thy life hath shone forth as the sun in the hearts of the faithful, emitting miracles; wherefore do thou illumine with the never-fading light us also who honour thine all-honourable memory.

The Versicle: The righteous shall flourish like the palm-tree; he shall grow like a cedar in Lebanon.

Do not cease supplicating for thy servants, so near unto thee, since thou (*mentioned by name*), hast enlightened them with thy spiritual life, that we all may joyfully honour thy honourable memory. [*Glory...Tone* 4:

Thou hast appeared, O most blissful (*mentioned by name*), an earthly angel and a heavenly man, fountain of emotion, current of mercy, abyss of wonders, stream of healings, divine olive-tree truly fruitful, with the oil of thy labours enlightening those that faithfully praise thee, O wonder-worthy one, and supplicating the Lover of man to deliver from afflictions those who lovingly celebrate thine all-honourable memory.

Both now...the Theotokion: Deliver from our necessities, O Mother of Christ the God that hast given birth unto the Creator of all, that we all may call unto thee: Hail thou, the only intercession for our souls.

The Stavro-theotokion. Similar to: As a virtuous...

Seeing Christ crucified and slaying the crafty one, the most pure Sovereign Lady sang the Compassionate One that hath come from her, as the Master, and, astonished at His long suffering, thus vociferated: O my greatly beloved Child! Do not forget Thy servants, do not tarry, O my consolation.

If there be Celebration, say the Theotokion of the resurrection. Tone 4: Look down upon the entreaties...

The Troparion, Tone 1: Having heard the voice of Thine apostle Paul, saying: We are foolish for Christ's sake, Thy servant *(mentioned by name)*, O Christ the God, did love on earth the life of the foolish for Thy sake. Wherefore in venerating his memory we entreat Thee, O Lord, to save our souls.

At the Matins, for God is the Lord, the same Troparion. After the 1st Stichologia, the Cathisma, Tone 5. Similar to: The Co-unoriginate Word...Let us honour with hymns the God-bearing *(mentioned by name)*, and as an adamant and a pillar immovable for the assaults of the enemy; for by his endurance He hath truly put the opposing enemy to shame and flight, and doth now supplicate for the salvation of our souls. *Twice.*

Glory...Both now...the Theotokion: Dreadful the wonder of conception and ineffable the manner of bringing forth were shewn in thee, O pure Ever-virgin; they frighten my mind and astound my thoughts; thy glory, O Theotokos, hath spread unto all for the salvation of our souls.

After the 2nd Stichologia, the Cathisma, Tone 4. Similar to: Speedily prevent...

By fasting and abstemiousness and by lying on bare ground

thou hast withered the passions of the body, but enlightened the soul, and in heaven hast received from Christ a great reward; wherefore, having pleased God, even after thy demise thou hast appeared as a worthy vessel of miracles unto those that have recourse unto the shrine of thy relics, O most blissful (*mentioned by name*). Supplicate Christ the God to grant the remission of sins unto those who lovingly venerate thy holy memory. *Twice.* [*Glory...Both now...the Theotokion:*

With thy divine birth hast thou, O pure one, renewed the mortal and corrupted by passions nature of the earth-born, and raised all from death unto the life of incorruption; wherefore as in duty bound we all bless thee, O most glorious Virgin, as thou didst foretell.

After Praise ye the name of the Lord...the Refrain: We praise thee, O holy and righteous (*mentioned by name*), and honour thy holy memory, for thou dost supplicate for us Christ our God. *The selected Psalm:* Blessed is the man that feareth the Lord...

After the Polyeleon the Cathisma, Tone 4. Similar to: Speedily prevent... Wonderful didst thou appear in thine endurance and hast pleased Christ in every way; thou hast, O most blissful (*mentioned by name*), strengthened thy soul with wise thoughts, having subjugated the fleshly subtleties unto the spirit; having further elected to do good in order to labour for God's sake, manfully didst thou say: The winter may be severe, but paradise is sweet; painful it is to work, but blissful is the meed. Wherefore, O most blissful one, supplicate Christ the God to save our souls. *Twice.*

Glory...Both now...the Theotokion: We magnify thee, O Theotokos, vociferating: Thou art the only blessed one, for from thee wast ineffably born Christ our God.

The Graduals, the 1st Antiphon of the 4th Tone. The Prokeimenon: The righteous shall be glad in the Lord, and shall trust in Him. *The Verse:* Give ear, O God, unto my voice when I cry unto Thee. Let every breath... *The Gospel (St. Matth.* 11, 27-30).

After the 50th Psalm, the Sticheron, Tone 8: O man of God, wonderful (*mentioned by name*)! Having climbed up the ladder of virtues, along the same hast thou ascended unto Jerusalem on high and there hast thou beheld Christ—the Desired One. For His sake hast thou attenuated thy body and hast exchanged the corruptible body for immortal life. Supplicate unceasingly for us also that unto our souls may be granted peace and great mercy.

The Canon, Tone 4. *Ode* 1. *The Heirmos:*

The red abyss of the sea with unmoistened steps having crossed on foot, the Israel of old hath, through the cruciform arms of Moses, obtained victory in the wilderness over the forces of Amalek.

Through participation in the light that is with God, thou, O holy and blissful (*mentioned by name*), wast light, and having, in consequence of thine extreme desire, departed unto Him, thou, O father, hast attained the realization of thy good hopes.

Inflamed by thy desire unto God, thou hast forsaken the world and, having met on the way Christ—the fellow-traveller, thou hast, O glorious father (*mentioned by name*), joyfully plodded with Him along the saving path.

Not desiring to become opulent in exhaustible riches, thou hast virtuously and wisely rejected the transient riches and glory, temporary food and worldly possessions. [*The Theotokion:*

Having learned thee to be a fair, select and all-honourable, the Son of God was become thy Son, O most unblemished one, and hath made the sons by grace of those, O Theotokos, who honour thee.

Ode 3. *The Heirmos:*

Delighted on Thine account is Thy church, O Christ, calling unto Thee: Thou art my strength, O Lord, both refuge and support.

With zeal hast thou stripped thyself for the spiritual deeds and hast vanquished, with the help from the Divine Spirit, the troops of the enemy.

With wounds, prayerful abstemiousness and blows hast thou, O holy father (*mentioned by name*), sorely hit off the worldly passions.

Having joyfully desired Thy life-bringing death, O Master, Thy blissful, O Jesus, (*mentioned by name*), hath starved to death the enemy. [*The Theotokion:*

Unto Him that delivereth men from the fearful fall through

disobedience, unto the cause of everything thou, O pure and most unblemished one, hast given birth.

The Cathisma, Tone 5. Similar to: The Co-unoriginate...

Illumined by the divine harmony, thou hast undeviatingly walked along the paths leading unto the divine rays of light, and, having evaded the attacks of the enemy, thou didst appear as a son of light and of day, O God-blissful, holy father (*mentioned by name*). [*Glory...Both now...the Theotokion:*

O most pure Mother of God, the city of Christ! Do deliver from dangers thy people calling unto thee, and resist the attacks of the intellectual, proud enemies, that we may vociferate unto thee: Hail thou, O blessed one! [*The Stavro-theotokion:*

By the cross of thy Son, O full of God's grace, the enchantment of idols hath been done away with, and the might of demons vanquished. Wherefore we, the faithful, dutifully ever hymn and bless thee, and confessing thee as truly the Theotokos, we magnify thee.

Ode 4. The Heirmos:

Elevated on the cross seeing Thee, the Sun of righteousness, the church stood up in her order worthily calling out: Glory to Thy power, O Lord.

Having joined the path of righteousness, thou, O holy (*mentioned by name*), hast entered the God-preserved divine city and art now enriched with the saving lustre.

Seeing in all the divine narratives one uniform, God-bearing meaning, thou, O holy (*mentioned by name*), hast put on divine vestment.

The grace of the Holy Spirit having found thy heart, O holy father (*mentioned by name*), as a perfectly clear tablet, hath written thereon perfect impassivity, faith and love unfeigned.

The Theotokion: He that sitteth on the most exalted cherubic throne, even our God the most glorified, having thee, O Mary God's Bride as a throne, hath rested in thine arms.

Ode 5. The Heirmos:

Thou, my God, didst come into the world as light, as a holy light that bringeth out of the darkness of ignorance those who in faith hymn Thee.

Having received the most resplendent light, thou, O worthy of glory (*mentioned by name*), appearedst as the sun and hast driven away the demoniac darkness.

Through the desire for Thee, O Christ, the all-righteous (*mentioned by name*) hath rejected the desires of the body, having cast them off as a worldly refuse.

Having strengthened thy soul by the divine power, thou hast found thine abode in the world in order to empty the passions, O God-wise father (*mentioned by name*).

The Theotokion: The care of corruptible things hath ceased, for the Virgin hath incorruptibly given birth, above nature and word, unto God the Word, and remaineth Virgin.

Ode 6. *The Heirmos:*

I will sacrifice unto Thee, O Lord, with the voice of praise—crieth out unto Thee the church, having been cleansed of the demons' blood with the blood that mercifully ran out of Thy side.

Directing thy mind entirely to God-wards in thine unceasing study, thou, O (*mentioned by name*), hast mercilessly rejected the solicitations of fleshly love or the acquirement of earthly goods.

Neither any defilement, nor spot hast thou, O blissful one, permitted to touch thee, whilst living in the midst of the world, but dost rather cleanse the defilement of the souls of those that have recourse unto thee, with thy venerable supplications.

Having thy thoughts above the fleshly subtleties, thou wast not affected, although bared in the midst of women, for thou hast put on the vestment of impassivity, O (*mentioned by name*).

The Theotokion: We proclaim Thee, O most holy Theotokos, both with our lips, thoughts and hearts; through thee we have been reconciled unto God, having been first rejected through the transgression of the forefather.

The Contakion from the Typicon; but if there be no Typicon, say this Contakion, Tone 8: Desirous of the heavenly beauty, the low delights of the body hast thou, O blessed (*mentioned by name*), left alone and passed away, after having led a life utterly void of any desire for the things of this vain world, like unto that of the angels; together with these do thou incessantly intercede before Christ the God for us all. [*The Oikos:*

How can I—sinner and defiled both in my soul and body—describe thine equal to angels' life, whilst thou wast in the flesh, and thy most glorious miracles? When even many and very wise are unable to succeed in declaring thy great endurance, humility and fervent love for Christ, yet trusting in thy meekness, O blissful one, I presume thus to vociferate unto thee: Hail thou, O most brilliant star, shining forth from the East of virtues and illumining the universe with thy miracles! Hail thou, that hast contemned thy parents' love, but loved with all thy heart Christ alone Who is the God of all, and followed after Him with an irrevocable desire! Hail thou, that hadst selected, according to the apostle, wild and foolish life! Hail thou, that hast changed the corruptible and unstable things by the hope of future reward. Hail thou, that in thine endurance wast like unto ancient Job! Hail thou, O great sufferer of Christ, invincible thyself and yet ever vanquishing the devil with thy humility! Hail thou, that, like unto that ancient Lazarus the beggar, thou dost rest now in the bosom of Abraham! Hail thou, that, after thy departure from this world, art an ever ready intercessor and protector unto all those who are in the midst of dangers and temptations! Hail thou, that quickly preventest those invoking thee! Hail thou, O God-wise (*mentioned by name*)!

Ode 7. The Heirmos:

In the Persian furnace the youths, descendants of Abraham, burning rather with love of piety than with the flame of fire, have called out: Blessed art Thou in the temple of Thy glory, O Lord.

Actuated by Christ-like divine desire to save others, thou hast, O father (*mentioned by name*), joyfully and entirely given thyself up thereunto, vociferating: Blessed art Thou in the temple of Thy Glory, O Lord.

Having received the food sent down unto thee from heaven, thou, O blissful father (*mentioned by name*), hast fed on it those who with good grace accept thine injunctions, and relinquish the dragging down sin.

Following the traditions of the fathers, thou hast, O wise father (*mentioned by name*), commanded to shun the wicked and destructive teaching of Origen unto those that call out: Blessed art Thou in the temple of Thy glory, O Lord.

The Theotokion: Hail thou, the hallowed divine tabernacle of the Most High, for through thee the joy is vouchsafed unto those, O Theotokos, who call out: Blessed art thou among women, O all-spotless Sovereign-Lady.

Ode 8. *The Heirmos:*

Having spread his hands, Daniel did close the jaws of the lions in their den; and the force of the fire was deadened by the zealously pious youths who girded themselves with virtue and called out: Bless the Lord, all ye the works of the Lord.

Most brilliant star wast thou, bringing unto life those that are in the mud of passions, for thou dost make defiled women lead the chaste life, and drivest away all infirmities, vociferating: Bless the Lord, all ye the works of the Lord.

Being entire in thy mind, in meshes of thy wise miracles, thou hast, O holy (*mentioned by name*), caught many to be foolish for Christ's sake, knowing that they may be abused, and in thy purest soul vociferating: Bless the Lord, all ye the works of the Lord.

The Lord alone is perfect, and He doth glorify His own according to their worth; when thou wast carried unto thy grave, O blissful one, He did with angelic bright singing honour the one calling out: Bless the Lord, all ye the works of the Lord.   [*The Theotokion:*

He that delivereth us, even the Lord, hath shone forth from thee, O pure Virgin; Him supplicate, O Sovereign-Lady, to enlighten those that hymn thee, and to free from attacks us that vociferate: Bless the Lord, all ye the works of the Lord.

Ode 9. *The Heirmos:*

A stone cut out without hands from an untouched mountain—from thee, O Virgin, was separated—that corner-stone, even Christ, Who hath joined together the distant natures; rejoicing thereat, we magnify Thee, O Theotokos.

Having with all thy heart offered thyself unto the Trinity, and having obtained therefrom good effecting rays, thou, O (*mentioned by name*), wast resplendent, and dost exult together with the angels.

Having united thyself through the divine desire and enlightened by abstemiousness, thou, O God-blissful (*mentioned by name*), hast already participated of the future good things and of their enjoyment.

Through thy labours and sweat thou hast obtained joy that hath no end; being in the enjoyment thereof, O most blissful (*mentioned by name*), do uninterruptedly remember us also.

The Theotokion: Do thou that hast given birth unto the Redeemer and Benefactor of all, save me and disperse the clouds of my soul—thou, O holy Sovereign-Lady, the cloud of the Light, strengthening me against the passions that are agitating me. [*The Photagogicon*: Having in thy wandering gone far away from those near you in this world, with thy spotless life hast thou pleased Christ—the God of all; Him supplicate now for us, thy servants, that in faith celebrate thine all-honourable memory, O God-wise (*mentioned by name*). [*The Theotokion:* Do thou, O Virgin, that hast given birth unto the Hypastatic Wisdom, Word Ever-existing and Physician of all, heal the cruel and of long-standing eschars and sores of my soul, and appease the thoughts of my passionate heart.

With the Lauds, the Stichera, Tone 4. Similar to:
Thou hast given a sign...

Thou hast, O Most Kind Lord, given us a parable of endurance and valour in Thy righteous (*mentioned by name*), who doth shine forth in many miracles, his virtues, words and deeds, and who is adorned with chastity and meekness; wherefore we glorify Thine ineffable economy, O Jesu all-powerful and Saviour of our souls.   *Twice.*

Righteous and meek, truthful, unblemished and faithful, eschewing every evil thing, illumined with virtues and shining forth in piety, hast thou appeared, O blissful (*mentioned by name*); wherefore we praise thee and joyfully celebrate to-day thy holy and honourable falling asleep, O God-wise one.

Having put on chastity and right faith, as a most precious purple robe, and having been crowned with truth and meekness as with a divine crown, thou, O (*mentioned by name*), hast desired to reign with the sufferers for Christ's sake, and now dost stand before the King of Hosts, even Jesus, the all-merciful and Saviour of our souls.   [*Glory...Tone* 8:

The manifestation of thy virtues, O God-wise one, hath illumined the hearts of the faithful. For who would not wonder hearing of thine immeasurable humility and endurance? or of meekness unto all and of forbearing, of mercy unto the sorrowing and unto those in danger of speedy help, unto those going by water of undisturbed haven, and unto those travelling by land of good speed? Everything hast thou, O wonder-worthy, God-beseemingly prevented, and now art thou crowned with an unfading crown from the hands of the Almighty God. Him supplicate that our souls may be saved. [*Both now...the Theotokion:* O Sovereign-Lady, accept the prayers of thy servants, and deliver us from every want and woe!

APPENDIX.

It had been originally intended to give here in extenso the Readings (Paroimias) appointed for different sets of services, but, the book having grown so bulky, it was decided to merely indicate here chapters and verses of the different books of the English Bible of which the Readings are made up, and to give in extenso only the Readings from the Books of Proverbs, and the Wisdom of Solomon, which are either not found in the ordinary Bible, or do not exactly correspond with the Slavonian or Greek text.

I. *The Readings to a Prophet.*
1. *From the Wisdom of Solomon* (3, 1-9).

The souls of the righteous are in the hands of God, and there shall no torment touch them. In the sight of the unwise they seemed to die, and their departure is taken for misery, and their going from us to be utter destruction, but they are in peace. For though they be punished in the sight of men, yet is their hope full of immortality. And having been a little chastised, they shall be greatly rewarded, for God proved them and found them worthy for Himself. As gold in the furnace hath He tried them, and received them as a burnt offering. And in the time of their visitation they shall shine, and run to and fro like sparks among the stubble. They shall judge the nations and have dominion over the people, and their Lord shall reign for ever. They that put their trust in Him shall understand the truth; and such as be faithful in love shall abide with Him; for grace and mercy is to His saints and visitation for His elect.

2. *From the Wisdom of Solomon* (5, 15-23; 6, 1-3).

The righteous live unto the ages; their reward is also with the Lord, and the care of them is with the most High. Therefore shall they receive a glorious kingdom and a beautiful crown from the Lord's hand, for with His right hand shall He cover them, and with His arm shall He protect them. He shall take to Him His jealousy for complete armour, and make the creature His weapon for the revenge of His enemies. He shall put on righteousness as a breastplate and true judgment instead of an helmet. He shall take holiness for an invincible shield. His severe wrath shall He sharpen for a sword, and the world shall fight with Him against the unwise. Then shall the right-arming thunderbolts go abroad, and from the clouds, as from a well-drawn bow, shall they fly to the mark. And from the hailstones full of wrath and cast as out of a stone bow the cities shall fall down, and the water of the sea shall rage against them, and the floods shall cruelly drown them. Yea, a mighty wind shall stand up against them, and like a storm shall blow them away; thus iniquity shall lay waste the whole earth, and ill dealing shall overthrow the thrones of the mighty. Hear therefore, O ye kings, and understand; learn ye that be judges of the ends of the earth. Give ear, ye that rule the people and glory in the multitude of nations, for power is given you of the Lord and sovereignty from the Highest.

3. *From the Wisdom of Solomon* (*pages* 49-50).

The same Readings are used at the services to a Monk and Monks, Monk-Martyr and Monk-Martyrs, to a Confessor, and to a Foolish for Christ's sake.

II. 1. *The Readings to an Apostle*: 1st *General Epistle of St. John*, 3, 21-24; 4, 1-6 (*ending* "heareth not us.")
2. *The Readings to an Apostle*: 2nd *General Epistle of St. John*, 4, 11-16.
3. *The Readings to an Apostle*: 3rd *General Epistle of St. John*, 4, 20-21; 5, 1-5.

III. 1. *The Readings to two or more Apostles*: 1st *General Epistle of St. Peter*, 1, 3-9.
2. *The Readings to two or more Apostles*: 2nd *General Epistle of St. Peter*, 1, 13-19.
3. *The Readings to two or more Apostles*: 3rd *General Epistle of St. Peter*, 2, 11-22 (*ending* "should live unto righteousness.")

IV. *The readings to one Hierarch:*

1. *The Reading from the Book of Proverbs* (3, 13-16; 8, 6, &c.).

The memory of the righteous man calleth forth for praises, and the blessing of the Lord is upon his head. Blessed is the man that findeth wisdom, and the man that getteth understanding. For the merchandise of it is better than the merchandise of silver, and the gain thereof than fine gold. She is more precious than costly stones; everything that is honoured cannot be compared unto her. Length of days and years of life are in her right hand; and in her left hand riches and honour. Out of her mouth truth proceedeth, and law and mercy she carrieth on her tongue. Hear me, then, O children, for I will speak of excellent things; and happy is the man that will keep unto my ways, for my paths are the paths of life, and the desire is fashioned of the Lord. Wherefore I entreat you and put forth my voice before the sons of men, for I with wisdom set up everything; I have called forth counsel, understanding and knowledge. Counsel is mine and sound wisdom, mine is understanding and strength is mine. I love them that love me; and those that seek me shall find grace. Understand, then, O ye simple, the cunning, and ye uninstructed—direct your hearts unto it. Hearken unto me again, for I will speak of honourable things, and the opening of my mouth shall be right things, for my mouth shall speak truth and wickedness is an abomination to my lips. All the words of my mouth are in righteousness; there is nothing froward or perverse in them. They are all plain to him that understandeth, and right to them that find knowledge. For I will teach you the truth, so that your hope may be in the Lord and ye may be with the Spirit.

2. *The Reading from the Wisdom of Solomon* (6, 12-16; 7, 30; 8, 2-4. 7-9. 21; 9, 1-4. 10. 11. 13).

The mouth of the righteous man bringeth forth wisdom, and the lips of the wise man know the grace. The mouth of the wise man teacheth wisdom, and the truth delivereth from death. If a righteous man happeneth to die, hope is not lost, for the son of a righteous man is born unto life, and in his good things doth he acquire the fruit of righteousness. There is ever light unto the righteous and of the Lord they obtain both grace and glory; the tongue of the wise acknowledgeth the good, and in their hearts resteth wisdom. The Lord loveth the hearts of the righteous, and acceptable unto Him are all undefiled in the way. The wisdom of the Lord doth illumine the countenances of the wise. She preventeth them that desire her, in making herself first known unto them. She is easily seen of them that seek her. Whoso seeketh her early shall have no great travail; and whoso watcheth for her shall quickly be without care. For she goeth about seeking such as are worthy of her, shewing herself favourably unto them in the ways, and meeteth them in every thought. Vice shall never prevail against wisdom. Wherefore I was a lover of her beauty; I loved her, and sought her out from my youth. I desired to make her my spouse, yea, the Lord of all things Himself loved her. For she is privy to the mysteries of the knowledge of God and a lover of His works. Her labours are virtues, for she teacheth temperance and prudence, justice and fortitude; which are such things, as men can have nothing more profitable in their life. If a man desire much experience, she knoweth things of old, and conjectureth aright what is to come. She knoweth the subtleties of speeches and can expound dark sentences; she foreseeth signs and wonders, and the events of seasons and times; unto all she is a counsellor of good things, since there is immortality in her, and she is a comfort in cares and grief. Wherefore I prayed unto the Lord, and besought Him, and with my whole heart I said: O God of my fathers, and Lord of mercy, who hast made all things with Thy word, and fashioned man in Thy wisdom that he should have dominion over the creatures which Thou hast made, and order the world according to equity and righteousness! Give me wisdom that sitteth by Thy throne, and reject me not from among Thy children, for I am Thy servant and son of Thine handmaid. O send her out of Thy holy heavens, and from the throne of Thy glory, that being present she may labour with me, that I may know what is pleasing unto Thee. And she shall lead me soberly in my doings and preserve me in her glory. For the thoughts of mortal men are miserable, and our devices are but uncertain.

3. *The Reading from the Wisdom of Solomon* (4, 10-12; 6, 21; 7, 15-17. 22. 26. 29; 2, 1. 10-17. 19-22).

When the righteous man is praised the people rejoice, for his memory is undying, since he is acknowledged both of God and man, and his soul pleased the Lord. Love therefore, O ye men, wisdom, and ye shall live; desire her and you shall be instructed, for the very beginning of her is love and the keeping of the law. Honour wisdom, that ye may reign for evermore. I will tell you and will not hide God's mysteries from you, for He it is that leadeth unto wisdom and directeth the wise; in His hands is all wisdom and knowledge of workmanship; and wisdom, which is the worker of all things, will teach you all, for in her is a spirit understanding and holy, brightness of everlasting light, and image of the goodness of God. She maketh people friends of God and prophets, she is more beautiful than the sun, and above all order of stars; being compared with the light, she is found before it. She hath freed from diseases those that pleased her, and hath set them in the right paths; she hath given unto them understanding to keep in holiness, saved them from those lying in wait, and granted them strength of power, so that all may understand that the most powerful of all is piety, and that vice shall never prevail against wisdom, nor judgment shall pass away without convicting the evil. But the ungodly reasoning with themselves not aright, said: let us oppress the righteous man, let us not spare the widow, neither need we be ashamed of the ancient gray hairs of the aged. Let our strength be the law, and let us lie in wait for the righteous, because he is not of our turn, and he is clean contrary to our doings; he upbraideth us with our offending the law and objecteth to our infamy the transgressions of our education; he professeth to have the knowledge of God, and he calleth himself the child of the Lord. He was made to reprove our thoughts; he is grievous unto us even to behold, for his life is not like other men's, his ways are of another fashion; we are esteemed of him as counterfeits, he abstaineth from our ways as from filthiness, he pronounceth the end of the just to be blessed. Let us see if his words be true, let us prove what shall happen in the end of him. Let us examine him with despitefulness and torture, that we may know his meekness and prove his patience; let us condemn him unto a shameful death, for by his own saying he shall be respected. Such things did they imagine and were deceived, for their own wickedness hath blinded them. As for the mysteries of God, they knew them not, neither did they discern that Thou art the Only God that hast the power of life and death, that savest in the time of tribulation and deliverest from every evil, that thou art compassionate and merciful, granting unto the just Thy grace, and setting Thy might against the haughty.

V. *The Readings to two or more Hierarchs:* 1st *as the* 1st *of IV.*

2. *The Reading from the Book of Proverbs* (10, 31-32; 11, 1-10).

The mouth of the just bringeth forth wisdom; but the froward tongue shall be cut out. The lips of the righteous know what is acceptable; but the mouth of the wicked speaketh frowardness. A false balance is an abomination to the Lord, but a just weight is His delight. Where pride cometh, there cometh shame also; but with the lowly is wisdom. The integrity of the upright shall guide them; but the perverseness of transgressors shall destroy them. Riches profit not in the day of wrath, but righteousness delivereth from death. When a righteous man dieth, remorse is felt, but the ruin of the wicked calleth forth derision. The righteousness of the upright straighteneth the paths, but the transgressors shall fall in their own wickedness. The righteousness of the just men shall deliver them, but the wicked are caught in their own naughtiness. When a righteous man dieth, the hope perisheth not, but the praise of the wicked shall perish. The righteous is delivered out of trouble, and the wicked cometh in his stead. In the mouth of the ungodly there is a snare for their neighbours, but the feeling of the righteous is profitable. When it goeth well with the righteous, the city prospereth, and at the ruin of the wicked there is rejoicing. By the blessing of the upright the city is exalted, but it is overthrown by the mouth of the wicked. He that is void of wisdom despiseth his neighbours, but a man of understanding holdeth his peace.

3. *The Reading from the Wisdom of Solomon* (4, 7-15.)

Though the righteous happen to die, yet shall he be in rest. For honourable age is not that which standeth in length of time, nor that which is measured by number of years. But wisdom is the gray hair unto men, and an unspotted life in old age. He pleased God, and was beloved of Him, so that living among sinners he was translated. Yea, speedily was he taken up, lest that wickedness should alter his understanding, or deceit beguile his soul. For the bewitching of naughtiness doth obscure things that are honest, and the wandering of concupiscence doth undermine the simple mind. He being made perfect in a short time, fulfilled a long time; for his soul pleased the Lord; therefore hasted He to take him away from among the wicked. This the people saw, and understood it not, neither did they lay this up in their minds, that His grace and mercy is with His saints, and that He doth visit His chosen.

VI. *The Readings to one Martyr:* 1st *Isaiah* (43, 9-14; *beginning*, "Thus saith the Lord," *and ending,* "Thus saith the Lord...the Holy One of Israel.")
The Readings to one Martyr: 2nd as the 1st in I.
The Readings to one Martyr: 3rd as the 3rd in V.

The same for the services to Martyrs, Hieromartyr, and Hieromartyrs, Female Martyr and Martyrs, Nun-martyrs, and Unmercenaries, except that the 3rd in these cases is the 2nd of I.

To the glory of the Holy, One-substanced, Life-giving and Indivisible Trinity of the Father, and of the Son, and of the Holy Ghost, in the reign of the Right-faithful Autocrat, our Great Sovereign, Emperor Nicholas Alexandrovitch of all the Russias, in the time of his Consort, the Right-faithful Lady, Empress Alexandra Feodorovna, of his Mother, the Right-faithful Lady, Empress Mary Feodorovna and of his Heir, the orthodox Lord, Cesarevitch and Grand Duke Michael Alexandrovitch; in the time of the orthodox Lord, Grand Duke Vladimir Alexandrovitch, of his Consort the Grand Duchess Mary Pavlovna, and of the orthodox Lords, Grand Dukes: Cyril, Boris and Andrew Vladimirovitchi; in the time of the orthodox Lord, Grand Duke Alexis Alexandrovitch, of the orthodox Lord Grand Duke Serge Alexandrovitch and of his Consort the orthodox Lady, Grand Duchess Elisabeth Feodorovna; in the time of the orthodox Lord, Grand Duke Paul Alexandrovitch and of the orthodox Lord, Grand Duke Demetrius Pavlovitch; in the time of the orthodox Lady, Grand Duchess Alexandra Josephovna, of the orthodox Lord, Grand Duke Nicholas Constantinovitch, of the orthodox Lord, Grand Duke Constantine Constantinovitch, and of his Consort the Grand Duchess Elisabeth Mavrikievna, and of the orthodox Lord, Grand Duke Demetrius Constantinovitch; in the time of the orthodox Lady, Grand Duchess Alexandra Petrovna, of the orthodox Lord, Grand Duke Nicholas Nicholaevitch, of the orthodox Lord, Grand Duke Peter Nicholaevitch, and of his Consort, the orthodox Lady, Grand Duchess Militza Nicholaevna; in the time of the orthodox Lord, Grand Duke Michael Nicholaevitch, of the orthodox Lords, Grand Dukes: Nicholas, Michael, and George Michaelovitchi, of the orthodox Lord, Grand Duke Alexander Michaelovitch and of his Consort, the orthodox Lady, Grand Duchess Xenia Alexandrovna, and of the orthodox Lord, Grand Duke Serge Michaelovitch; in the time of the orthodox Ladies, Grand Duchesses: Olga, Tatiana and Mary Nicholaevny, of the orthodox Lady, Grand Duchess Olga Alexandrovna, of the orthodox Lady, Grand Duchess Helena Vladimirovna, of the orthodox Lady, Grand Duchess Mary Pavlovna; in the time of the orthodox Lady, Grand Duchess Mary Alexandrovna and of her Consort; in the time of the Queen of the Hellenes Olga Constantinovna and of her Consort, of the Grand Duchess Vera Constantinovna, of the Grand Duchess Anastasia Michaelovna; and with the blessing of the Right Reverend Tikhon, Lord Bishop of Alaska and of the Aleutan Islands, this translation of the General Menaion, or the Book of Services common to the Festivals of our Lord, of the Holy Virgin, and of the different Orders of Saints, from the 16th edition of the Most Holy Governing Synod of Russia of 1862, hath been printed in the capital city of London, at the Dryden Press office, in its first impression in the year of the world 7408, and in the year from the incarnation of God the Word 1899, in the month of June, the sixty-second year of the reign of Queen Victoria.

Lightning Source UK Ltd.
Milton Keynes UK
UKHW020725310822
408116UK00005B/523